Prehistoric Men

Cover: Air view of the early village site of Çayönü in south-eastern Turkey, showing the exposures made during four campaigns by the Joint Prehistoric Project of Istanbul University and The University of Chicago. Age, ca. 7250–7000 B.C. *Photo courtesy of the Air Force of the Republic of Turkey.*

**Earlier editions of this book were published by
The Field Museum of Natural History**

Drawings by Susan Richert Allen and Philipp Herzog

Prehistoric Men

EIGHTH EDITION

Robert J. Braidwood

Oriental Institute and Department of Anthropology
University of Chicago

SCOTT, FORESMAN AND COMPANY   Glenview, Illinois

Dallas, Tex.   Oakland, N.J.   Palo Alto, Cal.   Tucker, Ga.   Brighton, England

The author and publisher wish to thank the following authors and publishers for permission to redraw the art on the following pages: p. 19, A. H. Schultz, "Die Körperproportionen der erwachsenen catarrhinen Primaten, mit spezieller Berücksichtigung der Menschenaffen," *Anthropol. Anz.,* 10 (1933), 154–185. p. 26, J. B. Birdsell, *Human Evolution,* © 1972 by Rand McNally and Company, Chicago, Fig. 8-9, p. 326. Redrawn by permission of Rand McNally College Publishing Company. pp. 111, 112, Figs. 10, 16-2, 17-9, and 23-3, *L'Anthropologie,* 70, 5-6 (1966). Redrawn by permission of Jean Perrot and Masson & Cie, Paris. p. 157, Fig. 13, *Iraq* II, 1 (1935). Redrawn by permission of Sir Max Mallowan and the British School of Archaeology in Iraq. p. 181, George Vaillant, "Excavations at Zacatenco," 32 (1930), and "Excavations at Arbillilo," 35 (1935). Redrawn by permission of the American Museum of Natural History.

Library of Congress Catalog Card Number: 74-82642
ISBN: 0-673-07851-5

Preface

Prehistoric Men first appeared in the Field Museum of Natural History's "Popular Series: Anthropology, Number 37" in 1948. I was invited to write it by an old friend, the late Dr. Paul S. Martin of the Museum, under whom I had spent a happy summer excavating in New Mexico in 1940. The book went through six editions for the Museum, after which the Museum generously agreed to release it to Scott, Foresman and Company for wider distribution.

Dr. Martin's invitation clearly implied that the book should be written for a popular audience. I took this implication seriously. The preface for the first six Museum editions began:

Like the writing of most professional archeologists, mine has been confined to so-called learned papers. Good, bad, or indifferent, these papers were in a jargon that only my colleagues and a few advanced students could understand. Hence, when I was asked to do this little book, I soon found it extremely difficult to say what I meant in simple fashion. The style is new to me, but I hope the reader will not find it forced or pedantic; at least I have done my very best to tell the story simply and clearly.

Since 1948 much has been learned of the past, and each edition of this book has grown larger to account for new and more complicated evidence. I'm afraid the style may have slipped back into jargon a bit, but it is my sincere hope that the book remains readable.

As this book has grown, many kind colleagues have given me the benefit of their knowledge and interpretations. Although there are too many to name individually, they will recognize their own guiding hands and know my gratitude to them. Particularly, however, I should like to recall my indebtedness to two non-archeologists, Mrs. Irma Hunter and Mr. Arnold Maremont, who first gave me sound advice, as intelligent laymen, on how best to tell the story.

The archeology I really know at first hand is that of the later prehistory of southwestern Asia. Even though this book is in no sense meant to be a universally balanced account of prehistory, I have increasingly felt too out of contact with earlier prehistory to do justice to portions of the original coverage. For this revision, therefore, I asked two old friends, Professor Hallam L. Movius, Jr., and Professor Sherwood L. Washburn, to suggest a pair of younger scholars who would be willing to counsel me on the archeology of Pleistocene ice-age times and on the human fossil record. Dr. Elizabeth McCown of Berkeley agreed to help with the chapter on human fossils and Professor Harvey M. Bricker of Tulane went over Chapters 4 and 5 (on early prehistoric archeology) for me. In fact, McCown and Bricker provided me with redrafts of these chapters with much new material. I have, however, recast portions of their drafts in my own style—hence, any possible errors in fact or emphasis are mine, not theirs. Needless to say, I am enormously indebted to them both.

I've already told you that my specific archeological experience and competence (such as it is) concerns the later prehistory of the Near East. It is probably fair to say that the central theme of the book is primarily this—how the stage was set, through the ages of prehistoric time, for the appearance of the urban civilizations of the Western cultural tradition. I give much attention to the transition from a hunting-collecting way of life to that of settled village-farming communities in southwestern Asia, which appears to have begun there some 12,000 years ago. Then, having set down my understandings of the available evidence for the appearance of urban and literate civilization in Mesopotamia by about 3,000 B.C., I have attempted a completely new chapter of short sketches on comparable developments—up to the appearance of early civilizations—in other parts of the world. Finally, I turn briefly to Britain as a single illustration of a region far removed from the then center of the civilizational achievement, to watch "the end of prehistory."

The prehistoric archeologist is in no danger of unemployment. New discoveries and new techniques for the interpretation of the evidence of mankind's past appear almost daily. The newer finds and techniques necessitate reconsideration of older evidence. I have not attempted to subject you here to many details of methodology or to the esoteric heights of the so-called new archeology— there will be time for that should you decide to go further into archeological studies. Slowly but surely we are moving toward fuller understandings of those beings whose history holds the greatest fascination for all of mankind—human beings themselves.

Robert J. Braidwood
March 1974

The scientist is right in thinking he corrects intellectual error and advances truth; yet to him history is peripheral or dead. . . . The humanist is justified in remarking that history is strewn with the relics of scientific theories once thought to be infallible.

Howard Mumford Jones, 1973

Contents

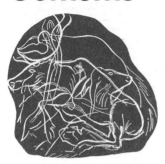

1
How we learn about the prehistoric past

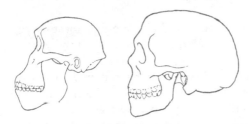

Prehistory means the time before written history began. Actually, more than 99 percent of the human story is prehistory. Human beings are certainly well over a million years old, but they did not begin to write history (or anything) until about 5000 years ago.

The people who lived in prehistoric times left us no history books, but they did unintentionally leave a record of their presence and their way of life. This record is studied and interpreted by different kinds of scientists.

Scientists Who Find Out About the Prehistoric Past

The scientists who study the bones and teeth and any other parts they find of the bodies of prehistoric people are called *physical anthropologists*. Physical anthropologists are trained, much like doctors, to know all about the human body. They study living people, too; they know more about the biological facts of human "races" than anybody else. If the police find a badly decayed body in a trunk, they ask a physical anthropologist to tell them what the person originally looked like. The physical anthropologists who specialize in prehistory work with fossils, so they are sometimes called *human paleontologists*.

Archeologists

There is a kind of scientist who studies the things that prehistoric people made and did. Such a scientist is called an *archeologist*. It is the archeologist's business to look for the stone and metal tools, the pottery, the graves, and the caves or huts of the people who lived before written history began.

But there is more to archeology than just looking for things. In Professor V. Gordon Childe's words, archeology "furnishes a sort of history of human activity, provided always that the actions have produced concrete results and left recognizable material traces." You will see that there are at least three points in what Childe says:

1. The archeologist has to find the traces of things left behind by ancient people, and
2. Only a few objects may be found, for most of these were probably too soft or too breakable to last through the years. However,
3. The archeologist must use whatever he can find to tell a story—to make a "sort of history"—from the objects and living places and graves that have escaped destruction.

What I mean is this: Let us say you are walking through a dump yard, and you find a rusty old spark plug. If you want to think about what the spark plug means, you quickly remember that it is a part of an automobile motor. This tells you something about the person who threw the spark plug on the dump. He either had an automobile, or he knew or lived near someone who did. He couldn't have lived so very long ago, you'll remember, because spark plugs and automobiles are less than a century old.

When you think about the old spark plug in this way, you have just been making the beginnings of what we call an archeological *interpretation;* you have been making the spark plug tell a story. It is the same way with the man-made things we archeologists find and put in museums. Usually, only a few of these objects are pretty to look at; but each of them has some sort of story to tell. Making the interpretation of his finds is the most important part of the archeologist's job. It is the way he gets at the "sort of history of human activity" which is expected of archeology.

Some Other Scientists

There are many other scientists who help the archeologist and the physical anthropologist find out about prehistoric people. The geologists help us tell the age of the rocks or caves or gravel beds in which human bones or man-made objects are found. There are other scientists with names which all begin with "paleo" (the Greek word for "old"). The *paleontologists* study fossil animals. There are also *paleobotanists* and *paleoclimatologists,* who study ancient plants and climates. These scientists help us know the kinds of animals and plants that were living in prehistoric times and so could be used for food by ancient people; what the weather was like; and whether there were glaciers. Also, when I tell you that prehistoric men and women did not appear until long after the great dinosaurs had disappeared, I go on the say-so of the paleontologists. They know that fossils of humans and of dinosaurs are not found in the same geological period. The dinosaur fossils come in early periods, the fossils of people much later.

Since World War II even the atomic scientists have been helping the archeologists. By testing the amount of radioactivity left in charcoal, wood, or other vegetable matter obtained from archeological sites, it has been possible to assess the approximate age of the sites. Shell has been used also, and even the hair of Egyptian mummies. The dates of geological and climatic events have also been discovered. Some of this work has been done from drillings taken from the bottom of the sea.

It has also proved possible to assess the time when certain volcanic rocks were formed. If a bed of such rocks was formed later than (and hence sealed in) an archeological or human fossil site, then we may say that the site must be at least earlier than the "date" of the covering rock bed. Unfortunately, we do not always find such volcanic beds where we'd like to find them—nicely sealing in our own sites. The method depends on measuring the amount of argon in the rock, the result of potassium-argon transformation. Measurements of less than about 100,000 years ago are difficult to make so the method deals mainly with traces of early people.

Such dating by radioactivity has considerably changed the dates which the archeologists used to give. If you find that some of the dates I give here are more recent (or more ancient) than the dates you see in other books on prehistory, it is because I am using one of the new dating systems.

How the Scientists Find Out

So far, this chapter has been mainly about the people who find out about prehistoric people. We also need a word about *how* they find out.

All our finds came by accident until about a hundred years ago. People digging wells, or digging in caves for fertilizer, often turned up ancient swords or pots or stone arrowheads. People also found some odd pieces of stone that didn't look like natural forms, but they also didn't look like any known tool. As a result, the people

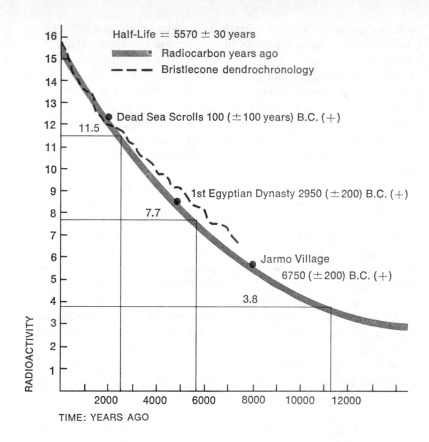

Radiocarbon Chart—The rate of disappearance of radioactivity as time passes*

*It is very important that the limitations of the radioactive carbon age determination system be kept in mind. (1) As the statistics involved in the system are used, there are two chances out of three that the "date" of a sample falls within the span of the plus-minus tolerance expressed in the full determination. For example, 6750 ± 200 B.C. means there are only two chances in three that the real "date" fell between 6950 and 6550 B.C. (2) The "best now obtainable" value of the half life of C14 is 5730 ± 40 yrs. Nevertheless, so many determinations have already been issued in the "old" or Libby value that there is agreement among the laboratories that the 5570 ± 30 yr. value shall be retained. Some archeologists have ignored this agreement, and quote their "dates" in 5730 ± 40 yr. half-life terms. This naturally causes confusion. (3) There is increasing evidence that the natural production of radioactive carbon in the earth's atmosphere (by cosmic rays) has not been constant, as was first assumed. This means that a determination is really given in terms of *radiocarbon years ago,* and that these are *not* necessarily equivalent to true calendar years ago. The black dashed line in the chart above indicates that dendrochronological ages (indicated by tree rings of bristlecone pine) are actually older than ages in radiocarbon years, as we go back in time. We assume that the dendrochronological years are equivalent to true calendar years. Thus, beyond about 2000 years ago, radiocarbon determinations (and radiocarbon years) are short or later than calendar (dendrochronological) years. Unfortunately, the dendrochronology only goes back about 7000 years, so that we cannot recalibrate our radiocarbon age determinations earlier than that. See also the note on page 86. Corrections for the possible contamination of samples *in situ* remains a problem. Hence any single radioactive age determination is not really a "date" in a true time sense. A group of consistent determinations from several sites for a given type of archeological material is more impressive.

4

who found them gave them queer names, such as "thunderbolts." The people thought the strange stones came to earth as bolts of lightning. We know now that these strange stones were prehistoric stone tools.

Many important finds still come to us by accident. In 1935, a British dentist, A. T. Marston, found the first of two fragments of a very important fossil human skull in a gravel pit at Swanscombe, on the River Thames, England. He had to wait nine months, until the face of the gravel pit had been dug eight yards farther back, before the second fragment appeared. They fitted! Then, twenty years later, still another piece appeared. In 1928, workmen who were blasting out rock for the breakwater in the port of Haifa began to notice flint tools. Thus the story of cave-dwellers on Mount Carmel, in Palestine, began to be known.

Planned archeological digging is only about a century old. Even before this, however, a few realized the significance of objects they dug from the ground; one of these early archeologists was our own Thomas Jefferson. An early digger of mounds was a German grocer's clerk, Heinrich Schliemann. Schliemann made a fortune as a merchant, first in Europe and then in the California gold rush of 1849. He became an American citizen. Then he retired and had both money and time to test an old idea of his. He believed that the heroes of ancient Troy and Mycenae were once real Trojans and Greeks. He proved it by going to Turkey and Greece and digging up the mounds that contained the remains of both cities.

Schliemann had the great good fortune to find rich and spectacular treasures, and he also had the common sense to keep notes and make descriptions of what he found. He proved beyond doubt that many ancient city mounds can be *stratified*. This means that there may be the remains of many towns in a mound, one above another, like layers in a cake. (The only trouble with that analogy—as I can tell you from well-learned experience—is that the layers in the mounds aren't always horizontal, while the cake layers usually are!)

You might like to have an idea of how mounds come to be in layers. The original settlers may have chosen the spot because it had a good spring and there were good fertile lands nearby, or perhaps because it was close to some road or river or harbor. These settlers probably built their town of stone and—in many parts of the world—of *sun-dried mud-brick*. Finally, something would have happened to the town—a flood, or a burning, or a raid by enemies—and the walls of the houses would have fallen in or the sun-dried bricks would have melted down as mud in the rain. Nothing would have remained but the mud and debris of a low mound of *one* layer.

The second settlers would have wanted the spot for the same reasons the first settlers did—good water, land, and roads. Also, the second settlers would have found a nice low mound to build their houses on, a protection from floods. But again, something would finally have happened to the second town, and the walls of *its* houses would have come tumbling down. This would make the *second* layer. And so on.

In Syria I once had the good fortune to dig on a large mound that had no less than fifteen layers. Also, most of the layers were thick, and there were signs of rebuilding and repairs within each layer. The mound was more than a hundred feet high. In each layer, the building material used had been a soft, unbaked mud-brick, and most of the debris consisted of fallen or rain-melted mud from these mud-bricks.

This idea of *stratification* was already a familiar one to the geologists by Schliemann's time. They could show that their lowest layer of rock was oldest or earliest, and that the overlying layers became more recent as one moved upward. Schliemann's digging proved the same thing at Troy. His first (lowest and earliest) city had at least nine layers above it; he thought that the second layer contained the remains of Homer's Troy. We now know that Homeric Troy was layer VIIa from the bottom; also, we count eleven layers or sublayers in total.

Schliemann's work marks the beginnings of modern archeology in southwestern Asia. Scholars soon set out to dig on ancient sites from Egypt to Central America.

Archeological Information

As time went on, the study of archeological materials—found either by accident or by digging on purpose—began to show certain things. Archeologists began to get ideas as to the kinds of objects that belonged together. If you compared a mail-order catalogue of 1890 with one of today, you would see a lot of differences. If you really studied the two catalogues hard, you would also begin to see that certain objects "go together." Horseshoes and metal buggy tires and pieces of harness would begin to fit into a picture with certain kinds of coal stoves and furniture and china dishes and kerosene lamps. Our friend the spark plug, and radios, and electric refrigerators, and light bulbs would fit into a picture with different kinds of furniture and dishes and tools. You aren't old enough to remember the kind of hats that women wore in 1890, but you've probably seen pictures of them, and you know very well they couldn't be worn today.

This is one of the ways that archeologists begin the study of their materials. The various tools and weapons and jewelry, the pottery, the kinds of houses, and even the ways of burying the dead tend to fit into a picture. Some archeologists call all of the things that go together to make such a picture an *assemblage*. The assemblage of the first layer of Schliemann's Troy was even more different from that of the seventh layer than our 1890 mail-order catalogue is from the one of today.

The archeologists who came after Schliemann began to notice other things and to compare them with occurrences in modern times. The idea that people will buy better mousetraps goes back into very ancient times. Today, if we make good automobiles or radios, we can sell some of them in Siam or even in Timbuktu. This means that some present-day types of American automobiles and radios form part of present-day "assemblages" in both Siam and Timbuktu. The total present-day "assemblage" of Siam (especially the rural parts) is quite different from that of Timbuktu or that of America, but they have at least some automobiles and some radios in common.

Now these automobiles and radios will eventually wear out. Let us suppose we could go to some remote part of Siam or to Timbuktu in a dream. We don't know what the date is in our dream, but we see all sorts of strange things and ways of living in both places. Nobody tells us what the date is. But suddenly we see a 1960 Ford; so we know that in our dream it has to be at least the year 1960, and only as many years after that as we could reasonably expect a Ford to keep in running order. The Ford would probably break down in twenty years' time, so the Siamese or Timbuktu "assemblage" we're seeing in our dream has to date at about A.D. 1960–1980.

Archeologists not only "date" their ancient materials in this way; they also see over what distances and between which peoples trading was done. It turns out that there was a good deal of trading in ancient times, probably all on a barter and exchange basis.

Everything Begins to Fit Together

Now we need to pull all these ideas together and see the complicated structure the archeologists can build with their materials.

Even the earliest archeologists soon found that there was a very long range of prehistoric time which would yield only very simple things. For this very long early part of prehistory, there was little to be found but the flint tools which wandering, hunting, and gathering people made, and the bones of the wild animals they ate. Toward the end of prehistoric time there was an increasing tendency toward settling down—even more so with the coming of agriculture—and all sorts of new things began to be made. Archeologists soon got a general notion of what ought to appear with what. Thus, it would upset a French prehistorian digging at the bottom of a very early cave if he found a fine bronze sword, just as much as it would upset him if he found a beer bottle. The people of his very early cave layer simply could not have made bronze swords, which came later, just as did beer bottles. Some accidental disturbance of the layers of his cave must have happened.

With any luck, archeologists do their digging in a layered, stratified site. They find the remains of everything that would last through time, in several different layers. They know that the assemblage in the bottom layer was laid down earlier than the assemblage in the next layer above, and so on up to the topmost layer, which is the latest. They look at the results of other "digs" and find that some other archeologist 200 miles away has found ax-heads in his lowest layer exactly like the ax-heads of their fifth layer. This means that their fifth layer must have been lived in at about the same time as was the first layer in the site 200 miles away. It also may mean that the people who lived in the two layers knew and traded with each other. Or it could mean that they didn't necessarily know each other, but simply that both traded with a third group at about the same time.

You can see that the more we dig and find, the more clearly the main facts begin to stand out. We begin to be more sure of which peoples lived at the same time, which earlier and which later. We begin to know who traded with whom, and which peoples seemed to live off by themselves. We begin to find enough skeletons in burials so that the physical anthropologists can tell us what the people looked like. We get animal bones, and a paleontologist may tell us they are all bones of wild animals; or he may tell us that some or most of the bones are those of domesticated animals, for instance, sheep or cattle, and therefore the people must have kept herds.

So far, so good, as these kinds of evidence come to hand. In the jargon, we've been establishing the "time-space systematics" of the general region of our concern. As archeologists, we cannot ignore this step; we must know where we are, so to speak, and how various parts of our evidence are interrelated in both time and space. Once we have this time-space systematics level of study reasonably blocked out, however, we can then turn to the how and why questions, the so-called processual studies. Here we become concerned with such things as the subtle hints our evidence gives of man-nature relationships, of how these change with time and with possibly changing environments and developing technologies, types of settlements, and population changes. More important than anything else—as our structure grows more complicated and our materials increase—is the fact that "a sort of history of human activity" does begin to appear.

We must do all this without one word of written history to aid us. Everything we are concerned with goes back to the time *before* people learned to write. That is the prehistorian's job—to find out what happened before written history began.

2
The changing world in which our prehistoric ancestors lived

Humans, or at least human-like beings, have been around, we'll say, at least three million years. The potassium-argon age determinations we spoke of earlier suggest a figure for still earlier sub-human-like fossils of around five million years. But, since we still have to face the problem of when we shall speak of fully identifiable men and women, let us take the three million years as a good round figure to work with. It is very hard to understand how long a time three million years really is. If we were to compare three million years to one day, we'd get something like this: The present time is midnight, and Haus was born just fifty-seven seconds ago. Earliest written history began about two minutes, twenty seconds ago. Everything before 11:57 P.M. was in prehistoric time.

Or maybe we can grasp the length of time better in terms of generations. As you know, primitive peoples tend to marry and have children rather early in life. So suppose we say that twenty years will make an average generation. At this rate there would be 150,000 generations in three million years. But our United States is just approaching ten generations of age, twenty-five generations take us back before the time of Columbus, Julius Caesar was alive just 100 generations ago, David was king of Israel less than 150 generations ago, 250 generations take us back to the beginning of written history. And there were 149,750 generations before written history began. You are around 150,000 generations removed from your australopithecine ancestors.

Changes in Environment

The earth probably hasn't changed much in the last 5,000 years (250 generations). Men and women have built things on its surface and dug into it and drawn boundaries on maps of it, but the places where rivers, lakes, seas, and mountains now stand changed little until very recently, when large-scale tampering with bulldozers began. That tampering has been widespread, however, so that most of the changes that have occurred within the last 5,000 years have probably depended as much on human activities as upon nature.

In earlier times the earth looked very different. Geologists call the last great geological period the *Pleistocene*. According to the latest results of the potassium-argon age determination method, the Pleistocene began somewhat over three million years ago. It was a time of great fluctuation and change in climates, land forms, and environments. Sometimes we call it the Ice Age, for in the Pleistocene there were at least three or four times when large areas of earth were covered with glaciers. The reason for my uncertainty is that, while there seem to have been four major mountain or alpine phases of glaciation, there have been only three general continental phases in the Old World. Even if there were four continental phases, correlation of these with the alpine phases has been very difficult.*

Glaciers are great sheets of ice, sometimes over a thousand feet thick, which are now known only in Greenland and Antarctica and in high mountains. During several of the glacial periods in the Ice Age, the glaciers covered most of Canada and the northern United States and reached down into England and northern Germany in Europe. Smaller ice sheets sat like caps on the Rockies, the Alps, and the Himalayas. Save for the Antarctic, however, Pleistocene continental glaciation happened only north of the equator, so remember that "Ice Age" is only half true.

As you know, the amount of water on and about the earth does not vary. These large glaciers contained millions of tons of water frozen into ice. Because so much water was frozen and contained in the glaciers, the water level of lakes and oceans was lowered. Flooded areas were drained and appeared as dry land. There were times in the Ice Age when there was no English Channel, so that England was not an island, and a land bridge at the Dardanelles probably divided the Mediterranean from the Black Sea.

*This is a very complicated affair, also one on which not all authorities are in agreement. I follow the scheme now used by my colleague Karl Butzer. Details may be noted in his book, *Environment and Archaeology*. The chart on p. 12 suggests something of the complications involved. For some time it has been known that the alpine glaciations (e.g., Würm, Riss, etc.) were paired or double-phased affairs. It seems clear that for the earlier ranges of the Pleistocene, the safest thing is to refer to them as the *basal, lower,* and *middle Pleistocene*.

GENERAL TERMS		NORTHERN EUROPEAN TERMS	ALPINE TERMS	APPROX. TIME
POST-GLACIAL OR HOLOCENE				— 10,000
PLEISTOCENE	UPPER	WEICHSEL	WÜRM	
				— 75,000
		Last Interglacial		— 125,000
	MIDDLE	WARTHE	RISS	
		?	?	— 200,000
		SAALE	(MINDEL ?)	— 265,000
		Great Interglacial		
	LOWER	ELSTER	(MINDEL ?)	— 430,000
		?	(GÜNZ ?)	— 800,000
		"Cromerian" Interglacial		— 1,000,000
	BASAL	EARLIER	(GÜNZ ?)	
		Villafranchian		— 3,000,000

The Pleistocene Succession

INDICATING NAMES OF GLACIATIONS AND EARLIEST (VILLAFRANCHIAN) FOSSIL ANIMALS.

A very important thing for people living during the time of a glaciation was the region adjacent to the glacier. They could not, of course, live on the ice itself. The questions would be how close could they live to it, and how would they have had to change their way of life to do so.

Glaciers Change the Weather

Great sheets of ice change the weather. When the front of a glacier stood at Milwaukee, the weather must have been bitterly cold in Chicago. The climate of the whole world would have been different, and you can see how animals and people would have been forced to move from one place to another in search of food and warmth.

On the other hand, it looks as if only slightly over half of the whole Ice Age was really taken up by times of glaciation. In between came the *interglacial* periods. During these times the climate around Chicago was as warm as it is now, and sometimes even warmer. As the ice sheets melted during the interglacial phases, the levels of the seas and of lakes rose. The geologists can identify the now dry beaches of much higher Pleistocene sea and lake levels. It may interest you to know that the last great glacier melted away less than 10,000 years ago. Some geologists think we may be living in an interglacial period and that the Ice Age may not be over yet. So if you want to make a killing in real estate for your several hundred times great-grandchildren, you might buy some land in the Arizona desert or the Sahara.

We do not yet know just why the glaciers appeared and disappeared. It surely had something to do with an increase in rainfall and snowfall and a fall in temperature. It probably also had to do with a general tendency for the land to rise at the beginning of the Pleistocene. We know there was some mountain building at that time. Hence, rain-bearing winds nourished the rising and cooler uplands with snow. An increase in all three of these factors—if they came together—would have needed to be only slight. But exactly why this happened we do not know.

The reason I tell you about the glacial and interglacial phases of the Pleistocene is so that I may emphasize for you the changing world in which prehistoric people lived. Their surroundings—the animals and plants they used for food, and the weather they had to protect themselves from—were always changing. On the other hand, this change happened over so long a period of time and was so slow that individual people could not have noticed it. Glaciers, about which they probably knew nothing, moved in hundreds of miles to the north of them. The people must simply have wandered ever more southward in search of the plants and animals on which they lived. Or some may have stayed where they were and learned to hunt different animals and eat different foods. Prehistoric men and women had to keep adapting themselves to new environments and those who were most adaptive were most successful.

The truly unique thing about humans is that gradually, throughout their long prehistory, their adaptations to environments—and to environmental changes—have been accomplished by the tools that they have made and by the ways in which they have acted as social groups. What we call *cultural evolution* has gradually replaced *biological evolution* as the distinguishing characteristic of humans throughout the long range of their prehistory.

Other Changes

Changes did, of course, take place in the people themselves as well as in the ways they lived. The major biological changes seem to have taken place during the earlier parts of the Pleistocene, however. As time went on, we find the traces of the better tools and weapons people were making. Then, too, we begin to find signs of how they started thinking of things other than food and the tools to get it with. We find that they painted on the walls of caves, and decorated their tools; we find that they buried their dead.

At about the time when the last great glacier was finally melting away in the more northern regions, people in the Near East began making a basic change in human economy. They began to plant grain, and they learned to raise and herd certain animals. This meant that they could store food in granaries and "on the hoof" against the bad times of the year. This first really basic change in mankind's way of living has been called the *food-producing revolution*. In the New World (Mesoamerica) the same great discovery was being made, independently, on the basis of a quite different set of food plants, and without animals. Stirrings in the same direction seem to have been beginning in south and east Asia and in Africa. By the time these changes happened a modern kind of climate was beginning, but it does not appear to most authorities that climatic change determined the event itself in the Near East or in Mesoamerica. People had already grown to look completely as they do now. Know-how in ways of living had developed and progressed, slowly but surely, up to a point. It was impossible for people to go beyond that point if they only hunted and fished and gathered wild foods. Once the basic change was made—once the food-producing revolution became effective—technology leaped ahead and civilization and written history followed after a relatively *very* short time (say 5,000 years), considering prehistory's enormously long prelude.

As with almost all else I shall tell you in this book, remember that new evidence keeps making us change the picture we draw. I said earlier that *most* authorities reject climatic and environmental change as determining factors in bringing about the appearance of food production. Recently, however, Professor Herbert E. Wright, long one of my old field companions, began scouting the idea again on the basis of new evidence. We'll say more of this later.

3
Prehistoric humans themselves

Both my readers and I are particularly fortunate that my colleague and old friend Professor Sherwood L. Washburn has provided us with a new preface to this chapter:

Knowledge of human evolution is progressing rapidly. Because of the importance of Darwin's theory and the controversies over it, people often get the impression that the issues have remained much the same over many years. But since the first edition of this book, the number of fossil humans has more than doubled! Twenty years ago the ages of the fossil-bearing rocks were based on the opinions of geologists. Informed opinions, but still human opinions. Now there are methods of determining the age based on declining radioactivity of certain rocks. The ages are far greater than previously thought. Only a few years ago experts debated the relation of humans to apes and monkeys. But recently new techniques have made it possible to directly compare the genetic base (DNA) of the various creatures. Just as Darwin and Huxley thought, the African apes (chimpanzees and gorillas) are our closest living relatives. The difference is not in the conclusion, but in the methods. Today the differences are measured in laboratories in ways which are quite independent of the opinions of the people making the tests. And these methods will surely be improved, making the measurement of genetic distances easier and more accurate. Even as I write, the newspapers have announced a new find of human limb bones more than three million years old, and more human skulls have been found east of Lake Rudolf in Africa. We must think of the evidences for human evolution as rapidly increasing, and a brief chapter such as this needs revision almost as soon as it is written. But while the experts are worrying, and possibly disagreeing, over the precise time of separation of humans and apes, over the number of kinds of very early humans; or over the causes of human evolution, we must remember that the most fundamental points have not changed. All the evidence shows that humans evolved from very different kinds of creatures. All the evidence shows that human evolution did take place, and the new techniques are determining dates and measuring genetic distances in a way that very recently no one even dreamed would be possible. Since the first edition of this book we have entered the era of molecular biology, radiometric dating, and continental drift. The basis for understanding human evolution is far more objective than even half a dozen years ago, and it is remarkable, considering the intervening technical advances, that Darwin and Huxley were so right.

Do We Know Where Humans Originated?

For a long time some scientists thought the "cradle of mankind" was in central Asia. Other scientists insisted it was in Africa, and still others said it might have been in Europe. Today we have enough information to state that it probably existed in a wide tropical belt across the Old World. Our closest living relatives, the great apes, live in the forests of tropical areas across Africa and in the Far East. It is probable that it was in these same areas that humans and apes separated; here the first *hominids* (human-like creatures) evolved as forest-fringe animals feeding in open, savannah-like spaces.

The earliest now available hominid fossils and tools have been found in Africa, in *Pliocene* (the epoch immediately preceding the Pleistocene) deposits. Sites yielding early Pleistocene tools and fossil hominids exist in south Africa (Taung, Sterkfontein, Swartkrans, Kromdraai, Makapansgat) and in east Africa (Olduvai, East Rudolf, Omo, Lothagam, Kanapoi). These sites contain tools dating back two and one half million years and fossils back five million.

We will presently speak of at least three distinctive types of early hominids which have been found at these sites: a gracile *Australopithecus*, a robust *Australopithecus*, and a type we'll tentatively call *Homo "habilis."** In the Far East, also, an *Australopithecus (Meganthropus)* has been found and dated to not less than 1.9 million years ago.

Let me say it another way. How old are the earliest traces of distinctly human-like beings we now have? Some five million years. The best available evidence now comes from Africa, but this may only be because most human paleontological work has been concentrated there.

---

*The names given to fossils do not always stick. The term *Homo habilis,* applied first to a fossil find made by the Leakeys in east Africa, has not yet been universally accepted as a name for fossils of the same general type found in other parts of Africa. Hence, I tend to put the *habilis* within quotation marks.

Humans and Apes

Many people used to get extremely upset at the ill-formed notion that "humans descended from apes." Such words were much more likely to start fights or "monkey trials" than the correct notion that all living animals, including humans, ascended or evolved from a single-celled organism which lived in the primeval seas hundreds of millions of years ago.

It is easiest to begin the discussion of the origin of humans with an understanding of the relationship of modern men and women to other living animal species. Humans are classified as primates along with the great apes, the Old World monkeys, the New World monkeys, and the prosimians because of morphological similarities such as a relatively large brain, highly developed vision, reduction of face and nose, and well-developed hands. Humans are closer to the great apes than to the other primates. At some time in the past these two (both of the superfamily *Hominoidea*) must have shared a common ancestor. Our closest living relative is the chimpanzee, as has been shown by several lines of evidence—molecular studies, anatomical studies, and primate field studies.

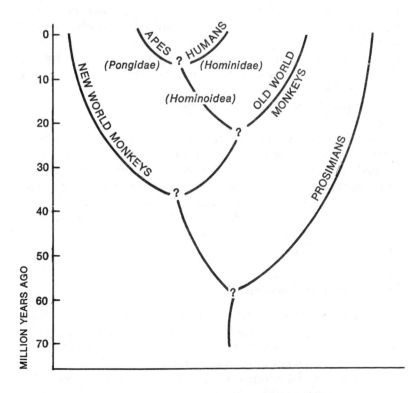

Time Sequence of the Branching of the Primate Order

Many molecular studies have been made comparing humans with chimpanzees. Studies of the genetic base—DNA—show the strands of chimpanzees and humans to be almost identical, with only a 2.5 percent difference. The blood cell hemoglobin of humans and chimpanzees is identical. Finally, immunochemical evidence indicates that chimpanzees are the primates most similar to humans, followed by gorillas, orangutans, gibbons, Old World monkeys, New World monkeys, and prosimians.

Professor Vincent Sarich, after studying immunochemical differences in albumins, has been able to establish an evolutionary clock suggesting the amount of time necessary to develop these differences. His estimates of the possible time of separation of African apes from monkeys are twenty to thirty million years. For the separation of humans and apes, he suggests six to twelve million years.

Anatomical studies of the methods of locomotion, the use of muscles, the pelvis and legs, the hands and feet, and the face all show similarities which result again in the chimpanzee being classed as the ape most like humans. Humans and apes are most alike in the trunk and arms. The shoulder region is especially similar and unique, in that no other animal can raise its arm over its head in the way a human and an ape can. The greatest differences between humans and apes are seen in the legs and pelvis, as apes do not walk upright in the way humans do, but use the knuckles of their hands as well as their feet in walking. Differences are also seen in the skull and face, with the greatest difference, of course, in the brain. The human brain, three times the size of the ape brain, makes possible speech, the development of hand skills, and greater intelligence.

Behavioral field studies of apes such as those done by Jane van Lawick-Goodall, George Schaller, and others allow comparisons to be made between humans and apes. Many similarities may be seen in social group and individual relationships. Mother-infant groups and juvenile play groups among apes are remarkably like those of humans. The use of simple tools by chimpanzees is greater than was at first believed and may give clues as to the behavior of our common ancestors.

The Family of the Hominidae

From here onward, our concern will be with beings in the hominid line, as distinct from beings in the pongid line (apes). The necessary anatomical changes that had to develop in order to progress from the common ape-human form toward distinct humans were: (1) efficient bipedal locomotion, (2) enlargement of the brain, and (3) some changes in face and teeth.

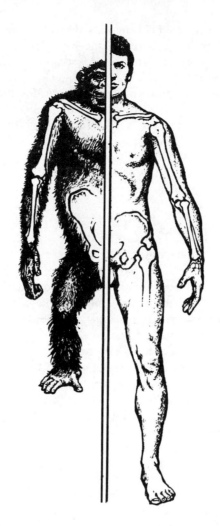

Morphological Comparison of Chimpanzees and Humans

The fossil form that is believed to represent the earliest known hominid is *Ramapithecus*. Scanty finds of this controversial ape-hominid have been dated from about fourteen million to ten million years ago. Finds have been made in western Europe, east Africa, India, and south China. Only jaw fragments have been found, but in the facial-dental complex, the fragments seem to foreshadow later hominids. Some scientists consider *Ramapithecus* an ape; others consider it to be on the direct line to *Australopithecus* and thus a hominid. The crucial period, then, in the biological evolution of humans is that from apes to humans. The time at which this bridge was crossed is controversial. In fact, there is a large gap in time, with no fossil evidence, between the *Ramapithecus* finds of ten to fourteen million years ago and the oldest australopithecines of four to five million years ago.

If one accepts the biomolecular evidence described above, humans and apes must have become separated by five million years ago; if one accepts the paleontological evidence alone, then the bridge was at least ten million years ago. More evidence is urgently needed. Professor Clark Howell speculates, from many lines of evidence, that the origin of the hominids was about ten million years ago.

Brains, Hands, and Tools

Whether all of the australopithecines were our ancestors or not, our proper ancestors must have been able to stand erect and to walk on their two feet. Four further important things probably were involved, next, before they could become humans. These are:
1. The increasing usefulness (specialization) of the thumb and hand, following upright posture.
2. The development of tools and their use in food getting.
3. The increasing size and development of the brain.
4. The development of simple language.

Nobody knows which of these is most important, or which came first. Most probably the growth of all four was very much blended together. If you think about each of the things, you will see what I mean. Unless your hand is more flexible than a paw, and your thumb will work against (or oppose) your fingers, you can't hold a tool very well. But you wouldn't get the idea of using a tool unless you had enough brain to help you see cause and effect. The increase in brain size and the internal reorganization were probably associated with basic behavioral changes. These changes probably resulted in language and tool production. And it is rather hard to see how your hand and brain would develop unless they had something to practice on—like tools. In Professor W. M. Krogman's words, "the hand must become the obedient servant of the eye and the brain." It is the *coordination* of these things that counts. With efficient bipedalism, which freed the hands for the making of tools, hunting at last became a more profitable way of life. Hunting has dominated human history, bringing about many changes in social and technical adaptations and in cooperative behavior. Less than 1 percent of hominid history has been dominated by agriculture.

Many other things must have been happening to the bodies of the creatures who were the ancestors of humans. Our ancestors had to develop speech. They had to get the idea of letting *certain sounds* have *certain meanings,* and thereby develop a sound code. The development of language was dependent on the increasing development of the brain. The anatomical requirements for making sounds and communication by sounds were already present, but the cortex of the brain had to develop in order to process the unique human "sound code."

All this must have gone very slowly. Probably everything was developing little by little, all together. Humans became humans very slowly.

When Shall We Call Humans Humans?

What do I mean when I say "humans"? People who looked pretty much as we do, and who used different tools to do different things, are humans to me. We'll probably never know whether the earliest ones talked or not. They could make sounds, but did they know how to make sounds work as symbols to carry meanings? But if the fossil bones look like our skeletons, and if we find tools which we'll agree couldn't have been made by nature or by animals, then I'd say we had traces of *humans.*

The fossil bones of the australopithecine-homo types in east and south Africa, which we shall describe shortly, are bound to come into the discussion. They are the best suggestion we have yet as to what our ancestors looked like. They were certainly closer to humans than to apes. Although their brain size was no larger than the brain size of modern apes, their body size and stature were quite small; hence, relative to their small size, their brains were large.

I ought to remind you, at this point, of the sadly fragmentary bits and pieces of fossils that are all that usually remain to us of the original beings the fossils represent. From these fragmentary fossils, the human paleontological colleagues make their reconstructions. The paleontologists must bear in mind the great variability we all can see when we think of all of the different types of our single living species, *Homo sapiens,* today. The matters of size and ruggedness of the fossil bones, as these might reflect the age and sex of the originals, are also at issue. Furthermore, any very precise method of dating—of assessing the chances for actual contemporaneity—is not available. It need not surprise us, then, that not all human paleontologists offer us the same names, classifications, and indications of the relationships of the originals. Some of our colleagues are splitters; some are lumpers. Hence don't be surprised if you find other suggestions of names and relationships than those we offer here.

The Earliest Humans We Know

The first finds of *Australopithecus* were made in south Africa in limestone quarries, the very first being at Taung in 1924 by Raymond Dart. This was a child's skull and was named *Australopithecus africanus*. Since then fragments of hundreds of individuals have been found in five south African sites. Tools have also been found in these sites which range in age from two to three million years. Two lineages or forms of *Australopithecus* exist—a small, gracile australopithecine and a larger, robust australopithecine. The pelves and vertebrae show they were bipeds and the skulls show that their brains had increased in size and that they had lost the large projecting canines. Therefore they could not be called pongid; they were hominid. They were both about five feet tall, but the robust form was more rugged, with a large lower jaw, extremely large molar teeth, and small canines. It also had much heavier markings for the muscular attachments than the gracile form.

Other important sites containing *Australopithecus*, as well as fossils of the genus *Homo*, are in the Rift Valley of east Africa. Three localities have yielded particularly valuable information on the early development of the hominid form. These are the Olduvai Gorge, the Omo Basin, and the region east of Lake Rudolf.

Olduvai Gorge, in Tanzania, which has received intensive study from the late Louis Leakey and his wife, Mary, has yielded hominids, with evidence of more than one type coexisting. There are many occupation sites at Olduvai. In 1959 the locality yielded a complete robust *Australopithecus* skull in a layer with stone tools and flakes. First called *Zinjanthropus*, it is now generally referred to as *Australopithecus boisei*, and the tools may well refer to the *Homo* type of the same time range. Many specimens have come from Olduvai, which spans a time period from two million to a half million years ago. The *Homo* type of fossil is the one generally referred to at Olduvai as *Homo "habilis."* Tools have been abundant, too.

More recently, work has been done by both Clark Howell and the French in the Omo Basin, where a continuous time span from four and a half to one and a half million years ago has been established. There have been seventy occurrences of hominid fossils found within a time range from three to one and a half million years ago, and tools have been found dating from two million years ago.

In the area east of Lake Rudolf, in Kenya, Richard Leakey and Glynn Isaac have recovered quantities of well-preserved hominids, as well as tools and other evidence of human habitation. They have found the oldest now known living site in the world—Koobi Fora—on the shores of Lake Rudolf. This site has been dated to $2.6 \pm .26$ million years ago by the potassium-argon dating method.

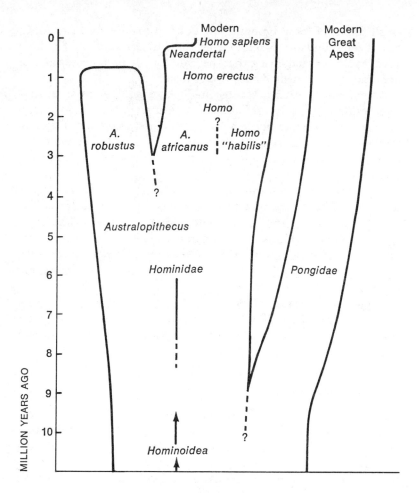

Phylogeny of Humans and the Great Apes

Both gracile and robust *Australopithecus* forms have been found at these various sites, along with that species of *Homo* which we've noted is distinct from *Australopithecus*. This last form, which dates from two million years ago, is known at present as *"Homo* sp. E. R. 1470."* The context in which it was found at Lake Rudolf is lower and older than that at the Koobi Fora living site. There is also evidence of it in the Omo Basin, and recently an older south African find has been suggested as another example of the same form. This form seems to have been larger-brained than the australopithecines, and was an efficient biped. It appeared early and was contemporaneous with the australopithecines.

In several other newly found sites in the Rift Valley system, small pieces of fossil hominid jaw bone, probably *Australopithecus*, have been found and dated to from three to five and a half million years ago, thus suggesting that the date for the first appearance of hominids will be pushed back even further.

As mentioned earlier, far distant in Java, another fossil australopithecine *(Meganthropus)* has been found from the same general time period, dating to not less than 1.9 million years ago. This find implies that this australopithecine form had an early and wide distribution—probably throughout the tropical world—by two million years ago.

We think that one form of *Australopithecus*, probably the gracile form, very likely continued to evolve and develop into *Homo* "habilis," the two perhaps being contemporaneous for a time. This *Homo* then undoubtedly developed into *Homo erectus*. The other (robust) form of *Australopithecus* became extinct. Certainly, however, the complete story of the *Australopithecus–Homo* "habilis" situation must wait until more evidence is discovered.

The australopithecine stage of human development lasted for a long time, from five million until about one and a half million years ago, when *Homo erectus* first appeared showing many advances over *Australopithecus*.

The *Homo erectus* Form

It was perhaps at this stage—say one and a half million years ago—that hominids began to develop language skills. It is probable that language came as slowly as improved tool use. Simple pebble tools were used by *Australopithecus* over long periods of time, and not until about 1.4 million years ago did hand axes and more developed and standardized types of tools begin to appear. The *Homo erectus* form was taller, had a larger brain, and a smaller face and teeth than the australopithecines. There is evidence of both tool advances and cooperative hunting. These facts point to a more complex method of communication which may well mark the period when language began to be of importance.

Fossils of *Homo erectus* have been found in Africa, Asia, and Europe, and range in time from one and a half million to a half million years ago. The first (originally called *Pithecanthropus*, now called *Homo erectus erectus)* finds were made in 1891–92 in Java by Dr. Eugene Dubois, a Dutch doctor in the colonial service. Finds have continued over the years. There are now bones enough to account for eight skulls. There are also four jaws and some teeth. Generally speaking, *Homo erectus* was about five feet six inches tall and didn't hold his head very erect. The skull was very thick and heavy, and had room for little more than two-thirds as large a brain as we have. *Homo erectus* had big teeth, a big jaw, and enormous eyebrow ridges. Later excavations in Java by von Koenigswald in 1937–38 produced two more skulls. Current work is being carried on by Tenku Jacob.

No tools were found in the geological deposits where these bones of *Homo erectus* appeared, but there are some tools in the same general area. The Java fossils have been dated at about one and a half to a half million years ago.

Peking Men and Some Early Westerners

Until the Lantian skull cap was found in 1963–64, the earliest known Chinese were those first called *Sinanthropus,* or "Peking man," because the finds were made near that city. They are now called *Homo erectus pekinesis.* In World War ii, the original bones were lost. Fortunately, there is a complete set of casts of the bones, and Chinese scholars have continued to find more bones.

The Peking people lived in a cave in a limestone hill, made tools, cracked animal bones to get the marrow out, and used fire. The cave was evidently occupied for a very long period of time from about 800,000 to 500,000 years ago. More than twelve skulls have been found and about 150 teeth, as well as complete skeletons.

The Peking people were not quite as tall as the Java people. Their skulls looked very much like the Java skulls, except that they had room for a slightly larger brain. The face was less rugged than was the Java face, but this isn't saying much.

Several jaws and pieces of skull of *Homo erectus* have been found in northwest Africa near the Mauritanian coast (Ternifine, Sidi Abderrahman, Rabat). They are dated to this same Middle Pleistocene time period. In east Africa, at Olduvai Gorge, several *Homo erectus* skulls plus a hip and thigh bone (known as "Hominid 9"), have been found. They seem to directly follow the early *Homo "habilis"* of the *Australopithecus* levels. The age of these fossils is at least 750,000 years. They were found with certain stone tools (Acheulean) which are quite distinctive from the earlier tools (Oldowan) found with *Australopithecus.* (We will return to these tools in the next chapter.)

A very large jawbone found near Heidelberg in Germany is the oldest hominid found in Europe. It resembles *Homo erectus* in that the jaw is very robust and massive, with no chin and rather small teeth. It dates from about 450,000 years ago. At the Vértesszöllös site in Hungary there have been found skull fragments with some characteristics of *Homo erectus,* along with many small tools and traces of fire. A discovery of a skull in Greece (Petralona) is consid-

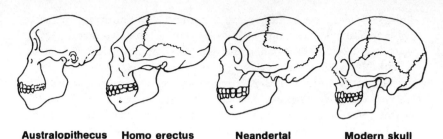

Australopithecus   Homo erectus   Neandertal   Modern skull

Human Skulls, Fossil to Modern, in Profile

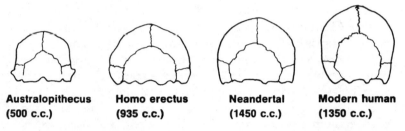

Australopithecus	Homo erectus	Neandertal	Modern human
(500 c.c.)	(935 c.c.)	(1450 c.c.)	(1350 c.c.)

Relative Sizes of Fossil to Modern Crania, Seen from Behind

ered by many to be another example of a *Homo erectus* type in Europe. Recently a new find by Henry de Lumley in a cave, La Caune de l'Arago, near Tautavel in France included a skull and several tools dating from about 200,000 years ago. The skull has the massive features and flat forehead of *Homo erectus,* but it also has some traits pointing to the next type of human fossil appearing in Europe: Neandertal.

Hence there are some traces of *Homo erectus* in Europe, but they do not compare in number to the examples we have of this human form in the Far East and in Africa. Perhaps *Homo erectus* wasn't as numerous in Europe or only existed there for a short time.

Transitional Forms

Europe has produced several skulls that seem to be intermediate; while possessing *Homo erectus* traits, they yet seem more modern. One of these is a find in Germany, at Steinheim. It consists of the fragmentary skull of a man. The bone is thick, but the back of the head is neither very low nor primitive, and the face is also not primitive. The forehead does, however, have big ridges over the eyes. The more fragmentary skull from Swanscombe in England (p. 5) has been much more carefully studied. Only the top and back of that skull have been found. Since the skull rounds up nicely, it has been assumed that the face and forehead must have been quite "modern."

It is clear that evolution continued in Europe from the Heidelberg fossil through the Swanscombe and Steinheim types to a group of pre-neandertaloids. There are traces of these pre-neandertaloids pretty much throughout Europe during the third interglacial period—say 100,000 years ago. Pre-neandertaloids have been discovered at Ehringsdorf in Germany and Saccopastore in Italy. Other fossils that also show these characteristics of both *Homo erectus* and an early form of the final step are the Montmaurin mandible, Abri Suard, Lazaret, and Fontéchevade in France. These are between 70,000 to 100,000 years old. It is thought by many that they were ancestral to the later Neandertals and show the transition from *Homo erectus* to the Neandertal form. I won't describe them for you, since they are simply less extreme than the neandertaloids proper—about halfway between the Steinheim and the classic Neandertal people.

Typical "Cave Men"

The next humans we have to talk about are all members of a related group—in the present terminology, the first of the final taxonomic group, *Homo sapiens*. The first *Homo sapiens neanderthalensis*, "Neandertal man" himself, was found in the Neander Valley, near Düsseldorf, Germany, in 1856. He was the first human fossil to be recognized as such. Some of us think that the neandertaloids proper are only those people of western Europe who didn't get out before the beginning of the last great glaciation, and who found themselves hemmed in by the glaciers in the Alps and northern Europe. Professor Howell believes that the pre-neandertaloids who happened to get caught in the pocket of the southwest corner of Europe at the onset of the last great glaciation became the classic Neandertals. Out in the Near East, Howell thinks, it is possible to see traces of people evolving from the pre-neandertaloid type toward that of fully modern humans. Certainly, we don't see such extreme cases of "neandertaloidism" outside of western Europe.

There are at least a dozen good examples in the main or classic Neandertal group in Europe. They date to just before and in the earlier part of the last great glaciation (85,000 to 40,000 years ago). Many of the finds have been made in caves. The "cave men" the movies and the cartoonists show you are probably meant to be Neandertals. I'm not at all sure they dragged their women by the hair, however; the women were probably pretty tough, too!

Neandertals had large bony heads, but plenty of room for brains. Some had brain cases even larger than the average for modern humans. Their faces were heavy, and they had eyebrow ridges of bone, but the ridges were not as big as those of any of the *Homo erectus* group. Their foreheads were very low, and they didn't have much chin. They were about five feet three inches tall, but were heavy and barrel-chested.

One important thing about the Neandertal group is that there is a fair number of them to study. Just as important is the fact that we know quite a bit about how they lived, and about some of the tools they made. The classic Neandertals were found at Spy, Engis, Gibraltar, La Ferrassie, Le Moustier, and many other sites. As we saw above, their taxonomic classification is now generally considered to be *Homo sapiens neanderthalensis* (which distinguishes them from what we've become—*Homo sapiens sapiens*).

Other People Contemporary with the Neandertals

The Neandertals seem to have been a specialization in a corner of Europe. What was going on elsewhere? We think that the pre-neandertaloid type was a generally widespread human form. Other more or less extreme, although generally related, human forms evolved from this type.

A question that always comes up is what happened to the European Neandertals? Their disappearance was very abrupt, but they were undoubtedly absorbed into the modern *Homo sapiens* population. Almost all of their morphological evidence and traits can be seen somewhere in the modern population around the Mediterranean today. By 30,000 years ago, they had been absorbed and had disappeared; modern humans had replaced the Neandertals.

Fossils of Neandertals or Neandertal-like people have been found over a wide area in Europe, Asia, and Africa. Many of them show evolutionary trends toward modern humans. Although the classic Neandertals were found only in Europe, many parts of the rest of the world had variations of this human form. In the Near East, transitional groups were found in caves in Palestine. In fact, our best suggestion of what people looked like just before they became fully modern comes from certain Palestinian caves.

The First Moderns

Professor T. D. McCown and the late Sir Arthur Keith, who studied the Mount Carmel bones, figured out that one of the two groups involved had traits that were as much as 70 percent modern. The second group—the less modern looking—didn't rate that high. There were two similar groups or varieties of humans in at least one other Palestinian cave at about the same time as the Mount Carmel finds. The time would have been about that of the onset of colder weather, when the last glaciation was beginning in the north—say 75,000 years ago.

There were several caves on Mount Carmel, but the modern group came only from the cave called Mugharet es-Skhul ("cave of the kids"). It has also been found at the Kafzeh cave, in Galilee. The other group, from several Palestinian caves, had bones of people of the type we've been calling pre-neandertaloid, which we noted were widespread in Europe and beyond. The tools which came with each of these finds were generally similar, and McCown and Keith, and other scholars since their study, have tended to assume that both the Skhul group and the pre-neandertaloid group came at exactly the same time. The conclusion was quite natural: here was a population of men and women in the act of evolving in two different directions. But the time may not be exactly the same. It is very difficult to be precise, within 10,000 years, for a time some 75,000 years ago.

Southwestern Asia is an area of interest to those concerned with where early modern humans first developed. The more modern Skhul and Kafzeh finds contrast with those of the Tabun and other Palestinian finds, and an important new group from Shanidar in Kurdistan. The latter are of a more generalized neandertaloid type.

In Africa, many neandertaloid fossils have been found. In the north, in Morocco at Jebel Irhoud and Haua Fteah, they date to about 40,000 years ago. In south Africa, "Rhodesian man" shows variations of Neandertal traits. In east Africa, Neandertal-like fossils have been found along the Omo.

In south China a Neandertal-like fossil has been found at Mapa. Neandertals have been found in Java, evidenced by eleven skulls of the so-called Solo type, but these also have characteristics of *Homo erectus*.

Soon after the first extremely cold phase of the last glaciation, we begin to get a number of bones of completely modern men and women in Europe. We also get great numbers of the tools they made, and their living places in caves. Completely modern skeletons begin turning up in caves dating back to about 40,000 years ago, the beginning of the second phase of the last glaciation. These skeletons belonged to people no different from many people we see today. Like people today, not everybody looked alike.

Differences in the Early Moderns

The main early European moderns have been divided into two groups, the Cro-Magnon group and the Combe Capelle-Brünn group. Cro-Magnon people were tall and big-boned, with large, long, and rugged heads. They must have been built like many present-day Scandinavians. The Combe Capelle-Brünn people were shorter; they had narrow heads and faces, and big eyebrow ridges. Of course we don't find the skin or hair of these people. But there is little doubt they were of the type generally called Caucasoid.

Variations in modern humans are seen all over the world today and probably existed as local differences in the past. From a place called Wadjak, in Java, we have "proto-Australoid" skulls which closely resemble those of modern Australian natives. Some of the skulls found in south Africa, especially the Boskop skull, look like those of modern Bushmen, but are much bigger. The ancestors of the Bushmen seem to have once been very widespread south of the Sahara Desert. On the basis of evidence available at the moment, the authorities tend to agree that African Negroes were forest people who apparently expanded out of the westcentral African area only in the last several thousand years. The Mongoloids would seem to have been present by the time of the "Upper Cave" at Choukoutien, the *Sinanthropus* find-spot, but well after Peking man.

Modern men and women had already superseded the Neandertals when the New World was populated. The first people into the New World across the Bering Strait were similar to the already modern people in east Asia. Several waves of people migrated into America, intermingled, and spread south into both continents. American Indians are all descendants from these early *Homo sapiens sapiens* types.

What the Differences Mean

What do all these differences mean? They mean that, at one moment in time, within each different area, people tended to look somewhat alike. From area to area, they tended to look somewhat different, just as they do today. People became accustomed to life in some particular area within a continent (we might call it a "natural area"). As they went on living there, they evolved toward some particular physical variety. It would, of course, have been difficult

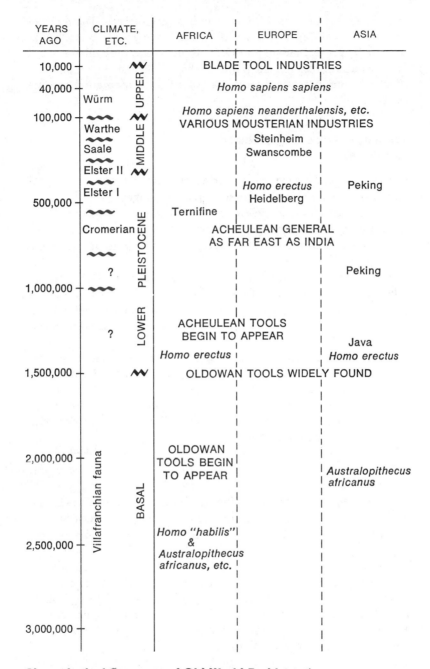

YEARS AGO	CLIMATE, ETC.		AFRICA	EUROPE	ASIA
10,000	〰	UPPER	BLADE TOOL INDUSTRIES		
40,000	Würm	UPPER	*Homo sapiens sapiens*		
100,000	〰 Warthe 〰 Saale 〰 Elster II 〰 Elster I 〰 Cromerian 〰 ? 〰	MIDDLE	*Homo sapiens neanderthalensis, etc.* VARIOUS MOUSTERIAN INDUSTRIES	Steinheim Swanscombe	
500,000		PLEISTOCENE	Ternifine ACHEULEAN GENERAL AS FAR EAST AS INDIA	*Homo erectus* Heidelberg	Peking
1,000,000					Peking
	?	LOWER	ACHEULEAN TOOLS BEGIN TO APPEAR *Homo erectus*		Java *Homo erectus*
1,500,000	〰		OLDOWAN TOOLS WIDELY FOUND		
2,000,000	Villafranchian fauna	BASAL	OLDOWAN TOOLS BEGIN TO APPEAR		*Australopithecus africanus*
2,500,000			*Homo "habilis"* & *Australopithecus africanus, etc.*		
3,000,000					

Chronological Summary of Old World Prehistory*

*In the column for climate, the glacials are given following Butzer (1971, Table 2), in mid-latitude European terms. 〰 indicates warmer interglacials. 𝗪 suggests that we cannot specify an exact moment of transition, as from the Lower to the Middle Pleistocene. The time scale is gradually compressed. Actually, *Australopithecus* fossils go back 5 million years and *Ramapithecus* more than 10 million.

to draw a clear boundary between two adjacent areas. The number of environmental niches to which humans are able to adapt is exceptionally great; humans continued to evolve as they filled each of the various niches. A neat point, however, is that their ability to adapt became increasingly a matter of cultural adaptation as time went on.

Summary of Present Knowledge of Fossil Humans

At this moment, the evidence bearing on human evolution (as presented above) appears to subdivide into four stages:

1. An australopithecine-*Homo* stage is the first, dating back to five million years ago, with several varieties of fossil hominids and with crude stone tools associated with at least some of them.
2. An early human *(Homo erectus)* stage followed, beginning at least with the Java, Olduvai, and Peking fossils perhaps a million years ago, and lasting down through the Heidelberg, Ternifine, and Vértesszöllös finds. This stage lasted to about 100,000 years ago.
3. Thereafter came first the transitional types such as Swanscombe, Steinheim, and Fontéchevade; then the Neandertals and their less extreme contemporaries.
4. Beginning about 40,000 years ago came the first traces of fully modern skeletons in Europe. The present tendency is to lump this entire stage under the term *Homo sapiens.*

Of course, the third or *transitional* stage noted here might be split between the second and the fourth. Thus we refer to *Homo sapiens neanderthalensis.*

There seems to be an increasing likelihood that the beings of the first stage will be accepted as "humans." There is no question that we are dealing with tool-making humans by the middle of this stage.

You will note a quickening of pace as the stages develop. People were learning ever better ways to adjust to the variety and to the changes in their environment. The fossil bones of their bodies show these adjustments, but the pace of the change is also amply demonstrated by the tools they made. That is the part of the story which the prehistoric archeologist must tell.

4
Cultural beginnings

Humans, unlike the lower animals, are made up of much more than flesh and blood and bones, for human beings have *culture*.

What Is Culture?

"Culture" is a word with many meanings. Doctors speak of making a "culture" of a certain kind of bacteria, and ants are said to have a "culture." Then there is the Emily Post kind of "culture"—you say a person is "cultured," or he isn't, depending on such things as whether or not he eats peas with his knife.

Anthropologists use the word, too, and argue heatedly over its finer meanings; but they all agree that every human being is part of or has some kind of culture. Since each particular human group has a particular culture, this is one of the ways in which we can tell one group of people from another. In this sense, a *culture* means the way the members of a group of people think and believe and live, the tools they make, and the way they do things. Professor Robert Redfield said that a culture is an organized or formalized body of conventional understandings. "Conventional understandings" means the whole set of rules, beliefs, and standards which a group of people lives by. These understandings show themselves in art, and in the other things a people may make and do. The understandings continue to last, through tradition, from one generation to another. They are what really characterize different human groups.

Some Characteristics of Culture

A culture lasts, although individual men and women in the group die off. On the other hand, a culture changes as the different conventions and understandings change. You could almost say that a culture lives in the minds of the people who have it. But people are not born with it; they get it as they grow up. Suppose a day-old Hungarian baby is adopted by a family in Oshkosh, Wisconsin, and the child is not told that he is Hungarian. He will grow up with no more idea of Hungarian culture than anyone else in Oshkosh.

So when I speak of ancient Egyptian culture, I mean the whole body of understandings and beliefs and knowledge possessed by the ancient Egyptians. I mean their beliefs as to why grain grew, as well as their ability to make tools with which to reap the grain. I mean their beliefs about life after death. What I am thinking about as culture is a thing which lasted in time. If any one Egyptian, even the Pharaoh, died, it didn't affect the Egyptian culture of that particular moment.

Prehistoric Cultures

For that long period of human history that is all prehistory, we have no written descriptions of cultures. We find only the tools people made, the places where they lived, the graves in which they buried their dead. Fortunately for us, these tools and living places and graves all tell us something about the ways the people lived and the things they believed. But the story we learn of the very early cultures must be only a very small part of the whole, for we find so few things. The rest of the story is gone forever. We have to make do with what we can find—with what these things can be made to tell us directly about themselves, and with what we can make them tell us indirectly about things we have not found.

Until very recently, we knew very little about the actual dwelling places of very early prehistoric people. Although there were some important exceptions, like the fallen-in cave in China where Peking man was found, very few of the cave dwelling sites or open-air dwelling sites known to archeologists could be dated to the long span of time before the last (Würm) glaciation. In the past decade or so, new ideas of what is important and new techniques of excavation have given us exciting new information from very early dwelling sites in Africa, Europe, and Asia. Some of the sites are caves and some of them are not, and we shall be talking about some examples later on.

A Special Note About Caves

Caves have been one of several possible kinds of dwelling places for humans since very early times. In places such as southwestern France, hotels, museums, houses, and barns are still built partly or completely within caves. Certainly, though, caves were more important in prehistoric times, when many generations of people lived in them.

Partly as a result of human occupation, many caves have deep layers of debris. The first people moved in and lived on the rock floor. They threw on the floor whatever they didn't want, and they tracked in mud; people seldom bothered to clean house in those days (although sometimes they did, as archeologists have discovered). Their debris—junk and mud and garbage and what not—became packed into a layer. But such an accumulation of junk is not the only reason why caves have deep layers of debris. The layers are composed for the most part of rock debris (clay, sand, gravel, large rocks, etc.) that fell from the roof and walls of the cave as a result of the destructive action of nature over time. As these weathering processes gradually attacked and wore away the rock forming the cave, the loosened fragments fell to the floor. All this happened whether people were living in the cave or not. When people *were* living there, their garbage and other debris became mixed with and incorporated within the natural debris, and an archeological level was created.

As time went on, and generations passed, the layer grew thicker. Then there might have been a break in the occupation of the cave for a while. Perhaps the game animals got scarce and the people moved away, or maybe the cave became flooded. Later on, other people moved in and began making a new archeological level of their own by once again contributing their refuse to the geological debris. Perhaps this process of layering went on in the same cave for a hundred thousand years. You can see what happened. The drawing on page 36 shows a section through such a cave. The earliest layer is on the bottom, the latest one on top. They go in order from bottom to top, earliest to latest. This is the *stratification* we talked about (pp. 5–6).

Although the archeological record provided by the layers of a stratified succession sometimes gets somewhat mixed up (by natural forces or by the activities of the early people themselves), it is usually an accurate source of information for the archeologist. The animal bones and shells, the fireplaces, the bones of men and women, and the tools they made all belong together if they come from one layer. We can get an idea of which things belong together and which lot came earliest and which latest. As a rule, the open-

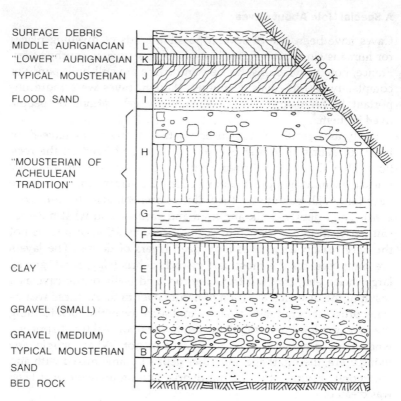

SURFACE DEBRIS		
MIDDLE AURIGNACIAN	L	
"LOWER" AURIGNACIAN	K	
TYPICAL MOUSTERIAN	J	
FLOOD SAND	I	
"MOUSTERIAN OF ACHEULEAN TRADITION"	H	
	G	
	F	
CLAY	E	
GRAVEL (SMALL)	D	
GRAVEL (MEDIUM)	C	
TYPICAL MOUSTERIAN	B	
SAND	A	
BED ROCK		

Section of Shelter on Lower Terrace, Le Moustier

air occupation sites do not have such long successions of layers, with their traces of development and change.

In most cases, prehistoric people lived only in the mouths of caves. They didn't like to live in the dark inner chambers, preferring rock shelters at the bases of overhanging cliffs if there was enough overhang to give shelter. When the weather was good, they no doubt lived in the open air as well. I'll go on using the term "cave" since it's more familiar, but remember that I really mean a rock shelter when I'm talking about where people actually lived.

Why So Little Has Lasted from Early Times

Although we know much more about very early dwelling places than we used to, many of the early stone tools that archeologists study have not been found exactly as the prehistoric people left them. The forces of nature rearranged the objects left on the surface of a dwelling area when, for one reason or another, the pre-historic inhabitants abandoned the site and moved away. Natural disturbance was particularly severe in Europe and other northern areas that were subject to glaciation and other effects of severe climate during the Pleistocene. Some habitation sites suffered the drastic fate of being overridden by glacial ice. The front of this enormous sheet of ice moved down over the country, crushing and breaking and plowing up everything, like a giant bulldozer. Among the things so moved or crushed or actually caught up and incorporated into the glacial ice would have been, of course, all the different tools, broken or whole, left on the original floor of the habitation site, as well as tent or shelter foundations, tent weights, graves, traces of fire, and everything else. When the glacial ice finally melted and dropped this load, we think of the result as a *secondary redeposition;* the objects found there are from disturbed or secondary contexts. We'll be returning to the matter of context very often.

A less spectacular but equally devastating disturbance that affected many sites (probably more than were overridden by glaciers) was the very slow downhill movement of newly thawed and mucky soil on a hill slope. This kind of soil flow, called *solifluction,* could take place in regions with severe climates hundreds of miles from glacial ice. If an ancient archeological site were located on a slope (even a slight one) affected by solifluction, all the tools, bones, traces of fire, and so forth would have been jumbled together and moved to the bottom of the slope in a more or less homogenized chaos. This mess might then eventually have been carried away by a stream into the valley bottom. Many early sites must have been destroyed by this process of secondary redeposition.

There were other ways, even in regions with less severe climates, in which natural forces could destroy the sites of early humans. Even a slight shift in the course of a river could cause the caving in and washing away of parts of the bank, including whatever dwelling places might have been located upon or under it. Erosion by the sea against a coastline might have done the same thing. Or the water level of the ocean or lakes might have risen, first disturbing by wave action and then flooding dwelling sites. Wind erosion could have been another destructive agent. Even the shallow caves or rock shelters in which early people often lived were not immune from natural disturbance; in many rock shelters, geologists have found evidence of erosional episodes during which some of the cave sediments and the man-made debris and tools included in them had been carried out of the shelter, usually by water action, and dispersed.

We have been talking so far about the disturbance of archeological sites by natural forces, but not all the stone tools, bones, and other objects so disturbed disappeared from view forever. Some did, of course—they were ground into tiny unrecognizable fragments, washed out to sea by a river, or carried into the sea by glacial ice, dropping to the bottom when the iceberg melted. But many of the early tools and bones were not moved so far away, especially if the disturbing agent was a river or solifluction or some combination of the two. Rather, archeologists have been able to find dense concentrations of objects incorporated in river gravels (presumably some hundreds of yards or even a few miles downstream from where the tools were originally washed into the river), or within the now stabilized solifluction debris at the bottom of slopes. These concentrations are regarded as archeological sites, even though they are in secondary context—the disturbed and mixed remnants of one or several sites that were originally in primary context upslope or upstream.

Although rich collections of stone tools can often be made from sites of such secondary context or redeposition, they are clearly not very satisfactory to the archeologist for cultural interpretation. It is unlikely that all the things, especially the small objects, that were present in the original primary context would be present in the secondary context. Furthermore, the stone tools were often damaged in transport, sometimes so severely that identification becomes difficult. Finally, there is no way of knowing which objects really belong together (many sites of different ages and cultures may have contributed tools to one river gravel). Thus we cannot tell in what relative order the tools were made and used, or what spatial relationships the tools originally had to huts, fireplaces, and other structures of the dwelling area.

In the past decade or so, archeologists have been finding and excavating more and more early sites with primary context—the undisturbed occupation floors at dwelling sites and at smaller special-purpose sites such as those where early humans killed and butchered game animals. Such sites provide much more information about life in earliest times, and they have begun to clear up some of the uncertainties and confusions that arose when archeologists had to deal mainly with collections of stone tools found in secondary contexts.

The Beginning of the Archeological Record

To a limited extent, the *use* of tools is almost certainly part of the primate heritage, and, if one is willing to define the matter rather generously, so is the manufacture of tools. Our closest living non-human relative is the chimpanzee. Dr. Jane van Lawick-Goodall's studies of wild chimpanzees show that occasionally they throw sticks and stones at other animals to intimidate them or drive them off. They also occasionally use sticks as clubs. Sometimes chimpanzees modify simple natural objects and use these to aid in some specific task. The best-known example of such an activity, which can be considered the manufacture and use of a tool, is "fishing" for termites by means of carefully modified twigs or grass blades. It is probable that long ago, before the beginning of the Pleistocene, the now extinct common ancestor of humans and the living apes engaged in the manufacture of simple tools also. What we do *not* find among the living non-human primates is the *regular and patterned manufacture of stone tools.* The meager evidence we have suggests that stone tool manufacture by primates began only within the human family, perhaps as late as about three million years ago. It is with the appearance of stone tools, which became so important for early cultures, that the record of *archeology* really begins.

The Road to Standardization

Reasoning from what we know or can easily imagine, there were probably three major steps in the prehistory of stone tool making. The first step would have been simple *utilization* of what was at hand. This step, as we have said, was probably taken long ago by the common ancestors of apes and humans, but the evidence for this is virtually nonexistent. A battered pebble found with the bones of *Kenyapithecus* at Fort Ternan in Kenya may be the result of such utilization, but this is not certain. *Kenyapithecus,* a fossil of the *Ramapithecus* type (see p. 19), was a primate that lived in east Africa about fourteen million years ago, and is considered by many to be a very early representative of the human family.

It used to be thought that the earliest stone tools were odd bits of flint and other stone found in the oldest Ice Age gravels in England and France. It is now thought that these odd bits of stone weren't actually worked by prehistoric people. The stones were given a name, *eoliths,* or "dawn stones." You can see them in many museums, but you can be pretty sure that very few of them were actually fashioned or used by humans. They occur in the wrong place at the wrong time, and they are not very similar to the earliest definite stone tools we now know about.

The second step would have been *fashioning*—haphazardly preparing a tool when there was a need for it. Very little archeological evidence is yet available for this step either. It probably did not last very long, and it may well have been at least partly contemporaneous with the earlier step of utilization. Perhaps some of the earliest stone tools we know about, dating to between three million and two million years ago, belong here. But the number of tools found in these earliest sites (for example, in the Omo Basin of southern Ethiopia) is very low. Moreover, the known sites are few. When we find out more about tool manufacture in this time range, we may well find that the third step had already been taken.

The third step would have been *standardization.* Here people began to make tools according to certain set traditions. Although it may have happened earlier, this kind of standardization had certainly been achieved by about two million years ago. Our best evidence of this so far comes from various of Louis Leakey's archeological sites in the Olduvai Gorge in Tanzania, but other sites in other regions tell the same story. The standardization achieved by the early tool-makers at this time makes it possible for archeologists to recognize what they call the *Oldowan* (after the Olduvai sites) tool-making tradition, to which we shall return after the explanation of some terms archeologists use.

Some More Archeological Terms

We have already explained (pp. 6–7) what archeologists mean by the term *assemblage.* But an assemblage is an all-inclusive concept, and in practice archeologists often have to make do with less than whole assemblages. Perhaps only a small part of the site was dug and only a sample of the assemblage, often a misleading sample, was recovered. Or, if the site happens to have been excavated many years ago, various objects may have been discarded because they were not then recognized or thought to be important. More often the archeologist was primarily interested, for the examination of some particular problem, in just one part of the assemblage. For very early sites, this usually meant all the stone tools, and for later sites all the pottery. A special term is applied to this kind of selection within an assemblage. It is useful to call all of the different tools found together in one layer and made of one kind of material an *industry.* The tools must be found together as people left them. Tools taken from the glacial gravels (or from windswept desert surfaces or river gravels or any geological deposit) are not "together" in this sense. Again, we might say the latter have only secondary or geological, not archeological or primary, context. *Archeological context* means finding things just as people left them. We can tell what tools go together in an industrial sense only if we have archeological context. Well-preserved cave and open-air deposits provide such context. The only artifacts found in many early sites are industries of stone tools alone. In this sense, then, industries (as I use the term) make up the incomplete traces of the original tool kits of prehistoric people.

We said earlier that standardization of tool manufacture was achieved when people began to make tools according to certain set traditions. By *tradition* I mean a set of habits for making one kind of tool for some particular job. Archeologists have recognized several such traditions or interrelated sets of habits for the production of stone tools in early prehistoric times. The earliest one is the *Oldowan* tradition; eventually another one called the *Acheulean* appeared. We will consider later what might be the meaning of the different tool-making traditions—what they are and what they are not.

The stone tool industries we shall be considering usually include both core tools and flake tools. The modification of an original, unworked piece of stone that produces any kind of chipped stone tool is always done by striking off or otherwise removing smaller pieces from the original larger piece. The general term for the smaller fragments so removed is *flake;* the larger piece is usually called a *core.* If the desired tool, or end-product of the manufacturing process, is what remains of the core after flakes have been properly struck off, the resultant tool is what archeologists call a *core tool.* If, on the other hand, the finished tool is made of a flake itself, this is obviously a *flake tool.* The very manufacture of a core tool would, of course, produce several to many flakes. Flakes that were simply left where they fell and never used for anything are called *waste flakes.* More likely, though, at least some of these flakes would have been turned into flake tools. A core that was used solely to produce flakes (from which to make flake tools) and then was thrown away would be called a *nucleus,* not a core tool. Such special nuclei are not very important in the very early part of the archeological record.

How did a flake, once it was removed from the core, become a flake tool? The simplest way is that it was just *used* as a tool—a knife, for example—without first being modified in any way. The use to which it was put might damage or alter the flake, dulling, crushing, or nicking the originally sharp edge. If these signs of damage by use are recognized by an archeologist, he will refer to the tool as a *utilized* flake. Such a piece was certainly a tool, but archeologists usually have something different in mind when they talk about a flake tool. They mean a flake whose properites were intentionally modified by the maker between the ti•.e it was struck from the core and the time it was first used. The modification in the shape of the flake (either of its gross outline or of something more limited, such as the trimming of one edge) was accomplished again by the removal from the larger piece (the flake) of smaller fragments (chips, spalls, etc.). Archeologists call this process of modification or rectification *retouching.* The result of such modification

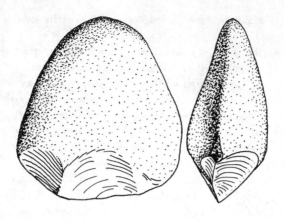

Bifacial Pebble Chopper from South Africa

(the scars visible on the flake) is called *retouch*. Although it may not be terribly logical to do so, the same terms are used also for core tools. Hence the sharp working edge of a pebble chopper or of a hand axe (tools that we'll discuss later) is identified by the location of retouch upon it. When an archeologist speaks of a stone tool, he means, unless he says otherwise, a retouched tool.

Oldowan Tools

The oldest stone tools known belong to the Oldowan tool-making tradition. Oldowan stone industries contain several different kinds of core tools and a few kinds of simple flake tools. Many of the core tools were made on water-rounded pebbles and are called *pebble tools,* but others were made on shattered, jagged hunks of stone. Whether Oldowan core tools were pebble tools or not depended largely on the kinds of rocks available for tool manufacture in the immediate vicinity of a particular site. A commonly occurring kind of core tool is called a *chopper* (though it probably had a wide range of uses). The tool illustrated here is made from a pebble and the retouch forming the cutting edge appears on both the upper and lower surfaces or *faces;* for this reason, it would be called a *bifacial pebble chopper.* Such tools occur frequently in Oldowan industries from east and south Africa that have been studied by Mary Leakey and other archeologists. In the very early Oldowan stone industries, flakes were often used just as they were struck from the core, but some were retouched to make more formal tools, especially various kinds of scrapers. Hammerstones and anvils used during tool manufacture also occur in Oldowan industries, and of course there are many waste flakes. Fragments of animal bones, broken in recurring formalized or patterned ways, may be crude bone tools, but archeologists still do not agree whether such objects represent a true bone tool industry or the accidental result of other processes unconnected with tool manufacture.

The oldest firmly dated Oldowan sites so far known occur in Africa, very often along with the australopithecine fossils we've already discussed (see p. 22), and are of early Basal Pleistocene age. Various sites between two and three million years old include those in the Olduvai Gorge itself and those of the lower Omo River valley in southern Ethiopia and in the region just east of Lake Rudolf in Kenya, but archeological details are few as yet. The earliest Oldowan sites in Morocco may also be this old.

At the moment, our best information about Oldowan sites and industries comes from the excavations of the Leakeys in the Olduvai Gorge itself, in Tanzania. There the earliest sites are a bit less than two million years old. Of a number of habitation sites, one of particular interest is that which the excavators call FLK I, an open-air site from the middle of geological Bed I. The living floor of the early occupants was covered with many stone artifacts and fragments of bone, which were not uniformly distributed. Remains of robust and gracile australopithecines were found there, but which of these two were the tool-makers remains unknown. In a central area of concentration (about twenty-one by fifteen feet), the tools were small and sharp (often utilized flakes), and the bone had been smashed into small splintered fragments. Mary Leakey thinks that this was the area in which meat was cut up into small chunks with the sharp flake knives and where the bones of the animals were smashed open to extract the marrow for eating. On the periphery of the living floor, outside the central concentration, the tools were larger, heavy-duty artifacts (including some choppers and other core tools). The animal bones in this area were less fragmentary, and they were often bones such as ribs and jaws that have little or no marrow in them. The preliminary cutting up of the carcasses may have taken place here. The less interesting, marrowless bones either were not carried into the central area of food consumption or were tossed from there to the margins of the camp site.

The Oldowan site called FLK I thus provides a very early example of the importance to the archeologist of living floors in primary context. Let us analyze what we are dealing with here. There are the stone tools and the animal bones themselves, but both are of different types. Even more important, one complex of bones/

tools is found in one area of the living floor (the center), and another complex of bones/tools in another area (the periphery). Here we begin learning about the possible subtle meanings of the interrelationships of things and their immediate environments. The whole matter appears simple and obvious when we spell it out. At the same time, to gain such an approach to understanding, archeologists must first have the luck to excavate sites which do preserve the potential information. Second, they must themselves carefully expose, extract, and record *all* of this information.

Basal Pleistocene Oldowan sites of about the same age as those at Olduvai Gorge have also been found in Morocco and Algeria in northern Africa. Oldowan tools have been found with australopithecine skeletal material at the famous sites of Sterkfontein and Swartkrans in south Africa (although at least the former site and perhaps both may be older than the Olduvai Gorge sites). Toward the end of the Basal Pleistocene, Oldowan tools were being made outside Africa. Several sites in Europe and the Near East appear to date from this time (possibly as old as the FLK I site at Olduvai or a bit younger), including an important cave site in southern France. At Vallonnet cave, on the Mediterranean coast near Nice, a small series of Oldowan tools including pebble choppers and utilized flakes occurs with the broken bones of various animals. Australopithecine skeletal remains have not yet been found at this or any other European site. There are very probably archeological sites of Basal Pleistocene age in the Far East and southeast Asia, but the dating is very uncertain, and we shall discuss this area of the world later.

Acheulean Tools

At various sites in Africa, archeological levels lying above those containing Oldowan industries have in them tools assigned to the *Acheulean* tool-making tradition. Early Acheulean stone industries include some of the same tool forms found in late Oldowan industries. Although archeologists are not yet sure of the details of the process, it is clear that in a general way the appearance of the Acheulean represents one part of the story of the developing complexity of human tool-making skills and habits.

Just as with the Oldowan, so with the Acheulean we see the manufacture and use of both core tools and flake tools. Older ideas of the Acheulean, based on collections of tools from secondary contexts, stressed the importance of the core tools. We now know that flake tools were important, too, even outnumbering core tools in many later Acheulean industries.

The most characteristic core tool of the Acheulean is a large, bifacially retouched, pointed implement commonly called a *hand axe*.* Hand axes come in different shapes—sometimes the pointed end is quite sharp and sometimes it is not. Hand axes of the early Acheulean (which in Europe used to be called the *Abbevillian*) are often rough, pear-shaped objects like the one in the illustration. The front view (or face) is like that of a pear with a bluntly pointed top, and the back view (or face—hence "biface") looks almost exactly the same. Look at them side on, and you can see that the front and back faces are the same and have been retouched or trimmed to a thin tip. The real purpose in trimming down the two faces was to get a good cutting edge all around. At a somewhat later time, Acheulean hand axes were thinner and the cutting edge was straighter and more regular. The outline of the front view thus became ovate, egg-shaped, or quite pointed. The large chip-scars of the ovate hand axe illustrated are shallow and flat. It is suspected that this resulted from the removal of the chips with a wooden club. The deep chip-scars of the earlier Acheulean hand axe came from beating the tool against a stone anvil.

We have very little idea of the way in which these hand axes were used. The name "hand axe" probably gives the wrong idea, for an axe, to us, is not a pointed tool. All of these early tools must have been used for a number of jobs—chopping, scraping, cutting, hitting, picking, and prying. Since the hand axes tend to be pointed, it seems likely that they were used for hitting, picking, and prying. But they have rough cutting edges, so they could also have been used for chopping, scraping, and cutting.

Another characteristic tool of the Acheulean stone industry, especially from sites in Africa and southern Europe, is called a *cleaver*. It is either a bifacial core tool or a tool made from a very large flake. Its overall shape is similar to a hand axe *except* that it is square-ended rather than pointed. The straight sharp edge of a cleaver is very like that of a modern steel hatchet. Early Acheulean stone industries usually include some choppers (which could be made from pebbles) and other simple core tools like those of the Oldowan, but these became less important through time.

The manufacture of flake tools was very important in the Acheulean tool-making tradition. Early on, simple flakes of various sizes and shapes were struck from cores in about the same way that they were in the Oldowan tradition. Later (during the phase called

---

*Some archeologists call such tools *bifaces*, which is of course accurate since they are made by bifacial retouch. However, other quite different bifacial tools could equally well be called bifaces and are so called by some archeologists. It is better, then, to avoid confusion and to use the more specific term *hand axe*, even though it may have little to do with the way the tool was used.

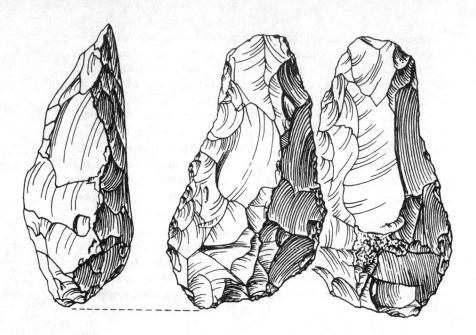

"Abbevillian" Hand Axe

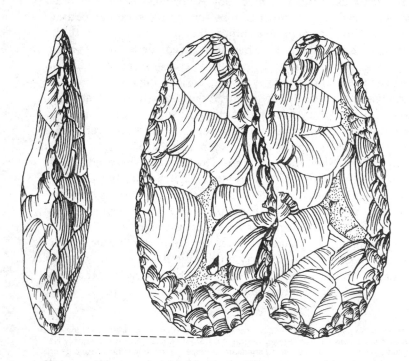

Acheulean Ovate Hand Axe

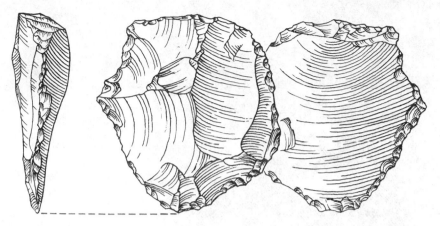

Levallois Flake

middle Acheulean in Europe), the tool-makers began to strike flakes from cores that were carefully prepared in advance in such a way as to *predetermine* the general size, shape, and thickness of the flake produced. The use of a prepared core (or nucleus) technique for striking off flakes was widespread during the latter part of the Acheulean tool-making tradition. In Europe, the prepared core technique is usually known as the *Levallois* technique, and the Levallois core is called a *tortoise core* because before the desired flake is struck off, the nucleus is chipped in such a fashion as to resemble the general shape of a tortoise shell. The Levallois flake struck from a tortoise core is usually large and thin with sharp cutting edges, and the broad preparatory removal chips are preserved on its upper surface. You can see them in the utilized Levallois flake shown in the illustration. The Levallois flake (as is the case with other flakes) might have been used without further modification or retouched to make one or another kind of patterned flake tool.

The flake tools most commonly found in Acheulean stone industries are various kinds of scrapers, flake knives, and flakes with notched or denticulate (saw-toothed) edges. These tools are similar to those we shall talk about later in Mousterian stone industries. As we said above, in many later Acheulean industries, flake tools are more numerous than hand axes or other core tools. Acheulean bone tools are rare, and there is still nothing that we can call a patterned bone tool industry. Recently, Professor François Bordes found, in a late Acheulean level at Pech de l'Azé II, a fragment of an ox rib bearing a meandering design of engraved lines. This frag-

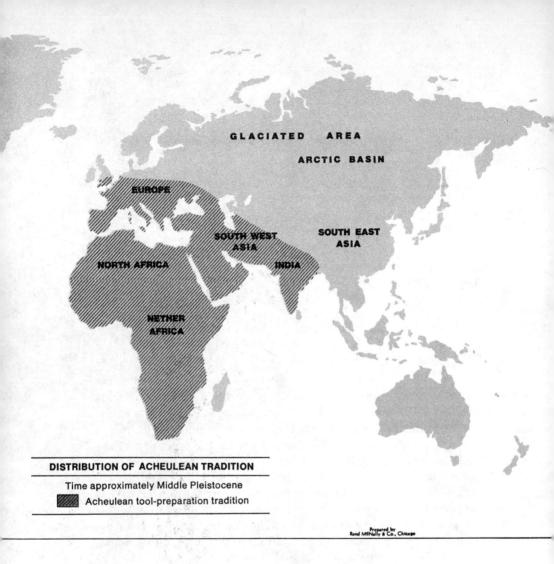

DISTRIBUTION OF ACHEULEAN TRADITION

Time approximately Middle Pleistocene

Acheulean tool-preparation tradition

Prepared by
Rand McNally & Co., Chicago

ment, apparently not a tool, may be the earliest example yet known of a decorated bone object. Although wooden tools are seldom preserved in sites so old, fragments of various kinds of wooden tools or weapons have been found in the early Acheulean site of Torralba in Spain and in the much later Acheulean site of Kalambo Falls in Zambia.

Tools of the kinds archeologists assign to the Acheulean toolmaking tradition are found in the southwestern part of the Old World—in Africa, southern Europe, southwest Asia, and most of the Indian subcontinent. With the possible exception of Java (about which archeologists are still arguing), they are not found in the rest of the Old World—not in most of the Soviet Union, in the Far East, in southeast Asia, or in Australia. You can understand, then, why the Acheulean is sometimes referred to as the "Western tradition of hand axe manufacture" (see map).

The time span during which Acheulean tools were made extends from the early Lower Pleistocene (for example, some sites at Olduvai Gorge and in north Africa) to at least the time of the Riss Glacial at the end of the Middle Pleistocene (for example, the site of Pech de l'Azé II). In parts of Africa, such as at Kalambo Falls in Zambia, tools that must be called Acheulean apparently continued to be manufactured well into the Upper Pleistocene. This is a very long span of time, probably over one million years, and both the stone tools and the people who made them changed considerably during that time. By now many Acheulean sites, both open-air and cave, are known, and we will look at several particularly interesting examples.

The adjacent sites of Torralba and Ambrona in Spain tell us of the activities of human groups who hunted elephants and other animals there during the time when the Mindel glaciation covered much of northern Europe. The stone tools of these hunters are assigned to the early part of the Acheulean tradition. The evidence suggests that the sites were temporary camps at which elephants and other game animals were killed, butchered, and eaten. Professor F. Clark Howell, who directed the excavations, found some signs that the elephants may have been driven or stampeded into the kill with the aid of fire. Stone tools used for butchering and the smashed bones of the animals are abundant. Some of the fragmentary wooden implements found at Torralba may have been simple wooden spears.

At Olorgesailie, in Kenya, several Acheulean living floors have been excavated; they were probably occupied sometime during the Middle Pleistocene. The sites vary in size and artifact content, but all were apparently located on sandy camping areas along small streams draining into a nearby lake. The hand axes, cleavers, flake tools, and other artifacts at Olorgesailie are assigned to the later Acheulean tradition. A wide range of animals are represented in the garbage bones—hippopotamus, horse, pig, elephant, etc. At one of the Olorgesailie sites, almost all the refuse bone is that of a large, extinct species of baboon. Dr. Glynn Isaac, one of the excavators, suggests that these bones may be the result of the massacre of a single baboon troop, an activity known to have been practiced by some recent African hunters.

We have been talking so far about open-air sites, but the people making Acheulean tools lived in caves as well. Pech de l'Azé II is an Acheulean cave site, and so is the Lazaret cave, near Nice on the French Riviera. The Lazaret cave was occupied by makers of late Acheulean tools at the very end of the Middle Pleistocene (late

Riss). Excavation and study of the cave by Professor Henry de Lumley and his co-workers showed that an artificial tent-like structure had been built by the inhabitants *inside* the cave near its mouth. The tent or hut, measuring about thirty-six by twelve feet, was enclosed on one side by the natural wall of the cave; the other three walls and the roof were probably skins supported by a framework of poles held in place by a low dry-stone wall. The interior of the hut seems to have been divided into two rooms by a hanging (skin?) partition. On the floor of the inner room were two fireplaces and sleeping areas, and another sleeping area was located in the outer room near the entrance. The Lazaret cave is a small site, but it is one of the most informative caves thus far excavated.

Early Tools in the East

The earliest tools in east and southeast Asia included choppers, both unifacially and bifacially flaked, and simple flake tools. Work done before World War II by Professor Hallam Movius and others emphasized that hand axes and other distinctive tools of the Western or Acheulean tradition were not found in eastern Asia. With some possible exceptions (as we have mentioned, Java remains a problem), this observation is still valid for the long span of time before the Upper Pleistocene. Movius called this tool-making tradition of eastern Asia the *chopper-chopping tool tradition* ("chopping tool" was his name for what we are calling bifacial choppers). This name is still used by some, but more recent work has shown how similar the Oldowan tools of Africa are to the earliest east Asian material, and many archeologists now include the Asian stone industries in the Oldowan tradition. The chopper-chopping tool tradition may have had its earliest roots in the pebble tool tradition of African type, or we may eventually discover that it represents the independent beginnings of stone tool manufacture in this part of the world.

There are several kinds of tools in this tradition, but all differ from the Western hand axes and flakes. There are broad, heavy scrapers and tools with an adze-like cutting edge. These last-named tools are called *hand adzes,* just as the bifaces of the West have often been called hand axes. The section of an adze cutting edge is $\angle$ shaped; the section of an axe is $<$ shaped.

There are also pointed pebble tools and a variety of simple flakes. Thus the tool kit of these early south and east Asiatic peoples seems to have included tools for doing as many different jobs as did the tools of the Western traditions. The prehistoric people in this general area used mostly quartz and tuff and even petrified

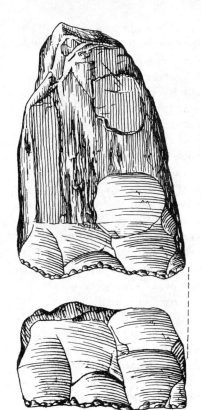

Anyathian Adze-like Tool

wood for their stone tools (see illustration of a hand adze from Burma made from a chunk of petrified wood).

Although these early stone industries of eastern Asia are similar enough to be grouped into one broad tool-making tradition, there are regional differences (depending at least in part on the kind of raw material available), and special regional names have been used—*Anyathian* for industries in Burma, *Patjitanian* for Java, *Tampanian* for Malaya, and others. At the present time, it is not possible to demonstrate that any of these early tools of eastern Asia are as old as similar Oldowan tools of Africa dating to the Basal Pleistocene, but it is to be expected that some day evidence of equal antiquity will be discovered. Certainly such tools were made and used as early as the Lower Pleistocene and continued in use during the Middle Pleistocene. What may at the moment be the earliest reasonably well dated tools in eastern Asia are a few flakes found just above a human skull at a site near Lantian in China; the skull and tools are apparently of early Lower Pleistocene age.

Also in China, near Peking, is the cave site of Choukoutien. This site, as we've already noted (p. 25), contained abundant early skeletal remains (the so-called Peking man), as well as tools and other items very useful to the archeologist. The deposits in the large cave were very thick, and people must have lived there over a very long period of time, beginning probably in the late Lower Pleistocene and extending possibly into the Middle Pleistocene. The Peking people had fire. They probably cooked their meat, or used the fire to keep dangerous animals away from the den. In the cave were bones of dangerous animals, members of the wolf, bear, and cat families. Some of the cat bones belonged to beasts larger than tigers. There were also bones of other wild animals: buffalo, camel, deer, elephant, horse, sheep, and even ostrich. Seventy percent of the animals Peking people killed were fallow deer. It's much too cold and dry in north China for all these animals to live there today. So this list helps us know that during at least part of the time people lived in the cave, the weather was reasonably warm and there was enough rain to grow grass for the grazing animals. At other times, the climate was colder than at present.

The Peking people also seem to have eaten plant food (as did early humans in general, although specific evidence is often lacking), for there are hackberry seeds in the debris of the cave. Tools were made of sandstone and quartz and sometimes of a rather bad flint. They belong in the Asian Oldowan tradition, and they include bifacial and unifacial choppers and various flake tools, including well-made flake scrapers. There are also many split pieces of heavy bone. The inhabitants probably split them so they could eat the bone marrow, but they may also have used them as tools.

Many of these split bones were the bones of the Peking people themselves. Each one of the skulls had already had the base broken out of it. In no case were any of the bones resting together in their natural relation to one another. There is nothing like a burial; all of the bones are scattered. Now it's true that animals could have scattered bodies that were not cared for or buried. But splitting bones lengthwise and carefully removing the base of a skull call for both tools and the people to use them. It's pretty clear who the people were. Peking man was a cannibal.

More Oldowan in the West?

We saw previously that over much of the western part of the Old World the tools made during the Lower and Middle Pleistocene could be assigned to the Acheulean tool-making tradition. However, this does not tell the whole story. At various sites of this age in Europe and southwestern Asia there are stone industries which have choppers and simple flake tools, but which do *not* have the hand axes or cleavers characteristic of the Acheulean. Except for the fact that they may be more varied and better made, such tools are similar to those of the Basal Pleistocene Oldowan tradition. Stone industries have been known for a long time in England, where they are called *Clactonian*, but some archeologists now prefer to emphasize their similarity with the earlier industries by calling them *Oldowan/Clactonian*. This implies that there were two separate tool-making traditions present in parts of the western Old World after the Basal Pleistocene. There are alternative explanations for these industries, which we will discuss later; for the moment, let us look at some of the relevant sites.

Vértesszöllös is an open-air site in Hungary that was occupied during a warm spell within the Mindel glacial episode. In addition to fragmentary human skeletal remains (see p. 25), Hungarian scientists have recovered many stone tools associated with several hearths on the living floors. Bones of game animals, including deer and bison, had been smashed to extract the marrow. Most of the tools were made from small rounded pebbles. The core tools were pebble choppers, unifacial and bifacial, and the flake tools were mostly simple scrapers and notched and denticulate pieces. Hand axes were absent. The stone industry was very similar to earlier Oldowan industries.

From a somewhat later date (Great Interglacial), tools occurring in secondary context in river gravels at Clacton-on-Sea in England show us a similar stone industry, including notched flake tools similar to some found at Vértesszöllös. What is different about the Clacton industry is that the choppers were made of irregular chunks of flint, rather than water-rounded pebbles. The choppers were good Oldowan forms, but because they were not pebble tools, they were not originally recognized as such. Once again there were no hand axes, and the flakes were not produced by the Levallois technique. One of the rare wooden implements of very early times was found at Clacton—the fire-hardened end of a wooden spear.

Stone industries without hand axes but with flake tools (and sometimes with choppers) continue to be found into the early Upper Pleistocene—for example, the open-air site of High Lodge in England (Riss) and the earliest level (Last Interglacial) in Tabun Cave at Mount Carmel in Palestine. A similar Last Interglacial industry, this time associated with human skeletal remains, has been found at the cave of Fontéchevade in France. The name *Tayacian* has been used for the latter two cave industries, but this should not disguise their similarity to other representatives of the Oldowan/Clactonian.

The Meaning of the Different Traditions

Before we continue our story further into the Upper Pleistocene, we should stop and consider an important but still controversial question. What do the traditions really mean? I see them as the standardization of ways to make tools for particular jobs. We may not know exactly what job the maker of a particular hand axe or flake tool had in mind. We can easily see, however, that he already enjoyed a know-how, a set of persistent habits of tool preparation, which would always give him the same type of tool when he wanted to make it. Therefore, the traditions show us that persistent habits already existed by this time for the preparation of various kinds of tools.

This tells us that one of the characteristic aspects of human culture was already present. There must have been, in the minds of these early tool-makers, a notion of the ideal kind of tool for a particular job. Furthermore, since we find so many thousands upon thousands of tools of one kind or another, the notion of the ideal kinds of tools *and* the know-how for making each kind must have been held in common by many tool-makers, and must have been passed on from one generation to another. I could even guess that the notions of the ideal type of one or the other of these tools stood out in the minds of their makers somewhat like a symbol of "perfect tool for good job." There is, indeed, reason to suggest that symbol using may have appeared much earlier. At the same time, might the appearance of such early standardized tool forms be taken as a hint of a further step—that crude word symbols were also being made? I suppose that it is not impossible.

Here, for the last time, I suppose I might wrestle again with the slippery matter of a definition of "human." As Professor Harvey Bricker remarks, we must each make our own decision as to who shall be let into our club. I myself am perfectly comfortable about calling the makers of *standardized* tools (our third step) humans, men and women, people. That would include the later australopithecines and that early *Homo "habilis."* I'd also suspect that when we learn more of them, we may well vote admission with full privileges to the beings who *fashioned* tools (our second step), although some of us may choose to hide behind the term "hominid." I can't imagine myself going much further back than that, to include the *utilizers* (our first step). I'd surely not call them anything beyond "hominid" or "pre-hominid." Remember, however, my gut feelings are archeological, artifactual. Probably most of my human paleontological colleagues would be more venturesome in this regard.

Traditions Are Tool-Making Habits,
Not Cultures, Tribes, Etc.

A stone tool-making tradition results from patterned or standardized ways of making stone tools that continued—always with some changes—through time. The recognition of such a tradition is really a generalization or abstraction made by archeologists in order to group together industries and assemblages of tools that are similar in certain defined ways. At this point, we must consider a question that is very important to modern archeologists: What is the relationship between such abstract *tool* groups and the *social* groups in which the real men and women who made and used the tools lived?

First, we can say that archeologists do not equate any of the early tool-making traditions we have talked about with any particular kind of social grouping that would be recognized by an ethnographer working today with living peoples. This means, for example, that, for archeologists, Acheulean tools were not made by any one clan, tribe, nation, or whatever. You can understand why this must be true if you look again at the map showing the distribution of the Acheulean tradition and consider the vast territory involved and the very different kinds of environmental conditions represented.

Second, our early tool-making traditions are not cultures (look again at the definition of a culture on p. 33). Recognition of a tradition gives us information about only part of the range of activities of the many cultures that existed during prehistory. Cultures within which Acheulean tools were made were, in other ways, certainly very different one from the other—in the climate and topography they had to cope with, in the plants and animals available for subsistence, and so on. Also, throughout the time when Acheulean tools were made, there were real biological (evolutionary) changes in the tool-makers, the men and women themselves. The early stages of the development of language probably belong here, but we can make no assumption of linguistic (or other communicational) unity over the whole area of Acheulean distribution.

Third, tool-making traditions cannot be equated with distinct human racial groupings. It used to be thought by many (but never all) archeologists that flake tools were made by one biological variety of humans and hand axes by another, but the evidence against this notion is now so strong that we need not consider it further.

After a review of what tool-making traditions are *not*, we are left with the position that the traditions are persistent habits for the production of tools. These habits persisted because, although they were not the totality of any one culture, they were one part of general cultural behavior—which means learned shared behavior. The "conventionalized understandings" about how to make tools were transmitted from one generation to another through learning. Changes in tool-making tradition, like changes in other aspects of culture, occurred as the understandings slowly changed and as new conditions made modifications advantageous.

All this is simple and straightforward, but a special problem presents itself when more than one tool-making tradition seems to be present in the same general area during the same broad span of time. This problem becomes a common one in later prehistory, but an example from what we have talked about so far is the apparent existence in Lower and Middle Pleistocene Europe of two tool-making traditions—Acheulean and Oldowan/Clactonian. Some stone industries contained hand axes, cleavers (sometimes), and certain kinds of flake tools. Other industries had rather different flake tools and choppers (usually), but no hand axes. Many archeologists believe that these differences represent two tool-making traditions—two *different* sets of conventionalized understandings that were transmitted through time within *different* local groups of tool-makers. This is the idea that has been suggested here.

There are, though, other archeologists who strongly disagree. They prefer what is often called a *functional* interpretation of the observed variability. According to this view, people of the same local group sharing the same set of conventionalized understandings would have made hand axes at one camp site at one time to answer a particular need and failed to make hand axes at a different camp site some weeks or months later because the tasks then at hand did not call for them.

It is easy to understand how this functional interpretation of differences in stone tool industries may often be the correct one, especially if one is dealing with some special-purpose site (such as a butchering site), or if only a small part of a living floor, representing only one of several activity areas, is represented in the particular industry being studied. But *all* difference is not functional difference, and each problem case must be examined separately. At a minimum, the archeologist must know the *full range* of variation from any one living floor. If he suspects that within a given local area two *different* stone industries may have been produced by the *same* human groups, he must try to learn if the industries were very closely contemporaneous. At the moment, the dating of very early archeological sites seldom if ever permits such a demonstration of contemporaneity. Based on what we now know, some so-called Oldowan/Clactonian sites of Europe and western Asia may have been incorrectly interpreted, but the conclusion that two tool-making traditions were present in this area during much of early prehistory is still the more likely one.

Early Upper Pleistocene Industries

During the earlier part of the Upper Pleistocene, at a time equivalent to the Last Interglacial and the first half of the Würm Glacial in Europe (say, roughly, 100,000 to 40,000 years ago), tool-makers in many parts of the Old World were making stone industries that were composed primarily of various kinds of flake tools. By this time, biological evolution had proceeded to the point where the tool-maker was already an early variety of *Homo sapiens*. It is clear that in many parts of the world this *Homo sapiens* was the heavy-faced, powerfully muscled "archaic" form we've met earlier, called Neandertal man in Europe. The term Neandertal has been extended in one form or another to other regions. And at some place (or places), the more modern form of *Homo sapiens* (people like us) was coming into being through the processes of biological evolution.

If archeological industries from the early Upper Pleistocene are compared with older ones, we see immediately a great increase in regional variation. We will presently note that by the end of the Pleistocene, differentiation was so pronounced that virtually every river valley or range of hills had its own peculiar archeological features. Earlier, however, in the time period we are now discussing, some geographically broader generalizations can be made, but we must not forget the great variation.

A major archeological complex recognized for this time period is called *Mousterian* (often with qualifiers such as *Mousterian of Acheulean Tradition, Levalloiso-Mousterian*, etc.). Mousterian stone industries have been found at sites in much of Europe, including European Russia, in the Near East and extending into parts of Soviet central Asia, and in north Africa, from the Mediterranean into the Sahara. The shared characteristic of Mousterian industries was the abundant, thus quantitatively important, use of flakes, produced usually by either the Levallois technique or what we call the *discoidal core* technique. The latter produced a rather different kind of flake (they are normally shorter and thicker than Levallois flakes), but less preparation of the core was required and a greater number of regular flakes could have been struck from it. It is also fair to say that in Mousterian industries the flake tools produced regularly (as opposed to occasionally) had more variety and complexity than flake tools in the earlier industries.

Probably the most commonly occurring Mousterian tools are medium-sized flake *side scrapers*. Compare the illustration of the side scraper with the end scraper illustrated on page 73, and imagine potential uses for it, such as the scraping of hides. There are also some small pointed tools and sometimes a few small hand

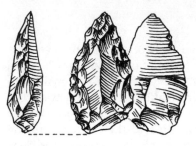

Mousterian Point

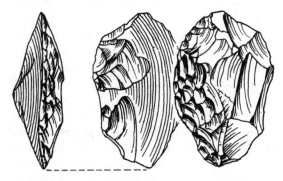

Mousterian Side Scraper

axes. The last of these tool types is often a flake worked on both of the flat sides (that is, bifacially). Flakes with notched or denticulated (saw-toothed) cutting edges occur, sometimes in great numbers. In most Mousterian industries, there are a few tools that become common in later, final Pleistocene industries—end scrapers, cutting and engraving tools called *burins,* perforators or punches, and special backed knives—but such tools are seldom numerous. There are also pieces of flint worked into the form of crude balls. The pointed tools may have been fixed on shafts to make short jabbing spears; the round flint balls may have been used as bolas. Actually, we don't *know* what either tool was used for. The points are illustrated (p. 73), as well as the side scrapers.

As we shall see in the next chapter, archeologists give a special name—*blades*—to long, narrow stone flakes. In the late Upper Pleistocene, the regular and customary production of blades from special cores was a characteristic of many stone industries. Although people making Mousterian tools sometimes produced long, narrow flakes (which are by definition blades), they did not do so regularly or systematically. It is true, however, that early Upper Pleistocene tool-makers at some sites in the Near East and north Africa were acquainted with the special technique required for the production of blades, and used it regularly. Archeologists do not call these industries Mousterian, however.

Bone tools have also been found from this period. Some are called *scrapers,* and there are also long, chisel-like leg-bone fragments believed to have been used for skinning animals. Larger hunks of bone, which seem to have served as anvils or chopping blocks, are fairly common. Compared with the use humans made of bone, antler, and ivory during the late Upper Pleistocene, this is all very meager, and it is not yet particularly meaningful to call this a varied and complex bone industry. Bits of mineral, used as coloring matter, have also been found. We don't know what the color was used for. There is still very little evidence of art or decoration, but body painting remains a likely possibility, as does the use of colored pigments in burial ritual.

At this point we may ask whether the Mousterian was a toolmaking tradition (as we have applied the term to the Acheulean, for example). The answer is, almost certainly not. Some Mousterian industries are very similar to late Acheulean ones, some are similar to late Clactonian ones, and some cannot be characterized in either fashion. The meaning of the differences between specific Mousterian industries is the subject of continuing hot debate among archeologists. Functional variation is certainly important here, but as with the earlier time period we discussed, it cannot supply the whole explanation. A quick or simple solution to the known problems is unlikely if for no other reason than that different local regions have very different archeological sequences and peculiarities.

The extremely complicated interrelationships of the different habits used by the tool-makers of this range of time are being systematically studied. Professor François Bordes and others have developed detailed methods of great importance for understanding these tool preparation habits, and he and others are constantly refining and extending these methods. The role of functional variation has been investigated for various assemblages of the Near East and Europe by Lewis and Sally Binford, Leslie Freeman, and others. For the moment, most would agree that the Mousterian is not a single tool-making tradition. It is, rather, a somewhat unfortunate cover term used by archeologists to designate stone industries, based primarily upon flake tools, in one part of the Old World during the earlier Upper Pleistocene.

As had their predecessors, people making Mousterian tools lived in open-air sites as well as in caves. Although archeologists have often paid little attention to them, Mousterian open-air sites are actually very numerous. An interesting example is known from the site of Molodova I in the Ukraine region of the Soviet Union. A ring-like pile of large mammoth bones, which enclosed an area of about twenty-six by sixteen feet, is thought to have been used by the occupants to weigh down the skin walls of a temporary hut or tent. Traces of a number of hearths were found inside this probable shelter. Hundreds of tools (especially side scrapers and denticulate flakes) and thousands of waste flakes and bone fragments littered the living floor both within the shelter and immediately around it. The bone fragments indicate the use of a wide variety of large game animals in addition to the woolly mammoth—woolly rhinoceros, horse, moose, elk, reindeer, and brown bear.

Mousterian cave sites are much better known because archeologists have long concentrated on excavating them. The old idea of prehistoric men was that they were cave men, hence caves were where archeologists looked. Some examples are Le Moustier in southern France, Tabun in Israel, Shanidar in Iraq, and Jebel Irhoud in Morocco. At all four of these caves, human skeletal remains were found with Mousterian tools, sometimes with clear evidence of intentional burial. These burials have been found on the floors of the caves; in other words, the people dug graves in the places where they lived. The holes made for the graves were small. For this reason (or perhaps for some other) the bodies were in a curled-up or contracted position. Flint or bone tools or pieces of meat seem to have been put in with some of the bodies. In several cases, flat stones had been laid over the graves. Burial of human dead is not the only evidence of ritual activity from Mousterian sites. At several cave sites in western Europe, skeletal remains reveal that cave bears were either arranged or buried by prehistoric people in a very unusual fashion. These earliest signs of ritual treatment of the dead, both human and animal, are perhaps more easily understood when we remember that we are dealing here with the beginning forms of *Homo sapiens* themselves.

Other African and Asian Industries of the Early Upper Pleistocene

In that part of the African continent lying south of the Sahara Desert and the Nile Valley, some stone industries belonging to the Acheulean tool-making tradition were still being made in the early Upper Pleistocene. One example is the apparently late Acheulean occupation at Kalambo Falls in Zambia. But sometime within the time period we are dealing with here, changes appeared in the African stone industries that impel archeologists to use different names for them. The changes were generally in the same direction we have noted for the northwestern part of the Old World—greater quantitative importance of flakes, the use (sometimes, not always) of more sophisticated techniques of flake production, and an increased variety and complexity of retouched flake tool forms. Core tools continue to appear in most of these industries, but they are no longer the large hand axes and cleavers of the Acheulean. In east and south Africa lived people whose industries show a development of the Acheulean tradition. Such industries are called *Fauresmith*. The tropical rain forest region contained people whose stone tools apparently show adjustment to this peculiar environment. Professor Desmond Clark considers this to have been the case with the so-called *Sangoan* industry of stone picks, adzes, core-bifaces of specialized Acheulean type, and bifacial points which were probably spearheads.

In eastern Asia, as we noted before, people had developed characteristic stone choppers and flake tools. This tool preparation tradition, basically Oldowan, lasted in some areas to the very end of the Pleistocene. The information we have about early Upper Pleistocene sites in this large area suggests again the increased importance of flake tools. In the late Upper Pleistocene, people moved into hitherto unoccupied regions and other changes took place, but these matters will be dealt with in the next chapter.

Culture at the Beginning of the Last Great Glacial

The few things we have found must indicate only a very small part of the total activities of the people who lived at the time. All of the things they made of wood and bark, of skins, of anything soft, are gone, except for those found in such rare cases as that of Kalambo Falls. The fact that burials were made is pretty clear proof that the people had some notion of a life after death. But what this notion really was, or what gods (if any) they believed in, we cannot know. The so-called bear cults might suggest some notion of hoarding up the spirits or the strength of bears killed in the hunt. Probably the people lived in small groups, as hunting and food-gathering seldom provide enough food for large groups of people. These groups possibly had some kind of leader or "chief." Very likely the rude beginnings of rules for community life and politics, and even law, were being made. But what these were, we do not know. We can only guess about such things, as we can only guess about many others; for example, how the idea of a family must have been growing, and how there may have been witch doctors who made beginnings in medicine or in art, in the materials they gathered for their trade.

The stone tools help us most. They have lasted, and we can find them. As they come to us, from this cave or that, and from this layer or that, the tool industries show a variety of combinations of the different basic habits or traditions of tool preparation. This seems only natural, as the groups of people must have been very small. The mixtures and blendings of the habits used in making stone tools must mean that there were also mixtures and blends in many of the other ideas and beliefs of these small groups. And what this certainly means is that there was no one *culture* of the time. Rather there must have been a great variety of loosely related cultures at about the same stage of advancement. We could say, too, that here we really begin to see, for the first time, that remarkable ability of people to adapt themselves to a variety of conditions. We shall see this adaptive ability even more clearly as time goes on and the record becomes more complete.

5
Early moderns

From some time in the second interstadial or pause of the last great glaciation (say some time after about 40,000 years ago), we have more accurate dates for archeological sites in the Old World. This is because we have now arrived at the span of time within which radiocarbon age determination can be used effectively to give us absolute or *chronometric* (i.e., time before the present) dates. Also, at least for much of the European-Mediterranean area, the geological record of climatic fluctuations is increasingly well understood. This record can be used for *relative* dating, telling us which sites were earlier or later than others, even though it does not give us a date in years. We will look later at one important regional archeological sequence dated by both relative and chronometric determinations.

Blade Tools: A New Tool Production Technique Appears

Something new was probably beginning to happen in the European-Mediterranean area about 40,000 years ago. A new technique was becoming popular in westernmost Asia, in Europe, and in parts of north Africa. This was the blade tool preparation technique.

A stone blade is really just a long, narrow, more or less parallel-sided flake, as the drawing shows (p. 67). It has sharp cutting edges,

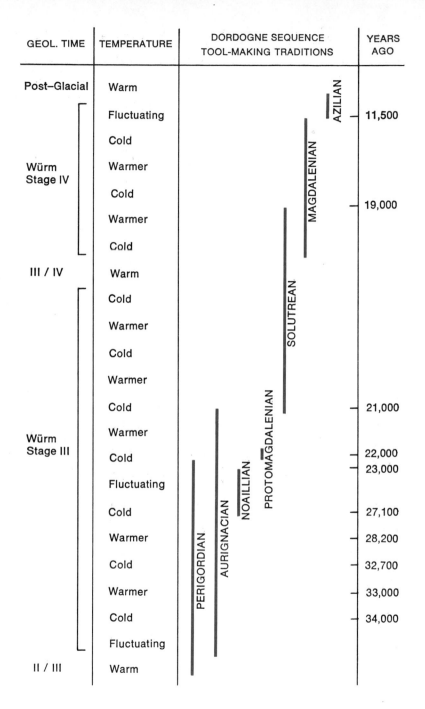

GEOL. TIME	TEMPERATURE	DORDOGNE SEQUENCE TOOL-MAKING TRADITIONS	YEARS AGO
Post–Glacial	Warm		
Würm Stage IV	Fluctuating	AZILIAN	11,500
	Cold	MAGDALENIAN	
	Warmer		
	Cold		19,000
	Warmer		
	Cold		
III / IV	Warm		
Würm Stage III	Cold	SOLUTREAN	
	Warmer		
	Cold		
	Warmer		
	Cold		21,000
	Warmer		22,000
	Cold	PROTOMAGDALENIAN	23,000
	Fluctuating	NOAILLIAN	
	Cold		27,100
	Warmer	AURIGNACIAN	28,200
	Cold	PERIGORDIAN	32,700
	Warmer		33,000
	Cold		34,000
	Fluctuating		
II / III	Warm		

The Dordogne Sequence of the Late Upper Pleistocene, with Temperature (Climate) Indicated

NOTE IRREGULAR VERTICAL SCALE

64

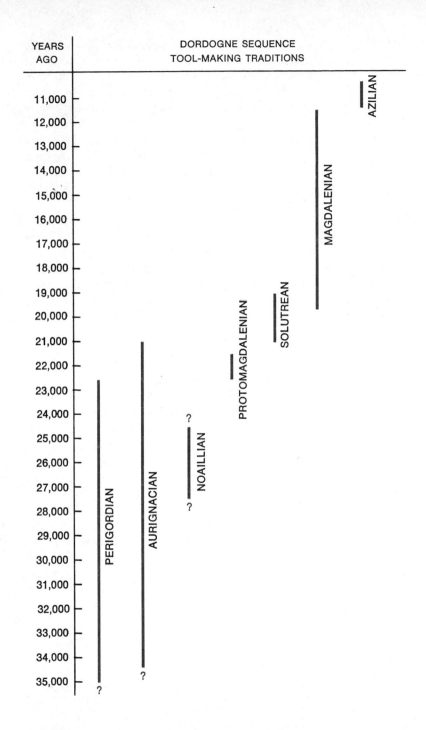

The Dordogne Sequence of the Late Upper Pleistocene

NOTE TRUE VERTICAL SCALE IN TERMS OF TIME

and makes a very useful knife. The real trick is to be able to make one. It is almost impossible to make a blade out of any stone but flint or a natural volcanic glass called *obsidian*. And even if you have flint or obsidian, you first have to work up a special prismatic blade core from which to remove blades. One way (though not the only one) is to strike with a hammer stone against a bone or antler punch which is directed at the proper place on the blade core. The blade core has to be well supported or gripped while this is going on. To get a good flint blade tool takes a great deal of know-how.

A difficulty in coming to agreement as to just when the blade tool technique became effective is that more or less parallel-sided long flakes had appeared occasionally in some early flake tool industries. The regular and customary production of blades from prismatic blade cores seems, however, to have been a late phenomenon. And there is a further element in the matter. As a rule, in the blade tool technique proper, the blade itself was treated as a blank or first step and was then worked further into one of the variety of special tools we'll describe presently.*

The Earliest Blade Tools

The earliest stone industry containing blade tools regularly and systematically produced from prismatic blade cores occurs at the cave site of Haua Fteah in Libya. This industry, which some call *Pre-Aurignacian,* apparently dates to the end of the Last Interglacial. Similar industries have been found at the Tabun cave in Israel and at a few sites in Syria and Lebanon. These Near Eastern industries have been given the name *Amudian,* and they were made at a time equivalent to the beginning of the Würm Glacial (about 75,000 years ago). As we saw before, blade industries were unusual in this time period (early Upper Pleistocene), when most other sites contained Mousterian flake industries. But this early use of the blade technique did not continue in these areas. For some reason, the habit of making blades in the Near East and Libya was interrupted. Blades only reappeared there at about the same time they were first made in Europe, some time about 40,000 years ago; that is, after the first phase of the last glaciation had ended.

We are not sure just where the earliest *persisting* habits for the

---

*Professor André Leroi-Gourhan once gave an interesting distinction between hand axes, flakes (of generally Mousterian type), and blades (of generally Magdalenian type). Given a one pound hunk of good raw flint, an experienced knapper could get eight inches of cutting edge with the hand-axe preparation technique, forty inches of cutting edge with the flake preparation technique, and from ten to forty *feet* of good cutting edge through the blade preparation technique. The figures may not be too accurate, but the order of the contrast is suggestive.

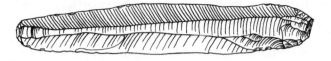

Plain Blade

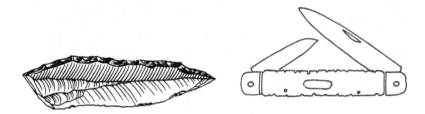

Backed Blade

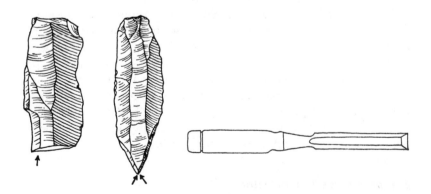

Two Burins

production of blade tools developed. Impressed by the very early momentary appearance of blades at Tabun on Mount Carmel, Professor Dorothy A. Garrod first favored the Near East as a center of origin. She spoke of "some as yet unidentified Asiatic centre," which she thought might be in the highlands of Iran or just beyond. We now know that an early blade industry in Iraqi Kurdistan, called the *Baradostian* by its discoverer, Professor Ralph Solecki, must date back at least about 35,000 years. At a nearby site in Iranian Kurdistan, Dr. Bruce Howe believes there may have been a gradual transition from the local Mousterian into the Baradostian. But we are not on sure ground yet. When the blade tools reappeared in the Syro-Palestinian area, they did so in industries which also included Levalloiso-Mousterian flake tools. From the point of view of form and workmanship, the blade tools themselves are not so fine as those which seem to have been making their appearance in western Europe about the same time. There is a characteristic Syro-Palestinian flake point, possibly a projectile tip, called the *Emiran*, which is not known from Europe. The appearance of blade tools, together with Levalloiso-Mousterian flakes, continued even after the Emiran point had gone out of use. In Libya, blades reappeared in an industry called the *Dabban*; the transition from Mousterian to Dabban happened about 38,000 years ago.

In southwestern Europe, the earliest industries in which the blade technique was regularly used (the early Perigordian) appeared somewhere between 40,000 and 35,000 years ago. Blade tool industries in central Europe (Aurignacian and others) may slightly predate 40,000 years ago. In both European regions, the stone industries in which blades occurred also contained, at least at first, some tools perfectly characteristic of Mousterian industries. It seems clear that the production of blade tools did not immediately swamp the set of older habits in Europe.

The bones of the blade tool-makers we've found so far indicate that anatomically modern human beings had now certainly appeared. Unfortunately, only a few fossil humans have so far been found from the very beginning of the blade tool range in Europe (or elsewhere). What I certainly shall *not* tell you is that conquering bands of fine, strong, anatomically modern people, armed with superior blade tools, came sweeping out of the East to exterminate the lowly Neandertalers. Even if we don't know exactly what happened, I'd lay a good bet it wasn't that simple.

European Blade Tool Industries

We know a great deal about different blade industries in Europe. Most of these come from occupation layers in cave sites (because archeologists have concentrated on caves), but by now we are beginning to get a lot of information from open-air sites, too. Just as was the case with Professor Bordes' studies of the developed flake tool industries, the blade tool industries lend themselves to elaborate typological studies and statistical analysis. Professor Hallam Movius and his associates and students are pioneering in these detailed studies. It is hoped that as more carefully excavated materials become available, the complications will become more meaningful to us.

You will realize that all this complication comes not only from the fact that we are finding more material. It is due also to the increasing ability of the prehistoric peoples of the time to adapt themselves to a great variety of situations. Their tools indicate this adaptiveness. We know there was a good deal of climatic change at this time. The plants and animals that people used for food were changing, too. The great variety of tools and industries we now find reflects these changes and the ability of the people to keep up with the times. An increase in the variety of activities—of different kinds of tasks which people undertook—was doubtless also involved. Now, for example, we find many examples of tools to *make* other tools. These tools also show their makers' increasing ability to adapt themselves.

The variation of the blade industries is very great, but archeologists have managed to group them into general tool-making traditions. Like the earlier ones we have mentioned, these traditions are persistent (though always somewhat changing) habits for the production of tools. They differ markedly from the older traditions (such as the Acheulean) in that they persisted for much shorter spans of time—in some cases no more than a few thousand years—and they were much more localized. Regional variation *within* recognized traditions was also greater than in the past, and relatively small geographical regions commonly had their own distinct archeological sequences that differed markedly from those in adjacent regions. Our fullest information about the European blade tool industries still comes from France (though other areas are catching up fast) because archeological research started earlier and was done more intensively in that country. If an archeologist wished to be reasonably accurate, he would probably have to discuss the blade tool industries of France alone in terms of five or six regional sequences, because what could be said about the foothills of the Pyrenees would not apply, for example, at all to the region around Paris.

Faced with a situation like this (which would also be true for Spain, Czechoslovakia, the Soviet Union, etc.), the only feasible course of action is to choose one region and use it as a partial but informative example. Writers of textbooks and others have long focused on what is now called the *Dordogne sequence*. (The Dordogne is the name of a river in southcentral France, and many of the classic French cave sites lie within or near its drainage basin.) The choice of the Dordogne sequence is still probably a good one, and we shall now consider briefly what it is.

The Dordogne Sequence

The Dordogne sequence is a record of archeological sites and their assemblages in a large part of southwestern France between about 35,000 years ago and the end of the Pleistocene. The succession of tool-making traditions and the details of the stone, bone, and antler industries apply reasonably well (but not without troublesome exceptions) to an area between Limoges and Toulouse, centered on the modern political unit or province also called Dordogne. North of Limoges toward the Loire and south of Toulouse toward the Pyrenees, some things still apply, but others do not. For northern, east-central, or southeastern France, the Dordogne sequence is often of little help in understanding what happened.

About seven tool-making traditions are represented in the Dordogne sequence. Some are better documented than others, and there is room for disagreement about terminology, but many scholars would recognize traditions called *Perigordian, Aurignacian, Noaillian, Protomagdalenian, Solutrean, Magdalenian,* and *Azilian.* (The Azilian carries on into postglacial times and is also considered a "Mesolithic" tradition.) The *relative* chronological placement of these industries, in terms of recognized climatic phases, is shown in the chart on page 64. Notice carefully that although one usually speaks of the second half of the Würm Glacial as composed of two cold stages (III and IV) separated from each other and from the earlier Würm by more temperate episodes (II/III and III/IV), the cyclical fluctuation of climate was actually far more complex. The sequence of climatic phases, simplified on the chart to indicate only temperature, has been worked out by French geologists, principally Dr. Henri Laville at the University of Bordeaux. It is this kind of *relative dating* sequence that archeologists use most of the time when they are trying to determine how one Dordogne industry relates to another chronologically. The chart also shows some chronometric dates, based on radiocarbon determinations. Note carefully that, because the climatic phases were not of equal length, this chart does not have a uniform vertical scale representing time. The line showing the duration of the Solutrean tradition is as long as that for the Perigordian, but the Solutrean lasted for about 2,000 years, whereas the Perigordian lasted over 11,000 years. Compare this

Tanged Point

Notched Blade

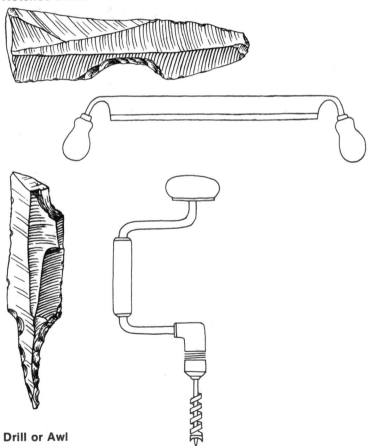

Drill or Awl

with the other chart, on page 65, that does have a uniform vertical time scale, and the true durations of the tool-making traditions are more easily apparent.

Some of the tradition names (Solutrean, Aurignacian) are familiar to the general reader because they have been known and written about for a century or more. Others, like the Noaillian (recognized and named as late as 1966 by Dr. Nicholas David), are not mentioned in the older textbooks. Because some aspects of the cultures represented by the Dordogne sequence have become so well known, the temptation has often been to let this sequence stand for *all* the later Upper Pleistocene blade tool industries of the Old World. The names of the traditions have been extended to apply to other industries in east Africa, Siberia, and even Alaska, implying a degree of similarity and contemporaneity that is far from the case. The last century's image of a unilinear, worldwide similarity in cultural evolution dies hard! The sites and assemblages of the Dordogne sequence give us information about the culture of early modern humans as it existed in one small region near the northwestern corner of the inhabited world; they are not a blueprint for the whole of that world.

Let us now look at some of the products and characteristics of the blade tool traditions.

Special Types of Blade Tools

The most characteristic tools that appeared at this time were made from blades.

1. The *backed* blade. This is a knife made of a flint blade, with one edge purposely blunted, probably to save the user's fingers from being cut (see p. 67). There are several shapes of backed blades, some of which are especially characteristic of Perigordian industries.

2. The *burin* or *graver*. The burin was the original chisel. Its cutting edge is *transverse*, like a chisel's. Some burins are made like a screwdriver, save that burins are sharp. Others have edges more like the blade of a chisel or a push plane, with only one bevel. Burins were probably used to make slots in wood and bone; that is, to make handles or shafts for other tools. They must also be the tools with which much of the engraving on bone (see p. 67) was done. There is a bewildering variety of different kinds of burins, and they are customarily found in all the blade tool industries.

3. The *tanged* point. These stone points were used to tip darts or light spears. They were made from blades, and they had a long tang at the bottom where they were fixed to the shaft.

End-Scraper on a Blade

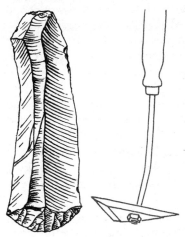

Laurel Leaf Point

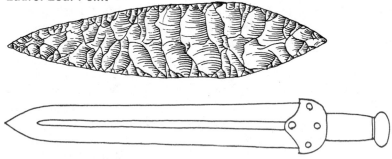

Shouldered Point

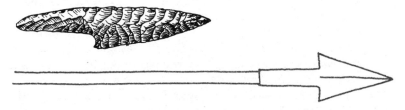

At the place where the tang met the main body of the stone point, there was a marked "shoulder," the beginnings of a barb. Such points had either one or two shoulders (see p. 71). The example illustrated is characteristic of Magdalenian industries, but there are somewhat similar Perigordian ones.

4. The *notched* blade. Along with the points for darts or light spears must go a tool to prepare the dart or spear shaft. To-day, such a tool would be called a draw-knife or a spoke-shave, and this is what the notched blades probably are. Modern spoke-shaves have sharp straight cutting blades and really "shave." Notched blades of flint probably scraped rather than cut (see p. 71).

5. The *awl, drill,* or *borer.* These blade tools were worked to a spike-like point. They must have been used for making holes in such materials as wood, bone, shell, and skin (see p. 71).

6. The *end-scraper on a blade* is a tool with one or both ends worked so as to give a good scraping edge. It could have been used to hollow out wood or bone, scrape hides, remove bark from trees, and a number of other things (p. 73).

There is one very special type of flint tool, which is best known from western Europe in the Solutrean. The most interesting Solutrean tools were not made of blades at all, although normal burins, drills, and other blade tools appear in Solutrean industries.

7. The *laurel leaf point.* Some of these tools are long and dagger-like, and must have been used as knives or daggers. Others were small, called *willow leaf,* and must have been mounted on spear or dart shafts. Another typical Solutrean tool is the *shouldered point.* Both the laurel leaf and shouldered point types are illustrated (see p. 73).

The industries characterized by tools in the blade tradition also yield some flake and core tools. We will end this list with two types of tools that appeared at this time. They were made from either thick flakes or amorphous chunks (cores). Both are characteristic Aurignacian tools.

8. The *keel-shaped round scraper* is usually small and quite round, and had chips removed up to a peak in the center. It is called "keel-shaped" because it is supposed to look (when upside down) like a section through a boat. Actually, it looks more like a tent or an umbrella. Its outer edges are sharp most of the way around, and it was probably a general purpose scraping tool (see p. 75).

9. The *keel-shaped nosed scraper* was made on a flake or chunk with a flat bottom, and has one nicely worked end or "nose." Such tools probably were used like push planes (see p. 75).

Keel-shaped Round Scraper

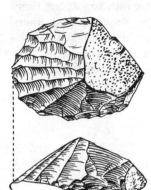

Top view

 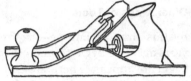

Side view

Keel-shaped Nosed Scraper

Top view

End view

The stone tools (usually made of flint) we have just listed are among the most easily recognized blade tools, although they show differences in detail at different times. There are also many other kinds. Not all of these tools appear in any one industry at one time. Thus the different industries in the Dordogne sequence and others each have only some of the blade tools we've just listed, and also a few flake tools. Some industries even have a few core tools. The particular types of blade tools appearing in one cave layer or another, and the frequency of appearance of the different types, tell which industry we have in each layer.

Other Kinds of Tools

By this time in Europe—say from about 40,000 to about 10,000 years ago—we begin to find other kinds of material, too. Bone tools begin to appear. There are knives, pins, needles with eyes, and little double-pointed straight bars of bone, called *gorges*, that were probably used for catching fish. The fishline would have been fastened in the center of the bar; when the fish swallowed the bait, the bar would have caught crosswise in the fish's mouth.

One quite special kind of bone tool of the Aurignacian is a long flat point for a light spear. It has a deep notch cut up into the breadth of its base, and is called a *split-based bone point* (p. 77). We have examples of bone beads from these times, and of bone handles for flint tools. Pierced teeth of some animals were worn as beads or pendants. There were even spool-shaped buttons or toggles.

Antler came into use for tools, especially in central and western Europe. We do not know the use of one particular antler tool that has a large hole bored in one end. One suggestion is that is was a thong-stropper used to strop or work up hide thongs; another suggestion is that it was an arrow-shaft straightener. French prehistorians have traditionally called it a *baton de commandement.*

Another interesting tool, usually of antler, is the spear- or dart-thrower, which is little more than a stick or shaft of antler with a notch or hook on one end. The hook fits into the butt end of the spear or dart, and the length of the spear-thrower allows one to put much more power into the throw (p. 77). It works on pretty much the same principle as the sling. Elaborately decorated antler examples are known from Magdalenian sites.

Very fancy harpoons of antler were also made in the latter half of the period in western Europe and are especially well known from the Magdalenian. These harpoons had barbs on one or both sides and a base which would slip out of the shaft (p. 77). Some had engraved decoration.

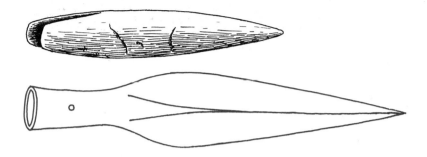

Split-based Bone Point

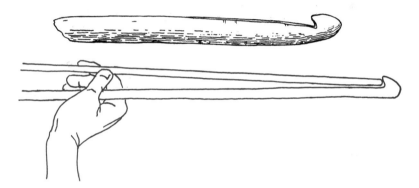

Spear-Thrower

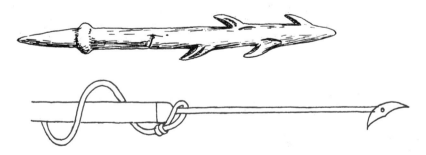

Bone Harpoon

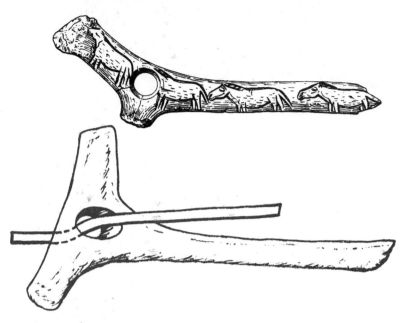

Thong-Stropper

Again let me invite you, by way of a favorite example of mine, to a way of thinking about the Dordogne region industries named on the charts (pp. 64–65). Think of the various tools as items in incomplete mail-order catalogues. Think of the similarities and differences there would be in a mail-order catalogue of 1900 and one of today. Many things, such as certain kinds of carpenter's tools, would not be greatly different. Other items would be considerably different, and many new materials would appear in the catalogue of today. In place of the dates on our catalogues, we have the stratigraphic position of the layers and their position in the climatic sequence to aid us in assessing the time relationships of the industries. But note also that some industries coexist in time on the chart (e.g., Perigordian and Aurignacian). For this, think of the similarities and differences you might note in comparing a modern American and a modern French mail-order catalogue. Finally, think of what the statistical studies hope to gain for us. Shall we be able to recollect the groups of items which belong together as part of one activity cluster? Can we, by these statistical studies, get all the kitchen items blocked together again, and so all the carpenter's items, all the plumber's items, and so on? The various items of the prehistoric activity clusters may not be nicely grouped for us to observe (as they are in the catalogues), so we need to attempt to reconstitute these groups.

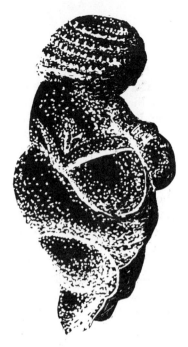

"Venus" Figurine from Willendorf

The Beginning of Art

In western Europe, at least, this period saw the beginning of several kinds of art work. It is handy to break the art down into two great groups: the movable art, and the cave paintings and sculpture. The movable art group includes the scratchings, engravings, and modeling which decorate tools and weapons. Knives, stroppers, spear-throwers, harpoons, and sometimes just plain fragments of bone or antler were often carved. There is also a group of large flat pebbles which seem almost to have served as sketch blocks. The surfaces of these various objects may show animals, or rather abstract floral designs, or geometric designs. There is a recent suggestion, by Mr. Alexander Marshack, that a group of bone artifacts with ordered scratches pertain to a system of calendrical notation based on the regularly changing phases of the moon.

Some of the movable art is not done on tools. The most remarkable examples of this class are little figures of women. These women seem to be pregnant, and their most female characteristics are much emphasized. It is thought that these "Venus" or "Mother-goddess" figurines may have been meant to show the great forces of nature—fertility and the birth of life.

Cave Paintings

In the paintings on walls and ceilings of caves we have some examples that compare with the best art of any time. The subjects were usually animals, the great cold-weather beasts of the end of the Ice Age: the mammoth, the woolly rhinoceros, the bison, the reindeer, the wild horse, the bear, the wild boar, and wild cattle. As in the movable art, there are different styles in the cave art. The really great cave art is pretty well restricted to southern France and Cantabrian (northwestern) Spain, but an interesting new group has recently been reported from Russia.

There are several interesting things about the Franco-Cantabrian cave art. It was done deep down in the darkest and most dangerous parts of the caves, although the people themselves lived only in the openings of caves. If you think what they must have had for lights—crude lamps of hollowed stone have been found, which must have burned some kind of oil or grease, with a matted hair or fiber wick—and of the animals that may have lurked in the caves, you'll understand the danger. Then, too, we're sure the pictures these people painted were not simply to be looked at and admired, for they painted one picture right over other pictures which had been done earlier. Clearly, it was the *act* of *painting* that counted. The painter had to go way down into the most mysterious depths of the earth and create an animal in paint. Possibly he believed that by doing this he gained some magic power over the same kind of animal when he hunted it in the open air. It certainly doesn't look as if he cared very much about the pictures he painted—as a finished product to be admired—for he or somebody else went down a short time later and painted another animal right over the original one.

The cave art of the Franco-Cantabrian style is one of the great artistic achievements of all time. The subjects drawn are almost always the larger animals of the time. In some of the best examples, the beasts are drawn in full color and the paintings are remarkably alive and charged with energy. They come from the hands of people who knew the great animals well—knew the feel of their fur, the tremendous drive of their muscles, and the danger one faced when hunting them.

Other artistic styles have been found in eastern Spain and in Africa and the eastern Mediterranean. They sometimes include lively drawings, often of people hunting with bow and arrow. The east Spanish art is found on open rock faces and in rock shelters. It is less spectacular and apparently more recent than the Franco-Cantabrian cave art.

Life at the End of the Ice Age in Europe

Life in these times was probably as good as a hunter could expect it to be. Game and fish seem to have been plentiful; berries and wild fruits probably were, too. From France to Russia, great pits or piles of animal bones have been found. Some of this killing was done as our Plains Indians killed the buffalo—by stampeding them over steep river banks or cliffs. Hunters making Perigordian tools drove horses off a cliff at the famous site of Solutré in eastern France; the remains of the thousands of butchered animals make up a tightly packed layer of bones several feet thick.

In western Europe, people lived in the openings of caves, under overhanging rocks, and in open-air sites. On the great plains of eastern Europe, very crude huts were built half underground. Dr. Bohuslav Klima's sites in the Pollau hills of Czechoslovakia are excellent examples. Comparable open encampment sites are reported from France, especially Magdalenian ones, and a hut foundation from Germany, as well. It is a question whether these sites were occupied year around. Parts of this time were cold, as we have seen from Laville's work with the Dordogne sequence. During much of the last great glaciation, northern Europe from Scotland to Scandinavia, northern Germany, and Russia, and also the higher mountains to the south, were certainly covered with ice. But people had fire, and the needles and tools used for scraping hides must mean that they wore clothing.

It is clear that the people were thinking of a great variety of things besides the tools that helped them get food and shelter. Such burials as we find have more grave-gifts than before. Beads and ornaments and often flint, bone, or antler tools are included in the grave, and sometimes the body was sprinkled with red ochre. Red is the color of blood, which means life, and of fire, which means heat. Professor Childe wondered if the red ochre was a pathetic attempt at magic—to give back to the body the heat that had gone from it. But pathetic or not, it is sure proof that these people were already moved by death as we still are moved by it.

Their art is another example of the direction the human mind was taking. And when I say human, I mean it in the fullest sense, for this is the time in which fully modern men and women appeared. It's not yet absolutely sure which particular group produced the great cave art, but in the Dordogne and surrounding regions, movable art objects of some kind appear associated with all seven named tool-making traditions. In France and elsewhere, a concern with art and decoration is a general characteristic of the cultures of the end of the Ice Age.

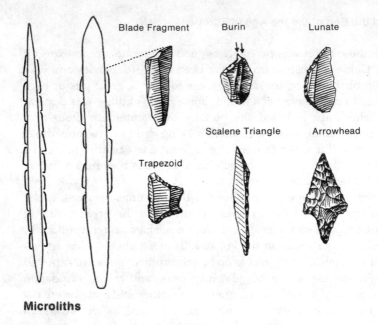

Microliths

Blade Fragment

Burin

Lunate

Scalene Triangle

Arrowhead

Trapezoid

Microliths

One peculiar set of tools seems to serve as a marker for the very last phase of the Ice Age in southwestern Europe. This tool-making habit is also found about the shore of the Mediterranean basin, and it moved into northern Europe as the last glaciation pulled northward. People began making blade tools of very small size. They learned how to chip very slender and tiny blades from a prepared core. Then they made these little blades into tiny triangles, half-moons *(lunates)*, trapezoids, and several other geometric forms. These little tools are called *geometric microliths*. They are so small that most of them must have been fixed in handles or shafts.

We have found several examples of microliths mounted in shafts. In northern Europe, where their use soon spread, the microlithic triangles or lunates were set in rows down each side of a bone or wood point. One corner of each little triangle stuck out, and the whole thing made a fine barbed harpoon. In historic times in Egypt, geometric trapezoidal microliths were still in use as arrowheads. They were fastened—broad end out—on the end of an arrow shaft. It seems queer to give an arrow a point shaped like a "T." Actually, the little points were very sharp, and must have pierced the hides of animals very easily. We also think that the broader cutting edge of the point may have caused more bleeding than a pointed arrowhead would. In hunting fleet-footed animals like the gazelle, which might run for miles after being shot with an arrow, it was an advantage to cause as much bleeding as possible, for the animal would drop sooner.

We are not really sure where the microliths were first invented. There is some evidence that they appeared early in the Near East. Their use was very common in northwest Africa, but this came later. Given the wide distribution of microliths in the Old World at the end of the Pleistocene, it is likely that they came into use in many areas within a very short span of time. It has frequently been suggested (but not very well documented) that the appearance of geometric microliths is the archeological expression of the invention and spread of the bow and arrow.

Remember that the microliths we are talking about were made from carefully prepared little blades, and are most characteristically geometric in outline. Each microlithic industry proper was made up, in good part, of such tiny blade tools. But there were also some normal-sized blade tools and even some flake scrapers in most microlithic industries. And in many there were tiny burins and tiny scrapers of nongeometric shape. Very small blade tools occur sometimes in earlier industries (for example, the Perigordian of the Dordogne sequence), but the great and widespread importance of geometric microliths is a new element at the end of the Ice Age.

Later Blade Tool Industries of the Near East and Africa

The habit of making blade tools of normal size apparently spread from Europe to central Siberia. We noted that blade tools were made in western Asia, too, at an early date. The western Asiatic blade tool industries do vaguely recall some aspects of those of western Europe, but archeologists quite properly use completely local names for them, such as *Emiran* and *Antelian* in Palestine and *Baradostian* and *Zarzian* in Kurdistan. Similar blade industries are known from the mountain valleys of Afghanistan, and there is some evidence from western India.

In north Africa, an early blade tool industry called Dabban (mentioned earlier) is known from coastal Libya at Haua Fteah, but the industries found at most north African and Saharan sites at the end of the Pleistocene are of a different kind called *Aterian*. Flakes (not blades) produced by the Levallois or discoidal core techniques were used to make Aterian tools, many of which had tangs, apparently for hafting. Other Aterian tools were bifacially flaked, leaf-shaped points. Later (mostly post-Pleistocene) industries in this north African area contained full-sized blade tools of the kinds we mentioned earlier for Europe. There were also geometric microliths. Recently, as part of the Nubian salvage effort (to reclaim the antiquities in the area flooded by the Aswan Dam in upper Egypt), several well-developed blade tool industries were discovered. Professor Philip Smith has named two he encountered the *Silsilian* and *Sebekian* industries. The last word has clearly not yet been written about the later Pleistocene of northeast Africa.

Blade tools, bifacial leaf-shaped points, and some other late stone tool types have also appeared in central and southern Africa. By early postglacial times, many industries of eastern and southern Africa were predominantly geometric microliths on bladelets, and eventually some coarse pottery appeared in east Africa. Professor Desmond Clark, who knows the prehistoric evidence from Africa very well, sees an increasing trend toward regional environmental specialization as time went on. New "niches," the forest fringes, the high grasslands, the dry savannas were the scenes of experimentation with new ways of living.

The Far East

By the end of the Pleistocene, large parts of Siberia had been occupied and, as we have mentioned, blade tool industries there were similar to those of Europe. In Mongolia and northernmost China, the very late Pleistocene industries were still predominantly based on flakes, and some contain choppers, but the presence of the true blade technique in some industries suggests that this part of the Far East was no longer completely divorced from the traditions of the western Old World. In Japan at the end of the Pleistocene one finds, among other things, exceptionally well made obsidian blade tools in forms very similar to those of Europe, the Near East, and Siberia.

Southern China and southeast Asia are very poorly known in the time period concerned. The stone industries seem to remain in the eastern chopper and simple flake tradition we mentioned before. Whatever may be our aesthetic impression of the stone tools, however, we must not imagine that the inhabitants of this part of the world were sunk in backwardness and sloth. One of the most interesting aspects of recent research on the prehistory of southeastern Asia is the evidence suggesting that the beginnings of food production may have been underway here at the end of the Pleistocene, as they were in the Near East.

Finally, it was in the latest part of the Pleistocene (at least 30,000 years ago) that people, making simple core and flake tools, entered the continent of Australia for the first time.

The New World Becomes Inhabited

Likewise, at some time toward the end of the last great glaciation—almost certainly less than 30,000 years ago—people began to move over the Bering Strait from Asia into America. As you know, the American Indians have been assumed to be basically Mongoloids. New studies of blood group types make this somewhat uncertain, but there is no doubt that the ancestors of the American Indians came by way of Asia. It has been generally agreed that the stone tool traditions of Europe, Africa, the Near and Middle East, and central Siberia did *not* move into the New World in their characteristically recognizable forms. With only a very few special or late exceptions, no core bifaces, flakes, or blade tools of western Old World types have been found in the Americas. We shall, however, postpone the story of the New World developments to a later chapter.

6
End and prelude

Up to the end of the last glaciation, we prehistorians have a relatively comfortable time schedule. The farther back we go, the less exact we can be about time and details. Elbowroom of five, ten, even fifty or more thousands of years becomes available for us to maneuver in as we work backward in time. But now our story has come forward to the point where more exact methods of dating are at hand. The radioactive carbon method, even allowing for its whimsicalities, reaches back into the span of the last glaciation. There are other methods, developed by the geologists and paleobotanists, which supplement and extend the usefulness of the radioactive carbon determinations. And, as our means of being more exact increase, our story grows more exciting. There are also more details of culture for us to deal with, which add to the interest.*

*This is *not* to say that we yet have really exact chronometric precision in the sense of true calendar years ago. Refer again to the chart on page 4, and its note. As I write this, there is evidence to correct, or "recalibrate," radiocarbon age determinations to calendar years, by means of the bristlecone pine dendrochronology, back to about 7000 years ago. The chart on page 4 suggests that by that time, radiocarbon age determinations run about a thousand years shorter (later) than the dendrochronology. How the dendrochronological curve will behave if it can be extended even earlier, we do not know, but Professor Hans Suess firmly believes it will stay on the early side of the determinations for some millennia at least.

Anyway, we have now arrived at a point in the story where this recalibration matter ought to be accounted for. There are two slightly differing recalibration tables. Also, many of the sites we shall be concerned with have only one or two radiocarbon determinations, and sometimes these determinations may look wildly improbable. After some consideration, I have decided not to attempt to recalibrate, but I will add a "(+)" after each radiocarbon determination I give, simply to remind you that the real date is probably some hundreds of years earlier than the determination. In fact, since I've grown used to thinking of dates in terms of the available radiocarbon determinations (in Libby half-life terms), I'll even add that "(+)" from now on to determinations older than 7000 years ago and to my "guess-estimates." Thus a determination of, say, 6750 ± 250 B.C.(+) probably has an age of about 7750 B.C.

Changes at the End of the Ice Age

The last great glaciation of the Ice Age was a complex affair; remember, for example, the climatic alternations we saw in the Dordogne sequence, with subphases after the end of the second major part. In Europe the second major part of this glaciation began slacking off somewhere around 14,000 years ago. By that time the glaciers had begun to melt back for the last time. (Remember, though, that some geologists aren't sure the Ice Age is over yet!) This melting sometimes went by fits and starts, and the weather wasn't always changing for the better, but we know that there was at least one time when European weather was even better than it is now.

The melting back of the glaciers and the weather fluctuations caused other changes, too. We know a fair amount about these changes in northwestern Europe. In an earlier chapter, we said that the whole Ice Age was a matter of continual change over long periods of time. As the last glaciers began to melt back, some interesting things happened to people.

In Europe, along with the melting of the last glaciers, geography itself was changing. Britain and Ireland had certainly become islands by 5,000 B.C.(+). The Baltic was sometimes a salt sea, sometimes a large freshwater lake. Forests began to grow where the glaciers had been, and in what had once been the cold tundra areas in front of the glaciers. The great cold-weather animals—the mammoth and the woolly rhinoceros—retreated northward and finally died out. It is possible that the efficient hunting of the earlier people of 20,000 or 25,000 to about 12,000 years ago had helped this process along (see p. 81). Europeans, especially those of the postglacial period, had to keep changing in order to keep up with the times.

As they have usually been presented, the archeological materials for the time from 10,000 to 6,000 B.C.(+) seem simpler than those of the previous 5,000 years. The great cave art of France and Spain had gone; so had the fine carving in bone and antler. Smaller, speedier animals were moving into the new forests. New ways of hunting them, or ways of getting other food, had to be found. Hence, new tools and weapons were necessary. Some of the people who moved into now deglaciated northern Germany were successful reindeer hunters. Then the reindeer moved still further north and east, and again new sources of food had to be found. These archeological materials have not yet been fully studied in terms of the subtle interrelationships which all the items in the assemblages bear to the evidence of their original environmental contexts. When these materials are given such new and more ecologically oriented interpretation, they may not seem so simple.

The Readjustments Completed in Europe

After a few thousand years, things began to look better. Or at least we can say this: by about 6,000 b.c.(+) we again get better archeological materials. The best of these come from the north European area: Britain, Belgium, Holland, Denmark, north Germany, southern Norway, and Sweden. Much of this north European material comes from bogs and swamps where it had become waterlogged and has kept very well. Thus we now have much more complete *assemblages** than for any time earlier.

The best known of these assemblages is the *Maglemosian*, named after a great Danish peat-swamp where much has been found. In the Maglemosian assemblage the flint industry was still very important. Blade tools, arrow points, and burins were still made, but there were also axes for cutting the trees in the new forests. Moreover, the tiny microlithic blades, in a variety of geometric forms, have also been found. There was a ground stone industry; some axes and clubheads were made by grinding and polishing rather than by chipping. The industries in bone and antler show a great variety of tools: axes, fishhooks, fish spears, handles and hafts for other tools, harpoons, and clubs. A remarkable industry in wood has been preserved. Paddles, sled runners, handles for tools, and bark floats for fishnets have been found. There are even fishnets made of plant fibers. Canoes of some kind were no doubt made. Bone and antler tools were decorated with simple patterns, and amber was collected. Wooden bows and arrows have been found.

It seems likely that many Maglemosian bog finds are remains of summer camps, and that in winter the people moved to higher and more forested regions. Nevertheless, an excellent excavation of a winter–early spring encampment was made at Star Carr in northern England. Childe called the people who made these assemblages the *Forest folk*; they probably lived much the same sort of life as did our pre-agricultural Indians of the northcentral states. They hunted small game or deer; they did a great deal of fishing; they collected

---

*I myself find "assemblage" a useful word when there are different kinds of archeological materials belonging together, from one area and of one time. An assemblage, for me, is made up of a number of "industries" (that is, all the tools in chipped stone, all the tools in bone, all the tools in wood, the traces of houses, etc.) and everything else that manages to survive, such as the art, the burials, the bones of the animals used as food, and the traces of plant foods; in fact, everything that has been left to us and can be used to help reconstruct the lives of the people to whom it once belonged. Our own present-day assemblage would be the sum total of all the objects in our mail-order catalogues, department stores and supply houses of every sort, our churches, our art galleries, and other buildings, together with our roads, canals, dams, irrigation ditches, and any other traces we might leave of ourselves, from graves to garbage dumps. Not everything would last, so that an archeologist digging us up—say 2,000 years from now—would find only the most durable items in our assemblage. Some of my colleagues who work in the earlier ranges of the Pleistocene where *only* chipped stone tools are found call them "assemblages" if they are found in good archeological context. This is what I myself use the word "industry" for.

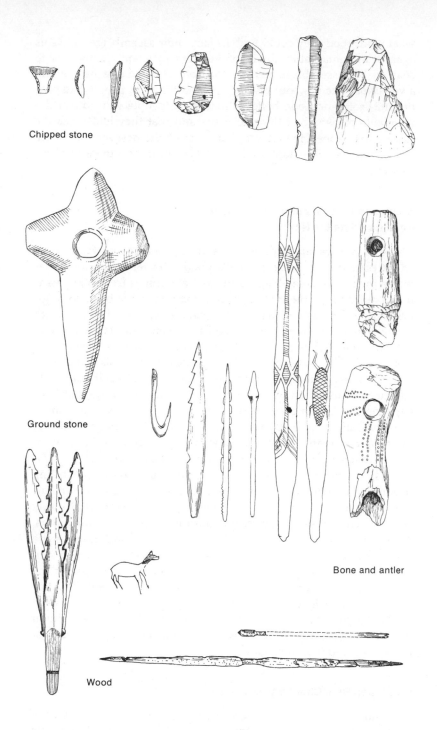

Chipped stone

Ground stone

Wood

Bone and antler

Sketch of Maglemosian Assemblage

what plant food they could find. In fact, their assemblage shows us again that remarkable ability of humans to adapt themselves to change. The assemblage includes the domesticated dog; he was still a very wolf-like dog, but his long association with people had now begun. Professor Coon believes that these people were direct descendants of people of the glacial age and that they had much the same appearance. He believes that most of the descendants of Ice Age survivors still extant are living today in the northwestern European area.

South and Central Europe Perhaps As Readjusted As the North

There is always one trouble with things that come from areas where preservation is exceptionally good: The very quantity of materials in such an assemblage tends to make things from other areas look poor and simple, although they may not have been so originally at all. The assemblages of the people who lived to the south of the Maglemosian area may also have been quite large and varied; but, unfortunately, relatively little of the southern assemblages has lasted. The waterlogged sites of the Maglemosian area preserved a great deal more. Hence the Maglemosian itself *looks* quite advanced to us, when we compare it with the few things that have happened to last in other areas. If we could go back and wander over the Europe of 8,000 years ago, we would probably find that the people of France, central Europe, and southcentral Russia were just as advanced as those of the north European-Baltic belt.

South of the north European belt the hunting–food-collecting peoples were living on as best they could during this time. One interesting group, which seems to have kept to the regions of sandy soil and scrub forest, made great quantities of geometric microliths. These are the materials called *Tardenoisian*. The materials of the Forest folk of France and central Europe generally are called *Azilian;* Dr. Movius believes the term might best be restricted to the area south of the Loire River. Professor H. T. Waterbolk once informed me that he doubted that really successful adjustments did take place in central Europe. In fact, Waterbolk is of the opinion that central Europe was pretty well depopulated before the earliest farmers moved into the region.

How Much Real Change Was There?

You can see that no really *basic* change in the way of life has yet been described. Childe saw the problem that faced the Europeans of 10,000 to 4,000 B.C.(+) as a problem in cultural readaptation to the postglacial forest environments. By 6,000 B.C.($+$) some quite successful solutions of the problem—such as the Maglemosian—had been made. The upsets that came with the melting of the last ice gradually brought about all sorts of changes in the tools and food-getting habits, but the people themselves were still just as much hunters, fishers, and food-collectors as they had been in 25,000 B.C.($+$). It could be said that they changed just enough so that they would not have to change. But there is a bit more to it than this.

In part because the spectacular Franco-Cantabrian art had now disappeared and in part due to certain accidents in the growth of ideas about prehistory, many prehistorians consider the materials of this time "inferior" or "degenerate." Professor Mathiassen of Copenhagen, who knows these archeological remains very well, puts the matter in another way. He speaks of the material as being neither rich nor progressive, in fact "rather stagnant," but he goes on to add that the people had a certain "receptiveness" and were able to adapt themselves quickly when the next change did come. My own understanding of the situation is that the Forest folk made nothing as spectacular as had the producers of the earlier Magdalenian assemblage and the Franco-Cantabrian art. On the other hand, they *seem* to have been making many more different kinds of tools for many more different kinds of tasks than had their Ice Age forerunners. I emphasize "seem" because the preservation in the Maglemosian bogs is very complete; certainly we cannot list anywhere nearly as many different things for earlier times as we did for the Maglemosians (p. 88). I believe this experimentation with all kinds of new tools and gadgets, this intensification of adaptiveness, this "receptiveness," even if it is still only pointed toward hunting, fishing, and food collecting, is an important thing.

Remember that the only possibly widespread artifactual marker we have handy for the *beginning* of this tendency toward receptiveness and experimentation is the little microlithic blade tools of various geometric forms. These, we saw, began before the last ice had melted away, and they lasted on in use for a very long time. I wish there were a better marker than the microliths, but I do not know of one. Remember, too, that as yet we can use the appearance of microliths as a marker only in Europe and about the Mediterranean.

Changes in Other Areas?

All this last section was about Europe. How about the rest of the world when the last glaciers were melting away? We are slowly beginning to learn more about this particular time in parts of the Old

World other than Europe, the Mediterranean basin, and the Middle East. People were certainly continuing to move into the New World by way of Siberia and the Bering Strait about this time. But for much of Africa and Asia, the story is still incomplete. Some day, we shall no doubt be able to fill in the scattered details we now have.

Some interesting new information has come as the result of the salvage archeology done in the area of southern Egypt, now flooded by the Aswan Dam. Besides developed and small Levalloisian tools of east African type, we now know that blade tools and microliths were being made by about 14,000(+) years ago (see p. 83). These are best represented at a place called Kom Ombo. Other microlithic industries, probably later, have appeared in the Kharga oasis. There appears to be good evidence at Kom Ombo that special adjustments were being made to riverside environments.

Real Change and Prelude in the Near East

The appearance of the microliths and the developments made by the Forest folk of northwestern Europe also mark an end. They show us the terminal phase of the old food-collecting way of life. It grows increasingly clear that at about the same time that the Maglemosian and other Forest folk were adapting themselves to hunting, fishing, and collecting in new ways to fit the postglacial environment, something completely new was being made ready in southwestern Asia. In other parts of the world, at about the same time, came other examples of the same new experiment.

Since my own career and competence (such as they are) have developed mainly in southwestern Asia, I'll concentrate on events there. Remember, however, it was not necessarily the center of the universe! Unfortunately, we do not yet seem to have as much understanding of the climate and environment of the late Ice Age in southwestern Asia as we have for most of Europe. There is also some difference of opinion on the matter, as we shall see. Probably the weather was never quite so violent or life quite so rugged as it was in northern Europe. We know that microliths made their appearance in western Asia by at least 12,000 b.c.(+), and probably earlier. They may serve us, short of anything better, as a mark for the beginning of the terminal phase of food collecting. Then, gradually, we begin to see the buildup toward the first *basic change* in human life.

This change amounted to a revolution just as important as the Industrial Revolution. In it people first learned to domesticate plants and animals. They began *producing* their food instead of simply gathering or collecting it. As food production became reasonably effective, people seem already to have settled down with a degree of permanence in village-farming communities. Open-air encampments with clusters of huts were far earlier (see p. 81), but the question of year-round and year-in, year-out permanence is at issue. Indeed, we seem now to be recovering increasing evidence of village-like settlements (year around?) before positive traces of effective food production. But with the appearance of the little farming villages in which traces of plant and animal domesticates do appear, a new way of life was actually under way. Professor Childe had good reason to speak of the "food-producing revolution," for it was indeed a revolution.

Questions About Cause

Although there is an increasing amount of speculation by some colleagues (perhaps too impatient to wait for adequate evidence?), we do not yet know *how* and *why* this great revolution took place. We are only just beginning to put the questions properly. I suspect the answers will concern some delicate and subtle interplay between humans and nature. Clearly, both the level of culture and the natural condition of the environment must have been ready before the change itself could come about. I mean this as simply as I write it, and not in an orthogenetic, or predetermined, sense.

It is going to take years of cooperative field work by both archeologists and the natural scientists who are most helpful to them before the *how* and *why* answers begin to appear. Both anthropologically and historically trained archeologists are fascinated with the cultures of people in times of great change. About 10,000 or 12,000(+) years ago, the general level of culture in many parts of the world seems to have been ready for change. In northwestern Europe, we saw that cultures "changed just enough so that they would not have to change." We linked this to environmental changes with the coming of postglacial times.

Perhaps because it had attracted archeological attention for so long, southwestern Asia was the first place in which we recovered substantial evidence of an actual food-producing revolution. We can see the important consequence of effective domestication of plants and animals in the spread of the settled village-farming community way of life. We *think* that there has been (although vast areas remain unsurveyed, and much destructive erosion has happened) an increase in the number of sites themselves, and that this indicates population increase. Certainly, also, within the village-farming community was the seed of civilization. The way in which effective domestication of plants and animals came about, however, must also be linked closely with the natural environment. Thus archeologists will not solve the *how* and *why* questions alone; both in the field and in the laboratory, they will need the help of interested natural scientists.

Preconditions for the Revolution

Especially at this point in our story, we must remember how culture and environment go hand in hand. Neither plants nor animals domesticate themselves; humans domesticate them. Furthermore, humans usually domesticate only those plants and animals which are useful. People cannot domesticate plants and animals that do not exist in the environment where the people live. Also, there are certainly some animals and probably some plants that resist domestication, although they might be useful.

This brings me back again to the point that *both* the level of culture and the natural condition of the environment, with the proper plants (and—in the Near East at least—animals) in it, must have been ready before domestication could have happened. Both the humans and the plant and animal forms—as well as end-glacial conditions—had happened several times earlier during the Pleistocene. But readiness is precondition, not cause. Why did effective food production happen first in the Near East, if indeed it did? Why did it happen independently in the New World, and only slightly later, too? Why also in the Far East and in southeastern Asia, where there are some claims it happened earliest? Why did it happen at all? Why are all human beings not still living as the Maglemosians did? These are the questions we still have to face.

Cultural Receptiveness and Promising Environments

Until the archeologists and the natural scientists—botanists, geologists, zoologists, and general ecologists—have spent many more years on the problem, we shall not have full *how* and *why* answers, if indeed we ever get them. I do think, however, that we are beginning to understand what to look for.

We shall have to learn much more about what makes human cultures receptive and experimental. Is "receptiveness" itself a useful notion here? Did change in the environment alone force the pace of change? Was it simply a case of Professor Toynbee's "challenge and response"? I cannot believe the answer is quite that simple. Were it so simple, we should want to know why the change hadn't come earlier, along with earlier environmental changes. We shall not know the answers, however, until we have excavated the traces of many more cultures of the time in question. We shall doubtless also have to learn more about, and think imaginatively about, the simpler cultures still left today. The "mechanics" of culture in general will be bound to interest us.

It will also be necessary to learn more about the environments of 10,000 to 12,000(+) years ago. Were they themselves in the process of significant change or were they relatively stable? In which regions of the world were the natural conditions most promising? Did these conditions include plants and animals which could be domesticated, or did they offer only new ways of food collecting? There is much work to do on this problem, but we are beginning to get some general hints.

Before I begin to detail the hints we now have from southwestern Asia, I want to do two things. First, I shall tell you of an old theory as to how food production might have appeared and also suggest some of the newer theories now under discussion. Second, I shall bother you with some definitions which should help us in our thinking as the story goes on.

An Old Theory As to the Cause
of the Revolution

The idea that change would result if the balance between nature and culture became upset is of course not a new one. For well over twenty-five years, one general theory prevailed as to how the food-producing revolution happened. This theory depended directly on the idea of natural change in the environment.

The 5,000 years following about 12,000 b.c.(+) must have been very difficult ones, the theory began. These were the years when the most marked melting of the last glaciers was going on. While the glaciers were in place, the climate to the south of them must have been different from the climate in those areas today. You have no doubt read that people once lived in regions now covered by the Sahara Desert. This is true; just when and exactly where is not entirely clear. The old theory went that, during the time of the glaciers, there was a broad belt of rain winds south of the glaciers. These rain winds would have kept north Africa, the Nile Valley, and the Middle East green and fertile. But when the glaciers melted back to the north, the belt of rain winds was supposed to have moved north too. Then the people living south and east of the Mediterranean would have found that their water supply was drying up, that the animals they hunted were dying or moving away, and that the plant foods they collected were dried up and scarce.

According to the old theory, all this would have been true except in the valleys of rivers and in oases in the growing deserts. Here, in the only places where water was left, the humans, animals, and plants would have clustered. They would have been forced to live in close propinquity to one another in order to live at all. Presently the people would have seen that some animals were more useful or made better food than others, and so they would have begun to protect these animals from their natural enemies. They would also have been forced to try new plant foods—foods which possibly had to be prepared before they could be eaten. Thus, with trials and errors, but forced to live close to plants and animals, people would have eventually learned to domesticate them.

The Old Theory Too Simple for the Facts

This theory was set up before we really knew anything in detail about the later prehistory of the Near and Middle East. We now know that the facts which have been found don't fit the old theory at all well. Also, I have yet to find an American meteorologist who feels that we know enough about the changes in the weather pattern to say that it could have been so simple and direct. And, of course, the glacial ice which began melting after 12,000(+) years ago was merely the last subphase of the last great glaciation. There had also been three earlier periods of great alpine glaciers, and long periods of warm weather in between. If the rain belt moved north as the glaciers melted for the last time, it must have moved in the same direction in earlier times. Thus, the forced neighborliness of humans, plants, and animals in river valleys and oases must also have happened earlier. Why didn't domestication happen earlier, then?

Furthermore, it does not seem to be in the oases and river valleys that we have yet found our first or only traces of either food production or the earliest farming villages. (I myself first thought that these traces would be restricted to the hilly flanks of the mountains of western Asia, but that notion was also too restrictive.) In fact, everything we now know suggests that the old theory was just too simple an explanation to have been the true one. The only reason I mention it—beyond correcting the ideas you may get in some older texts—is that it illustrates the kind of thinking we shall have to do, even if it is doubtless wrong in detail.

We archeologists shall have to depend much more than we ever have on the natural scientists who can really help us. I can tell you this from experience. I have had the great good fortune to have on my expedition staffs in Iraq in 1954–55, in Iran in 1959–60, and in Turkey since 1963, agronomists and botanists, geologists and geographers, and zoologists. Their studies added whole new bands of color to my spectrum of thinking about *how* and *why* the revolution took place and how the village-farming community began. But this is only a beginning; as I said earlier, we are just now learning to ask the proper questions.

A Flood of New Theories

Probably no focus of prehistoric archeological attention has attracted so much interest (or become so fashionable) since the end of World War II as the problem of the beginnings of food production. Naturally, this interest has led to much theorizing about cause, and the theories—particularly those depending on the "law-and-order" school of culture-process speculations—have bred like rabbits. (As regards the Near East, it has seemed to me that the theorists with the least familiarity with the region and its evidence have become the most ardent polemicists!)

We might note first that the matter of an environmentally determined change from food gathering to food production is still under consideration (see p. 94). We now have a suggestion that the late Pleistocene climate and environment of the Near East (and of the northern Mediterranean littoral) was of a cold, dry, treeless, artemisia (sagebrush) steppe type with a trend toward present conditions setting in only about 11,000(+) years ago. This is based on the analyses of pollen-bearing sediments recovered by Professors Herbert E. Wright and Willem van Zeist. Wright even ponders the idea that the late Pleistocene "refuge" of the present Mediterranean types of plant species might have been in north Africa, and he dismisses claims for a moist end-Pleistocene phase in Palestine as based on insufficient evidence.

You will note that this would mean that the early *post*-Pleistocene trend for at least parts of the Near East was toward *moister and warmer* conditions, not toward drier ones, as the old riverine-oasis theory of domestication held. Nor would it encourage the idea of no essential change at all, as I've myself believed. Wright's proposal is by no means universally accepted, but I know Wright as a responsible Pleistocene geologist and palynologist and I also know that he realizes the final evidence is not yet in hand.

I will not try to summarize the various culture-process theories for you; they are available in the volumes I cite in the bibliography. Some, such as Lewis Binford's tension-zone–demography scheme (ingenious as it may be as a pure mental exercise) already had no pertinence when they were written *if* Wright's palynological evidence was brought to bear. I myself am most sensitive to the type of reasoning behind Professor Kent Flannery's whimsically named

"Serutan," or systems theory, approach. Vastly oversimplified, systems theory in archeology *provokes* more adequate search for, recovery, and thoughtful interpretation of the overall evidence bearing on the web of interrelatedness of human activities with the natural environments in which they took place. (I'm sorry, but you must read that sentence twice and think about it!) Flannery develops his ideas most fruitfully in dealing with New World materials; he realizes that the Near Eastern evidence is still very meagre.* As I suggested in my Preface, however, at the very moment a new theory is being printed, new evidence to amend or outdate the theory is invariably being excavated. I know: the same thing always keeps happening to my own theories! We prehistoric archeologists are in no danger of unemployment.

About Stages and Eras

Now come some definitions, so I may describe my material more easily. Archeologists have always loved to make divisions and subdivisions within the long range of materials which they have found. They often disagree violently about which particular assemblage of material goes into which subdivision, about what the subdivisions should be named, about what the subdivisions really mean culturally. Some archeologists, probably through habit, favor an old scheme of Grecized names for the subdivisions: paleolithic, mesolithic, neolithic. I refuse to use these words myself although they sound very learned. They have meant too many different things to too many different people and have tended to hide some pretty fuzzy thinking. Probably you haven't even noticed my own scheme of subdivision up to now, but I'd better tell you in general what it is.

I think of the earliest great group of archeological materials, from which we can deduce only a food-gathering way of culture, as the *food-gathering stage.* I say "stage" rather than "age" because it is not quite over yet; there are still a few primitive people in out-of-the-way parts of the world who remain in the food-gathering stage. In fact, Professor Julian Steward would probably have preferred to call it a food-gathering *level* of existence, rather than a stage. This would be perfectly acceptable to me. I also tend to find myself using *collecting,* rather than *gathering,* for the more recent aspects or eras of the stage, as my favorite dictionary appears to attribute more sense of purpose and specialization to "collecting" than to "gathering."

Now, while I think we could make several possible subdivisions

---

*See particularly Flannery's 1973 paper, noted in the bibliography.

of the food-gathering stage—I call my subdivisions of stages *eras**—
I believe the only one which means much to us here is the last or
terminal subera of food collecting of the whole food-gathering stage.
The microliths seem to mark its approach, at least in the northwestern part of the Old World. It is really shown best in the Old
World by the materials of the Forest folk, the cultural adaptation to
the postglacial environments in northwestern Europe. We talked
about the Forest folk at the beginning of this chapter, and I used
the Maglemosian assemblage of Denmark as an example.

The food-producing revolution ushered in the *food-producing stage.*
This stage began to be replaced by the *industrial stage* only about
two hundred years ago. Now notice that my stage divisions are in
terms of technology and economics. We must think sharply to be
sure that the subdivisions of the stages, the eras, are in the same
terms. This does *not* mean that I think technology and economics
are the only important realms of culture. It is rather that, for most
of prehistoric time, the materials left to the archeologists have
tended to focus our deductions on technology and economics. For
the time toward the end of prehistory, deductions in other aspects
of culture should be increasingly possible as our finds grow more
complex and varied. So far, however, we are less sure of our interpretations in the other aspects of culture. It is far easier to identify
and interpret the traces of something meant to help you eat or
build than it is to interpret something meant to be prayed to. I do
not mean by this that there was no praying! Further, I myself feel
bullish about the future of archeological interpretation as it may be
applied to ever more of the total cultural spectrum. Such interpretation will not be easily done, however.

I'm so soon out of my competence, as conventional ancient history begins, that I shall only suggest the earlier eras of the food-
producing stage to you. This book is about prehistory, and I'm not
a universal historian.

The Two Earliest Eras of the Food-Producing Stage

The food-producing stage seems to appear in western Asia with
revolutionary suddenness compared to the long eons of time of the

---

*It is difficult to find words which have a sequence or gradation of meaning with re-
spect to both development and a range of time in the past, or with a range of time from
somewhere in the past which is perhaps not yet ended. One definition of stage in *Webster's Third New International Dictionary* is: "One of the steps into which the material development of man . . . is divided." I cannot find any dictionary definition that suggests
which of the words, *stage* or *era*, has the meaning of a longer span of time. Therefore, I
have chosen to let my eras be shorter, and to subdivide my stages into eras. Webster
gives era as: "A signal stage of history, an epoch." When I want to subdivide my eras, I
find myself using *suberas*. Thus I speak of the *eras* within a *stage* and of the *suberas*
within an *era*; that is, I do so when I feel that I really have to, and when the evidence is
clear enough to allow it.

food-gathering stage. This suddenness is seen by the relative speed with which the traces of new crafts appear in the earliest village-farming community sites we've dug. It is seen by the apparent spread and multiplication of these sites themselves, and the remarkable growth in human population we deduce from this apparent increase in sites. We'll look at some of these sites and the archeological traces they yield in the next chapter. When such village sites begin to appear, I believe we are in the *era of the primary village-farming community*. I also believe, however, that this is the second era of the food-producing stage.

The first era of the food-producing stage, I believe, was an *era of incipient cultivation and animal domestication*. I keep saying "I believe" because the actual evidence for this earlier era is so slight that one has to set it up mainly by playing a hunch for it. The reason for playing the hunch goes about as follows.

As the food-collecting era matured, we noticed a marked increase in the variety of different assemblages available, and these assemblages came from an ever broader variety of environmental situations. The whole habitable world became inhabited. My own tendency has been to see this as due to the increased ability of people to settle down and settle into a greater variety of specific environmental situations. This "in-settling" seems to have become even more intensified in the terminal subera of food collecting. People were learning to utilize a far greater variety of resources within any given environmental niche. As I understand him, this is what Flannery means by his "broad spectrum" collecting pattern. Perhaps this is what Mathiassen was thinking of when he spoke of "receptiveness." Certainly by now (say by 12,000(+) years ago), people's ingenuity at making cultural adaptations to a great variety of environmental situations was developing broadly over most of the world.

Professor Robert McC. Adams is of the opinion that this atmosphere of experimentation with new tools—with new ways of collecting a broader spectrum of subsistence needs from a given environment—is the kind of atmosphere in which we might well expect a breakthrough toward domestication to have been made. Where such breakthroughs might come, however, would have depended on the potential of certain environments, as we shall see presently. At the same time, it need not surprise us that the Forest folk of northwestern Europe had the domesticated dog, nor that the earliest now known domesticated dog is reported from Idaho, of about 11,000(+) years ago. In a very real sense, the whole latter part of the food-collecting era was becoming ready and "incipient" for the beginnings of cultivation and animal domestication.

Northwestern Europe was hardly the place for really effective beginnings in agriculture and animal domestication. These would have had to take place in one of those natural environments of promise, where a variety of plants and animals, each capable of domestication, was available in the wild state. Let me spell this out. Really effective food production must include a variety of items to make up a reasonably well-rounded diet. The food supply so produced must be trustworthy, even though the food-producing peoples themselves might remain happy to supplement it with fish and wild strawberries, just as we do when such things are available. So, as we said earlier, part of our problem is that of finding a region with a natural environment which includes—and did include, some 12,000(+) years ago—a variety of possibly domesticable wild plants and animals.

Nuclear Areas

Now comes the last of my definitions. A region with a natural environment which included a variety of wild plants and animals, both possible and ready for domestication, would be a central or core or *nuclear area* for our purposes here; that is, it would be when and *if* food production took place within it. It is pretty hard for me to imagine food production having ever made an independent start outside such a nuclear area, although there may be some possible nuclear areas in which effective food production never took place.

We know of several such nuclear areas and will speak of them briefly in a following chapter. In the New World, Middle America and the Andean highlands make up one or two; it is my understanding that the evidence now tends to suggest two. There is new evidence for a nuclear area somewhere in southeastern Asia, in the Malay peninsula or Burma, perhaps connected with the early cultivation of taro, breadfruit, banana, and mango. Possibly the cultivation of rice and the domestication of the chicken and of zebu cattle and the water buffalo belong to this southeast Asiatic nuclear area. On the other hand, Professor Ping-ti Ho makes a persuasive case for the domestication of millet, pigs, and rice in the Wei Valley in China. Professor Jack R. Harlan, as well as being in agreement with Ho, sees pearl millet and sorghum as independent cereal domesticates in a strip of sub-Saharan Africa. The nuclear area which, as I write this, I still believe was the scene of the earliest experiment in effective food production is southwestern Asia. Of course, I may be proved wrong by next Tuesday! Since I know it best, I shall use it as my example.

The Nuclear Near East

Events in the nuclear area of southwestern Asia are naturally of some added interest to the peoples of the Western cultural tradition. After all, our cultural heritage began there. The "nuclear" part of the whole area—for our purposes here—appears to be the piedmonts and hilly flanks of rainwatered grasslands which build up to the high mountain ridges of Iran, Iraq, Turkey, Syria, and Palestine. The map on p. 124 indicates the region. If you have a good atlas, locate the zone which surrounds the Karun-Tigris-Euphrates river systems and which proceeds down the eastern Mediterranean littoral. I myself was first persuaded that the nuclear area or "natural habitat zone of the potential domesticates" could be quite specifically located along the hilly flanks alone. It is now clear that the piedmonts and even the middle stretches of the river valleys may well yield parts of the story. I must remind you, also, that the beginnings of this area's "nuclearity" must depend at least in part on the resolution of the cold, dry, late Pleistocene proposition which Herbert Wright presents us with.

It does *not*, in any case, seem likely that the lower alluvial basin of the Karun-Tigris-Euphrates system (ancient Sumer, Akkad, and Elam) were part of the original nuclear area. The days of glory for this hot, dry region—Mesopotamia and its surroundings—came later, with the appearance of literate urban civilization. Professor James Henry Breasted, whose interests lay with these early literate peoples of ancient history, conceived of the Mesopotamian region as the righthand (eastern) end of his "fertile crescent." Breasted's crescent then arched up and over toward the west and southwest (locate the modern cities of Mosul and Aleppo in your atlas) into Syria and then down into Palestine toward Egypt.

Our region of interest here tends to rise above Breasted's crescent, into country of grassy piedmont hills and lower intermontane valleys, which (now at least) receive from ten to twenty or more inches of winter rainfall yearly. The Tigris, especially, has many tributaries which cut down through the piedmonts of the Zagros and Tauros ridges. The Lebanon and Judean ridges rise behind a narrow coastal plain on the Mediterranean side, but then fall to the Orontes-Jordan Valley (the northernmost extent of the Great Rift Valley), only to rise again farther inland. The picture you should have is of an arch-shaped zone, framed by ridges (with the Mediterranean on the west), and with a very great variety of environmentally diverse niches available, north to south, east to west, and upslope to downslope. This great environmental diversity doubtless has much bearing on the whole matter.

How far beyond the Zagros-Tauros-Lebanon-Judean frame of

ridges the nuclear area might have fingered is uncertain. The higher and colder plateaus of Persia and Anatolia were probably not so pertinent. But how far toward the northwest or northeast—perhaps even to the Macedonian foothills of the Balkan Mountains or to the northern slopes of the Koppet Dagh in Soviet Turkmenistan—did the upper boundary of the zone lie? We are not yet sure.

The Natural Environment of the Nuclear Near East

The more we learn of this general area, the more it seems surely to have been a nuclear area for the beginnings of food production. Nevertheless, this is where we archeologists need, and are now getting, the help of natural scientists. They are coming to the conclusion that the natural environments of the hilly-flanks zone today were approximately established some 8,000 to 10,000(+) years ago (if allowance be made for the destructive effects of erosion and deforestation of the last several thousand years). By 9,000(+) years ago, at least, Wright's cold, dry steppe condition was being replaced. There are still two kinds of wild wheat, a wild barley, several wild pulses, and wild sheep, goat, and pig in the region. We have discovered traces of each of these at about 9,000(+) years ago, as well as traces of wild cattle, each of which appears to be the probable ancestor of the domesticated form. In fact, at about 9,000(+) years ago, the two wheats, the barley, and at least the sheep and goat were already well on the road to domestication.

The wild wheats give us an interesting clue. They demand the winter–early spring rainfall pattern characteristic of this Mediterranean-type nuclear area. They are available together with the wild barley only within the hilly-flanks and piedmont zone. While the wild barley grows in a variety of elevations and beyond the zone, at least one of the wild wheats does not seem to grow below the hill country. As things look at the moment, the domestication of either wheat could have taken place *only* within this natural zone. Barley seems to have first come into cultivation due to its presence as a weed in already cultivated wheat fields. There is also increasing certainty that the animals which were first domesticated were most at home in this piedmont–hilly-flanks natural habitat in their wild state.

With a single exception—of that Idaho dog—the earliest positive evidence of domestication includes the two forms of wheat, the barley, the peas and lentils, and the goat, sheep, and pig. The evidence comes from within the hilly-flanks and piedmont zone. However, with the probable exception of the sheep and dog, it comes from what are evidently settled villages proper. It is thus from the era of the primary village-farming community, which I'll describe in the next chapter. We are still without positive evidence of domesticated grain in the first era of the food-producing stage, that of incipient cultivation and animal domestication, but there is some evidence for domesticated sheep and dogs in this first era.

The Era of Incipient Cultivation and Animal Domestication

I said above (p. 98) that my era of incipient cultivation and animal domestication is set up mainly by playing a hunch. Although we cannot really demonstrate it—and certainly not in the Near East—it would be very strange for food-collectors not to have known a great deal about the plants and animals most useful to them. We can imagine them remembering to go back, season after season, to a particular patch of ground where seeds or acorns or berries grew particularly well. Most human beings, unless they are extremely hungry, are attracted to baby animals, and many wild pups or fawns or piglets must have been brought back alive by hunting parties.

In the above senses, people have probably *always* been incipient cultivators and domesticators. But I believe that Adams is right in suggesting that this would be doubly true with the experimenters of the terminal subera of food collecting. We noticed that they also seem to have had an increasing tendency to settle down and settle into localized environmental situations. Now my hunch goes that *when* this experimentation and settling down and into took place within a potential nuclear area, where a whole constellation of potentially domesticable plants and animals was available, the change was easily made. The evidence certainly seems to be building up in this direction.

I shall remind you again that I am not able to explain exactly how the change came about. I fear we have much more to learn before we can fully describe and *explain* the appearance of food production.

Incipient Eras and Nuclear Areas

I have illustrated the development of food production in two complementary charts (pp. 106 and 107). The first chart briefly characterizes the eras or cultural levels of our interest, in different geographical regions of western Eurasia, from about 11,000 to 3,000 B.C.(+). The second chart shows the time and geographical positions of some of the more important sites from which our evidence comes.* You will see that my hunch means that eras of incipient cultivation tend to develop *only* within nuclear areas. In a nuclear area, the terminal subera of food collecting may even have been quite short—if, in fact, it existed at all. The era of incipience *may* have followed directly out of the more generalized era of food collecting. I do not know for how long a time the era of incipient cultivation and domestication would have lasted, but at least for several thousand years. Then it passed on into the era of the primary village-farming community.

Outside a nuclear area, the terminal subera of food collecting might have lasted for a long time; in a few out-of-the-way parts of the world, it still hangs on today. It would end in any particular place through contact with the ideas of people who had passed on into one of the more developed eras. In some cases, the terminal subera of food collecting was ended by the incoming of the food-producing peoples themselves. For example, the practice of food production was evidently carried into Europe by the actual movement of some numbers of peoples (we don't know how many) who had reached at least the level of the primary village-farming community. The Forest folk learned food production from them. There was no era of incipient cultivation and domestication proper in Europe, if my hunch is right. Remember, though, that we're not really sure of the boundaries of the nuclear area, and that portions of southeastern (Balkan) Europe might be on its fringes.

*As is the case with other chronological charts in this book, I have followed the usual archeological convention of considering the oldest material or information at the bottom of the chart, the latest (or youngest) at the top. The abbreviation "B.P." means "before present."

From left to right, these two charts follow a rough geographical line from northwestern Europe toward central and southeastern Asia. Since our interest here deals with the beginnings of food production, I've given some special attention, in the center of these charts, to "nuclear" southwest Asia. It may be noted that what was "nuclear" for the appearance of urban civilization (lower Mesopotamia) was evidently not quite the same region as was that for the appearance of the earliest village-farmers or for the first experiments at plant cultivation or animal domestication. As I understand the available evidence, the earliest effective food production took place in the piedmont and hill country which arcs about lower Mesopotamia (see map, p. 124).

The curved lines in red illustrate what have been called *sloping horizons*. The lines suggest the approximate times of appearance, in any given region, of the succession of eras or levels of cultural development, from that of the final food-collectors to that of urban civilization in lower Mesopotamia and Egypt. Since these charts only go to about 3000 B.C., urban civilization was yet to appear in any other region. Sloping horizons imply diffusion. The charts show, for example, that the early village-farming site of Jarmo in southwest Asia, with its domesticated wheat, barley, sheep, and goats, was in existence soon after 7000 B.C.(+). An equivalent type of village-farming site (e.g., Geleen, in Holland) did not appear in northwestern Europe until about 4500 B.C.(+). At 7000 B.C.(+), northwestern Europe was still at a level of terminal food collection.

The charts also suggest that the era or level of incipient cultivation and domestication was probably bound to the region of the natural habitat (or zone of nuclearity) of the potential plant and animal domesticates. The succeeding era or level, that of effective village-farming communities, did, on the other hand, diffuse widely. So also, much later, did the level of urban civilization.

Note that in the case of both charts, I have not recalibrated the dates; the (+) appears with the "B.P." and "B.C." columns in both cases.

Eras or Levels of Development from Food-Collection to Urban Civilization

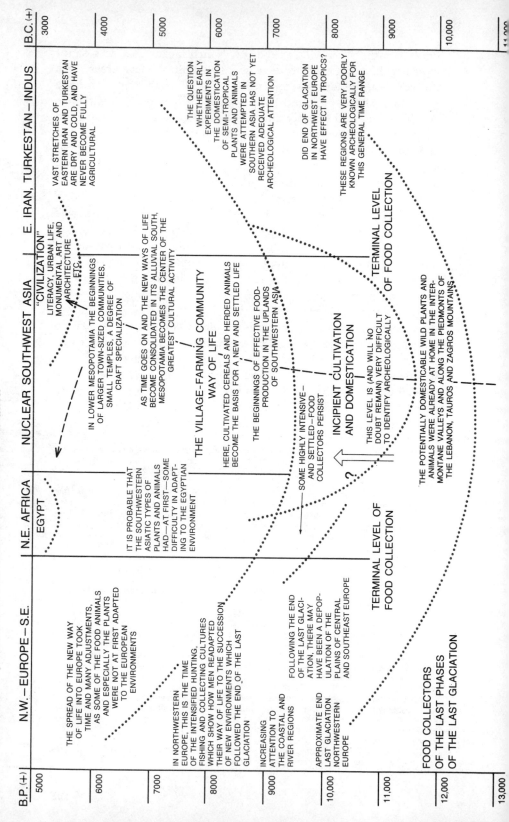

B.P. (+)	N.W.–EUROPE–S.E.	N.E. AFRICA	NUCLEAR SOUTHWEST ASIA	E. IRAN, TURKESTAN–INDUS	B.C. (+)

EGYPT

"CIVILIZATION"
LITERACY, URBAN LIFE, MONUMENTAL ART AND ARCHITECTURE ETC.

VAST STRETCHES OF EASTERN IRAN AND TURKESTAN ARE DRY AND COLD, AND HAVE NEVER BECOME FULLY AGRICULTURAL

THE SPREAD OF THE NEW WAY OF LIFE INTO EUROPE TOOK TIME AND MANY ADJUSTMENTS, AS SOME OF THE FOOD ANIMALS AND ESPECIALLY THE PLANTS WERE NOT AT FIRST ADAPTED TO THE EUROPEAN ENVIRONMENTS

IT IS PROBABLE THAT THE SOUTHWESTERN ASIATIC TYPES OF PLANTS AND ANIMALS HAD—AT FIRST—SOME DIFFICULTY IN ADAPTING TO THE EGYPTIAN ENVIRONMENT

IN LOWER MESOPOTAMIA THE BEGINNINGS OF LARGER TOWN-SIZED COMMUNITIES, SMALL TEMPLES, A DEGREE OF CRAFT SPECIALIZATION

THE QUESTION WHETHER EARLY EXPERIMENTS IN THE DOMESTICATION OF SEMI-TROPICAL PLANTS AND ANIMALS WERE ATTEMPTED IN SOUTHERN ASIA HAS NOT YET RECEIVED ADEQUATE ARCHEOLOGICAL ATTENTION

AS TIME GOES ON AND THE NEW WAYS OF LIFE BECOME CONSOLIDATED IN ITS ALLUVIAL SOUTH, MESOPOTAMIA BECOMES THE CENTER OF THE GREATEST CULTURAL ACTIVITY

IN NORTHWESTERN EUROPE, THIS IS THE TIME OF THE INTENSIFIED HUNTING, FISHING AND COLLECTING CULTURES WHICH SHOW HOW MEN READAPTED THEIR WAY OF LIFE TO THE SUCCESSION OF NEW ENVIRONMENTS WHICH FOLLOWED THE END OF THE LAST GLACIATION

THE VILLAGE-FARMING COMMUNITY WAY OF LIFE

HERE, CULTIVATED CEREALS AND HERDED ANIMALS BECOME THE BASIS FOR A NEW AND SETTLED LIFE

DID END OF GLACIATION IN NORTHWEST EUROPE HAVE EFFECT IN TROPICS?

THE BEGINNINGS OF EFFECTIVE FOOD-PRODUCTION IN THE UPLANDS OF SOUTHWESTERN ASIA

THESE REGIONS ARE VERY POORLY KNOWN ARCHEOLOGICALLY FOR THIS GENERAL TIME RANGE

INCREASING ATTENTION TO THE COASTAL AND RIVER REGIONS

SOME HIGHLY INTENSIVE—AND SETTLED—FOOD-COLLECTORS PERSIST

?

INCIPIENT CULTIVATION AND DOMESTICATION

FOLLOWING THE END OF THE LAST GLACIATION, THERE MAY HAVE BEEN A DEPOPULATION OF THE PLAINS OF CENTRAL AND SOUTHEAST EUROPE

TERMINAL LEVEL OF FOOD COLLECTION

THIS LEVEL IS (AND WILL NO DOUBT REMAIN) VERY DIFFICULT TO IDENTIFY ARCHEOLOGICALLY

TERMINAL LEVEL OF FOOD COLLECTION

APPROXIMATE END LAST GLACIATION NORTHWESTERN EUROPE

THE POTENTIALLY DOMESTICABLE WILD PLANTS AND ANIMALS WERE ALREADY AT HOME IN THE INTER-MONTANE VALLEYS AND ALONG THE PIEDMONTS OF THE LEBANON, TAUROS AND ZAGROS MOUNTAINS

FOOD COLLECTORS OF THE LAST PHASES OF THE LAST GLACIATION

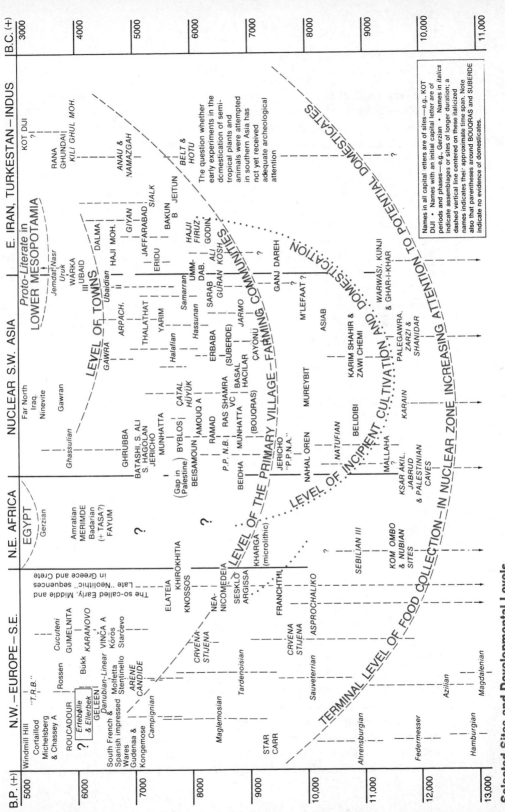

Selected Sites and Developmental Levels

Archeological Difficulties in Seeing
the Incipient Era

The way I see it, two things were required in order that an era of incipient cultivation and domestication could begin. First, there had to be the natural environment of a nuclear area, with its whole group of plants and animals capable of domestication. This is the aspect of the matter which we've said is directly given by nature. But such an environment with such a group of plants and animals in it undoubtedly existed well before 10,000(+) years ago in the Near East. It is also quite possible that the same promising conditions may have existed in regions which never developed into nuclear areas proper. Here again we come back to the cultural factor. I think it was that "atmosphere of experimentation" we've talked about once or twice before. I can't define it for you, other than to say that by the end of the Ice Age, the general level of many cultures was ready for change. Ask me how and why this was so, and I'll tell you we don't know yet; if we understood this kind of question, there would be no need for me to go on being a prehistorian!

Now since this was an era of incipience, of the birth of new ideas, and of experimentation, it is very difficult to see its traces archeologically. New tools having to do with the new ways of getting and, in fact, producing food would have taken some time to develop. It need not surprise us too much if we cannot find hoes for planting and sickles for reaping grain at the very beginning. We might expect a time of making do with some of the older tools, or with makeshift tools, for some of the new jobs, or turn the proposition the other way. Perhaps what we take to be stone "hoes" were meant only for grubbing out the roots of wild plants. What we call flint "sickles" may have been sickles at first, all right, but made for the reaping of *wild* grain. Some of the tools we tend to assume were used for agriculture may actually have been developed by collectors *for collecting.*

The present-day wild cousin of the domesticated sheep still lives in the mountains of western Asia. It has no wool, only a fine down under hair like that of a deer, so it need not surprise us to find neither the whorls used for spinning nor traces of woollen cloth in very early village levels. It must have taken some time for a wool-bearing sheep to develop and also time for the invention of new tools for weaving. It will be just as difficult (or even more difficult) to recognize the actual beginnings of animal domestication through artifacts, as for the beginnings of plant cultivation.

The *primary* and clinching evidence for the presence of cultivated plants or domesticated animals remains the actual carbonized kernels and the clear impressions of plants themselves, and the bones of the animals themselves. I distinguish these as primary evidence, as opposed to the *secondary* evidence of tools and other artifacts. Nevertheless, it is difficult even for an experienced comparative zoologist to tell which are the bones of newly domesticated animals and which are those of their wild cousins. This is especially so because the animal bones the archeologists find are usually fragmentary. Nor has there been, so far, absolutely complete agreement among all authorities about the identification and interpretation of the different available plant remains.

There were morphological (structural) changes in both plants and animals as full domestication was achieved, but such changes did not take place overnight. Even plants and animals under manipulation by humans and well along the road to fu effective domestication may not show sufficient morphological evidence of domestication to allow our specialists to recognize it. What they can identify as a domesticate is the already "finished product."

Furthermore, we are only now gathering a sort of library collection of the skeletons of the animals and an herbarium of the plants of those areas against which the traces which the archeologists find may be checked. In the nuclear area in the Near East, some of the wild animals have already become extinct. There are no longer any wild cattle or many wild horses in southwestern Asia. We know they were there from the finds we've made in caves of late Ice Age times, from some slightly later sites, and even from the hunting scenes shown on Assyrian reliefs.

Sites with Antiquities of the Incipient Era

So far, we know only a very few sites which would suit my notion of the incipient era of cultivation and animal domestication. I am closing this chapter with descriptions of two of the best Near Eastern examples I know. You may not be satisfied that what I am able to describe makes a full-bodied era of development at all. Remember, however, that I've told you I'm largely playing a kind of a hunch, and also that the archeological materials of this era will always be extremely difficult to interpret. At the beginning of any new way of life, there will be a great tendency for people to make do, at first, with tools and habits they are already used to. I would suspect that a great deal of this making do went on almost to the end of this era.

The Natufian, an Assemblage of the Incipient Era

The assemblage called the *Natufian* comes from the upper layers of a number of caves in Palestine. Traces of its flint industry have also turned up in Syria and Lebanon. Professor Enver Bostanci has found suggestive hints of a few Natufian-like tools at Beldibi, a cave on the southcentral coast of Turkey. In Palestine, the Natufian has various radiocarbon determinations which span two millennia, 10,000 to 8,000 B.C.(+).

Before World War II, the people who produced the Natufian assemblage were thought to have been only cave-dwellers, but now a number of open-air Natufian sites have been briefly described. In their best-known cave dwelling, on Mount Carmel, the Natufian folk lived in the open mouth of a large rock shelter and on the terrace in front of it. On the terrace they had set at least two short curving lines of stones, but these were hardly architecture; they seem more like benches or perhaps the low walls of open pens. There were also one or two small clusters of stones laid like paving, and a ring of stones around a hearth or fireplace. One very round and regular basin-shaped depression had been cut into the rocky floor of the terrace, and there were other, less regular, basin-like depressions. In the more recently reported open-air sites, of which M. Jean Perrot's Mallaha is so far the best known, the stone foundations for round houses have been found. It is already clear that further excavations at Mallaha will indicate a more developed Natufian assemblage than the one we now know. Furthermore, both Israeli and American colleagues are very actively engaged in exposing other Natufian sites.

Most of the finds in the Natufian layer of the Mount Carmel cave were flints. About 80 percent of these flint tools were microliths made by the regular working of tiny blades into various tools, some having geometric forms. The larger flint tools included backed blades, burins, scrapers, a few arrow points, some larger hacking or picking tools, and a special type—the sickle blade.

We know a sickle blade of flint when we see one, because of a strange polish or sheen which seems to develop on the cutting edge when the blade has been used to cut grasses or grain, or perhaps reeds. In the Natufian, we have even found the straight bone handles in which a number of flint sickle blades were set in a line.

Natufian Antiquities in Other Materials; Burials and People

The Natufian industry in bone was quite rich. It included, beside the sickle hafts mentioned above, points and harpoons, straight and curved types of fishhooks, awls, pins and needles, and a variety of beads and pendants. There were also beads and pendants of pierced teeth and shell. Utensils in ground and pecked stone (that is, rubbed down; not chipped, as with flint) were common. Mortars

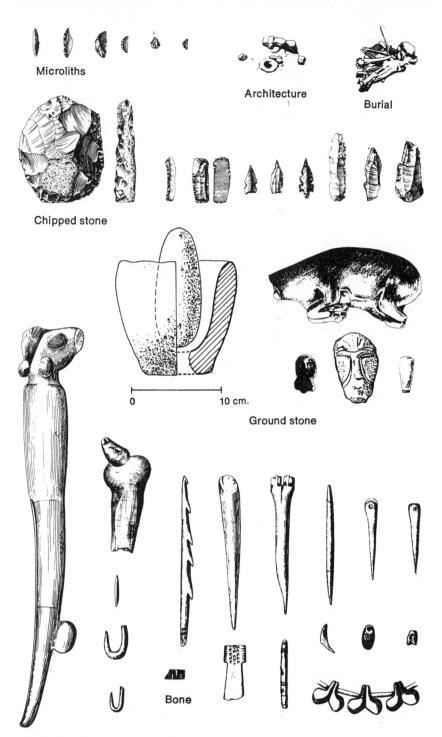

Microliths

Architecture

Burial

Chipped stone

0   10 cm.

Ground stone

Bone

Sketch of Natufian Assemblage

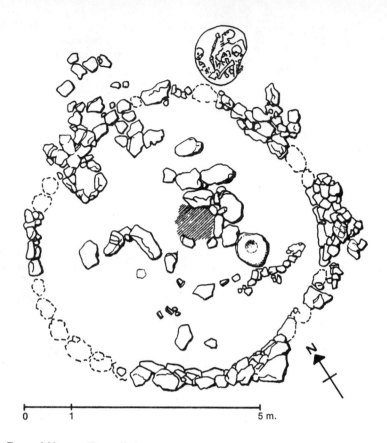

Mallaha Round House Foundation

and pestles showed traces of ochre stain in many cases, but some of these artifacts were doubtless used to grind food as well.

A number of Natufian burials have been found; some burials were grouped together in one grave. The people who were buried within the Mount Carmel cave were laid on their backs in an extended position, while those on the terrace seem to have been flexed (placed in their graves in a curled-up position). This may mean no more than that it was easier to dig a long hole in cave dirt than in the hard-packed dirt of the terrace. The people often had some kind of object buried with them, and several of the best collections of beads come from the burials. On two of the skulls there were traces of elaborate headdresses of shell beads.

Professor Ofer Bar-Yosef remarks that the Natufians seem to have favored areas of certain soil and vegetation types in Palestine. A simpler assemblage known mainly through its microliths alone occurs in other parts of the region. There are even questions of "base camps" vs. "exploitation camps" (temporarily occupied to take advantage of some seasonal food source).

The animal bones of the Natufian layers show beasts of a "modern" type, but with some differences from those of present-day Palestine. The bones of the gazelle outnumber those of the deer; since gazelles like a much drier climate than deer, Palestine must then have had much the same climate that it has today. Some of the animal bones were those of large or dangerous beasts: the hyena, the bear, the wild boar, and the leopard. The claim for a Natufian dog, once questioned, now seems acceptable. There are not yet, however, any other clear evidences of domesticated animals or plants. The study of the human bones from the Natufian burials is not yet complete. We may note, however, Professor Coon's assessment that these people were of a "basically Mediterranean type."

Why, then, do I believe that the Natufian assemblage indicates something of an incipient era? I am impressed by the sheer size of some of the open settlements, and by the attention given to simple but impressive architectural foundations. Both the variety and the number of new artifactual forms interest me. A few earlier stone grinding implements and flint sickles can be pointed to, both in southwestern Asia and in Nubian Egypt, but the number and variety of the Natufian examples especially intrigues me. So does the attention given to burials. In the end, of course, I also happen to know what is going to happen immediately following in time.

The Karim Shahir Assemblage

Unlike the Natufian, the Karim Shahir assemblage was first found in an open-air site. Now also known to have been present in at least one cave, it is best evidenced in what appear to have been at least semipermanent encampments. The first known instance, Karim Shahir itself, lies on top of a bluff in the Kurdish hill country of northeastern Iraq. It was dug by Dr. Bruce Howe of the expedition I directed in 1950–51 for the Oriental Institute and the American Schools of Oriental Research. Since then about a half-dozen sites with finds generally resembling those of Karim Shahir have been found along the Zagros flanks and piedmont. Zawi Chemi Shanidar, in northeastern Iraq, has a 8900 ± 300 b.c.(+) determination, while the same assemblage in the Shanidar cave itself has one of 8650 ± 300 b.c.(+). There is also early material on three Iranian sites—Asiab, Ganj Dareh, and Ali Kosh—but I believe only the Asiab materials can be anywhere near this early.

Karim Shahir itself has evidence of only one very shallow level of occupation. It was probably not lived on very long, although the people who lived on it spread out over about three acres. In spots,

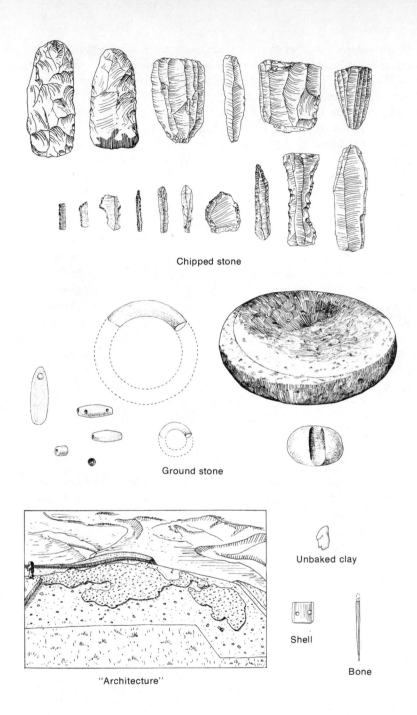

Chipped stone

Ground stone

"Architecture"

Unbaked clay

Shell

Bone

Sketch of Karim Shahir Assemblage

the single layer yielded great numbers of fist-sized cracked pieces of limestone, which had been carried up from the bed of a stream at the bottom of the bluff. We think these cracked stones had something to do with a kind of architecture, but we were unable to find positive traces of hut plans. At M'lefaat (an incompletely excavated open site in the northern piedmont in Iraq) and at Zawi Chemi, there were traces of rounded hut plans, and at Asiab, in the Iranian Zagros, the traces of a large round depression were found.

As in the Natufian, the great bulk of small objects of the Karim Shahir assemblage were in chipped flint. A large proportion of the flint tools were microlithic bladelets and geometric forms. The flint sickle blade was almost nonexistent, being far scarcer than in the Natufian. The people of Karim Shahir did a modest amount of work in the grinding of stone; there were milling stone fragments of both the mortar and the quern (hand mill) type, and stone hoes or axes with polished bits. Beads, pendants, rings, and bracelets were made of finer quality stone. We found a few simple points and needles of bone, and even two rather formless, unbaked clay figurines which seemed to be of animal form. Zawi Chemi yielded several well-made, crescent-shaped bone knives with flint blades.

The Karim Shahir phase has not yet yielded direct evidence of the kind of vegetable food its people ate. Actually, far less archeological excavation has yet been done on Karim Shahir-like sites than is the case with the Natufian. There is a considerable increase in the proportion of the bones of wild animals capable of domestication—sheep, goat, cattle, horse, wolf—as compared with animal bones from the earlier cave sites of the area, which have a high proportion of bones of wild forms such as deer and gazelle. There is also both some statistical and some microscopic evidence that the sheep of Zawi Chemi were actually domesticated, and Dr. Sandor Bökönyi reports goat domestication at Asiab.

Professor Frank Hole believes that his site of Ali Kosh, low in the Persian foothills overlooking the Mesopotamian plain, may include basal levels of a probably developed or advanced Karim Shahir type. Both wheat and barley are reported as domesticated in the earliest (Bus Mordeh phase) levels of the site, and there is a statistical suggestion that still-wild goats may have been herded. I myself am more inclined to think of this Bus Mordeh phase as of the next era of primary farming-villages.

No Other Incipient Era Assemblages in Southwestern Asia?

When we first began work in the upper piedmont of the Tauros in Turkey in 1963, we anticipated finding traces of the incipient era there, as well. So far, we have not found them—perhaps because, through circumstances beyond our control, our activities were restricted to higher portions of the piedmont than we would have chosen. We had hoped for traces of either a Natufian, a Karim Shahirian, or a quite different assemblage of an incipient type.

Since 1963, teams from both the Oriental Institute and the French C.N.R.S. (Centre National de la Recherche Scientifique) have investigated a site called Mureybit, on the banks of the middle Euphrates about fifty miles east of Aleppo. Mureybit is a mound of considerable size with a deep deposit in three phases, the earliest of which is now being identified as Natufian. Its round-house ruins of clay and wood yield a microlithic flint industry and ground stone tools, as well as traces of both wild einkorn wheat and wild barley, and the bones of wild cattle, the onager (wild ass), and the gazelle, The wild wheat is well south of its present distribution pattern and, curiously for a riverside site, there are few mussel shells and no fish bones.

Although the yield from the more recent French excavations is not yet published, my friend Jean Perrot assures me that the usage "Natufian" is doubtless justified. Somehow, the environment of the semi-arid stretch along the middle Euphrates (as I know it now) contrasts strangely with the green hill country of Mediterranean Palestine. Probably the Mureybit assemblage will prove to link more closely with the Natufian-like materials of the more arid Negev-Sinai region than with coastal Palestine proper. Certainly there is a convincing cluster of radiocarbon determinations from Mureybit for the time span of about 8600 to 7000 b.c.(+). Of another site, Bouqras, downriver from Mureybit, we yet know much less, but the basal levels again seem to be without evidence of food production.

Incidentally, in the flush of my own earlier "hilly flanks of the crescent–natural habitat zone" days, I wouldn't have dreamed anything as interesting as Mureybit could possibly be found on the middle Euphrates. In fact, the site's discovery was an accident of a survey undertaken at the request of the Syrian government in an area to be flooded. I've now learned my lesson. With so much of southwestern Asia still not adequately surveyed, I'd now not dream of saying that no more examples of the incipient era will yet turn up in any of the region's odd environment areas!

Were the Natufian and Karim Shahir Peoples Food-Producers?

It is clear that a great part of the food of the Natufian people must have been hunted or collected. Shells of land, freshwater, and sea animals may occur in their sites. The same is true as regards the Karim Shahir-type sites, save for seashells. At Asiab, which is beside a river, there are great quantities of river clamshells. We noted, however, that at Mureybit this is not true. But on the other hand, we have the sickles, the milling stones, the Zawi Chemi sheep and Asiab goats, and the general animal situation at Karim Shahir to hint at an incipient approach to food production. In the Karim Shahir-type sites, there was the tendency to settle down out in the open; this is echoed by the new open-air Natufian sites. The number of stone foundations certainly indicates that it was worth the peoples' while to have some kind of reasonably permanent structure, even if the site as a whole was short-lived. It is not inconceivable that the open sites were base camps and the cave sites were exploitation or hunting-party camps.

It is a part of my hunch that these things all point toward food production—that the hints we seek are there. But in the sense that the peoples of the era of the primary village-farming community, which we shall look at next, were fully food producing, the Natufian and Karim Shahir folk had not yet arrived. I think they were part of a general buildup to full-scale food production. They were possibly controlling a few animals of several kinds and perhaps one or two plants. If the basal level of Ali Kosh was actually as early as its excavators believe, such may have been the case at that site. The full possibilities of this "control" were prelude to a new way of life. I wish I could say whether the people of this area were living in their simple settlements all year around or not; some of our evidence seems to point toward seasonal occupation only.

This is why I think of the Karim Shahir and Natufian folk as being at a level, or in an era, of incipient cultivation and domestication. But we shall have to do a great deal more excavation in this range of time before we'll get the kind of positive information we need.

Villages Without Food Production?

Another curious twist of the recent evidence has to be noted here. A few years ago, I myself certainly followed Professor Gordon Childe's notion that where we had "village sites" in southwestern Asia, these would, of necessity, contain *primary* evidence of food production. That is, such sites would really yield the actual carbonized kernels or the clear impressions of domesticated plants and the bones of domesticated animals, whether the archeologists who excavated the sites had noticed this evidence or not. Any mound made up of a succession of layers of permanent-looking mud-walled houses would have been considered a "village site." Childe, of course, knew perfectly well about hut sites such as Klima's (see p. 81), but "village" seemed to mean more to him. The idea was that without effective food production, permanent year-around settlement for some generations would be practically unthinkable. And Childe's notion appeared to work out in practice. To the extent that we had early village sites in which their excavators had bothered to look for plant and animal remains, domestication and food production was indicated.

Now, of course, we see how much this picture seems to have changed. Both in the Natufian and in the Karim Shahirian regions, we have spoken above of open-air, mound-like sites. Some, such as Mureybit, are large (the Mureybit mound covers about thirty acres; whether the earliest phase itself spread over so large an area is not yet known). Is there any reason why we should not think of such settlement remains as having once been "villages"? It was Jean Perrot who, as early as 1963 in the analysis of his Mallaha materials, did a double take and announced that lack of primary evidence of food production was *not* necessarily due to an excavator's oversight. In other words, some early "villages" may not have owed their existence to produced food. Perrot feels sure that the Natufian "villages" fall into this category, and the Mureybit evidence points in the same direction. Indeed, in Palestine there is very good reason to believe that the original stands of wild wheat and barley were so lush that a bountiful yield was available for collectors.

However, before granting that the subsistence base of *every* "village" of this incipient era was simply one of intensified food collection, we have something to remember. I made the point earlier (see p. 109) that our botanical and zoological experts cannot identify domesticated forms until the morphological changes attending domestication really happen. I'd expect that in a fair number of our incipient era "villages," people were (quite unconsciously, of course) manipulating both plants and animals in directions which eventually led to full domestication.

The critical issue regarding "villages" is doubtless a matter of all-season, year-in year-out permanence. The "base camp" vs. "exploitation camp" suggestion is an interesting one, and must be examined further in the field. The ethnological record suggests that in certain very specialized situations, intensified food collection may indeed assure permanent settlement. Was such ever the case in southwest Asia, and on the basis of which food elements? While we noted that in Palestine the original stands of wild cereal are said to have been very lush, such is not claimed to have been so for the Zagros flanks region.

Recently, however, the agronomy expert of our 1963–64 field staff in southeastern Turkey, Professor Jack R. Harlan, reported on some experiments with stands of wild einkorn wheat still growing in the Çayönü region. A single, inexperienced man, Harlan was able to gather over four pounds of the grain, with a flint sickle, in one hour. This thrashed out to two pounds of clean grain in a wooden mortar and pestle. Chemical analysis showed the grain to be highly nutritious, containing some 24 percent protein, in contrast to 14 percent in modern bread wheat. Harlan estimates that an experienced prehistoric family, working for the three weeks of a normal harvest, could probably have acquired about a ton of clean grain equivalent. Moreover, the einkorn wheat is the smaller and less satisfactory of the two wild wheats.

We shall have to learn a great deal more before the matter becomes clear, and Perrot performed an important service in focusing attention on the matter.

Summary

I am sorry that this chapter has had to be so much more about ideas than about the archeological traces of the prehistoric people themselves. But the antiquities of the incipient era of cultivation and animal domestication will not be spectacular, even when we do excavate them in quantity. Few museums will be interested in these antiquities for exhibition purposes. The charred bits or impressions of plants, the fragments of animal bone and shell, and the varied clues to climate and environment will be as important as the artifacts themselves. It will be the ideas to which these traces lead us that will be important. I am sure that this unspectacular material—when we have much more of it, and learn how to understand what it says—will lead us to *how* and *why* answers about the first great change in human history. Until we do have much more evidence, I prefer to keep my fingers tightly crossed regarding many of the speculative "models" it is now so fashionable to propose in "explaining" the beginnings of food production.

I do think we can still confidently say that the earliest village-farming communities appeared in western Asia, in a nuclear area. We do not yet know why the Near Eastern experiment came first, or why it didn't happen earlier in some other nuclear area. Perhaps the level of culture and the promise of the natural environment were ready first in western Asia. Not by very much, however, for incipience appears to have gotten under way in Mesoamerica by 7000 b.c.(+); although the case for southeastern Asia does not at the moment appear to have been quite so early. The next sites we look at in the Near East will show a simple but effective food production already in existence. Without effective food production and settled village-farming communities, civilization never could have followed. How effective food production came into being by the end of the incipient era is, I believe, one of the most fascinating questions any archeologist could face.

It now seems possible, from certain of the Palestinian sites with derived varieties of the Natufian (Jericho and Nahal Oren; perhaps some of the Negev sites), that there were one or more local Palestinian developments out of the Natufian into later times. Mureybit seems to be telling us the same thing. In the same way, what probably followed after the Karim Shahir type of assemblage in Iraqi and Iranian Kurdistan (such as at Ali Kosh) was in some ways a reflection of the beginnings made at Karim Shahir, Zawi Chemi, and Asiab.

On page 103, I remarked that we cannot yet be certain how far to the northwest the original nuclear area extended. Hence I should at least mention here the very important late Pleistocene to approximately 5000 B.C.(+) sequence of the Franchthi cave in the Argolid peninsula of southern Greece. Still under excavation by Professor Thomas Jacobsen of Indiana University, and not yet fully reported, it is at least clear that whatever the details it yields, Franchthi is something for us to keep our eyes upon. One significant point is that by 7000 B.C.(+), the people of Franchthi were already acquiring obsidian from the island of Melos, which clearly implies so early a boat traffic to the Greek mainland.

7
The first revolution

As the incipient era of cultivation and animal domestication passed onward into the era of the primary village-farming community, the first basic change in human economy was fully achieved. In southwestern Asia, this change seems to have become fully effective by about 9000(+) years ago. I am going to restrict my detailed description to this earliest Near Eastern case. As I explained earlier, I have little firsthand knowledge about comparable experiments in the Far East, Africa, and the New World, although I do offer a brief summary chapter on them. But first, let us once again think of the contrast between food collecting and food producing as ways of life.

To point up the contrast, I freely admit that I am consciously idealizing and ignoring difficulties. I also realize that there is a contrary point of view—a sort of revival of the "noble savage" image of the lifeways of the hunter-collector. This contrary view also idealizes and ignores difficulties, speaking of hunting and collecting as a leisurely way of life, or of the "original affluent societies." Having spent several winter months in tent camps on both the Tauros and Zagros slopes (even with heavy Western clothes and purchased foods), I tend to wonder whether the special remaining ethnographic examples offered by this view have much validity. The "original affluent societies" (if indeed they were that) appear to me to be only those which remain in the Kalahari Desert and the Australian outback. Somewhere in between my extreme picture and the contrary one of the original affluent society may lie reality!

The Difference Between Food-Collectors
and Food-Producers

Childe used the word *revolution* because of the radical change that took place in the habits and customs of humans. Food-collectors—that is, hunters, fishers, berry- and nut-gatherers—had to live in small groups or bands, for they had to be ready to move wherever their food supply moved. Not many people can normally be fed in this way in one area, and small children and old folks are a burden. There is not enough food to store, and it is not the kind that can be stored for long.

Do you see how this all fits into a picture? Small groups of people living now in this cave, now in that, or out in the open, as they moved after the animals they hunted or the nuts and berries they collected; no permanent villages, a few half-buried huts at best; no breakable utensils or pottery; no signs of anything for clothing beyond the tools that were probably used to dress the skins of animals; no time to think of much of anything but food and protection and disposal of the dead when death did come; an existence which took nature as it found it, which did little or nothing to modify nature—all in all, a savage's existence, and a very tough one. People who spend their whole life following animals just to kill them to eat, or moving from one berry patch to another, are themselves really living just like animals.

Against this extreme picture of the hunter-collector's life, let me try to draw another—that of people's lives after food production had begun. Meat was stored "on the hoof," grain "in the bin," as Childe put it (Flannery's "banking"). People built reasonably permanent houses; it was worth their while, because they couldn't move far from their fields and flocks. In the neighborhood enough food could be grown and enough animals bred so that many people were kept busy. They all lived close to their flocks and fields, in a village. The village was already of a fair size, and it was growing, too. Everybody had more to eat; they were presumably all stronger, and there were more children. Children and old men could shepherd the animals by day or help with the lighter work in the fields. After the crops had been harvested the younger men might go hunting and some of them would fish, but the food they brought in was only an addition to the food in the village. Undoubtedly the women did much near-at-hand wild plant collecting, as they still do in Kurdish hill villages. The villagers wouldn't starve, even if the hunters and fishermen came home empty-handed.

There was more time to do different things, too. They began to modify nature. They made pottery out of raw clay, and textiles out of hair or fiber. Eventually people who became good at pottery making traded their pots for food and spent all of their time on pottery alone. Other people were learning to weave cloth or to make new tools. There were already people in the village who were becoming full-time craftsmen.

Other things were changing, too. The villagers must have had to agree on new rules for living together. The head of the village had problems different from those of the chief of the small food-collectors' band. If somebody's flock of sheep spoiled a wheat field, the owner wanted payment for the grain he lost. The chief of the hunters was never bothered with such questions. Even the gods had changed. The spirits and the magic that had been used by hunters weren't of any use to the villagers. They needed gods who would watch over the fields and the flocks, and they eventually began to erect buildings where their gods might dwell, and where the people who knew most about the gods might live.

Was Food Production a Revolution?

If you can see the difference between these two admittedly over-drawn pictures—between life in the food-collecting stage and life after food production had begun—you'll see why Professor Childe spoke of a revolution. By revolution, he did not mean that it happened overnight or that it happened only once. We don't know exactly how long it took. Some people think that all these changes may have occurred in less than 500 years, but I doubt that. The incipient era was probably an affair of some duration. Once the level of the effective village-farming community had been established, however, things did begin to move very fast. By 6000(+) years ago, the descendants of the first villagers had developed plow agriculture in the relatively rainless Mesopotamian alluvium and were living in towns with temples. Relative to the three million years of food gathering which lay behind, this had been achieved with truly revolutionary suddenness.

Gaps in Our Knowledge of the Near East

If you'll look again at the chart (p. 107), you'll see that I have few sites and assemblages to name in the incipient era of cultivation and domestication, and not many in the earlier part of the primary village-farming level either. Thanks in no small part to the intelligent cooperation given foreign excavators by the various Near Eastern government antiquities services, our understanding of the sequence in these countries grows more complete as political circumstances allow. I use several sequences on the Zagros-Tauros flanks as my main yardstick here. But I am far from being able to

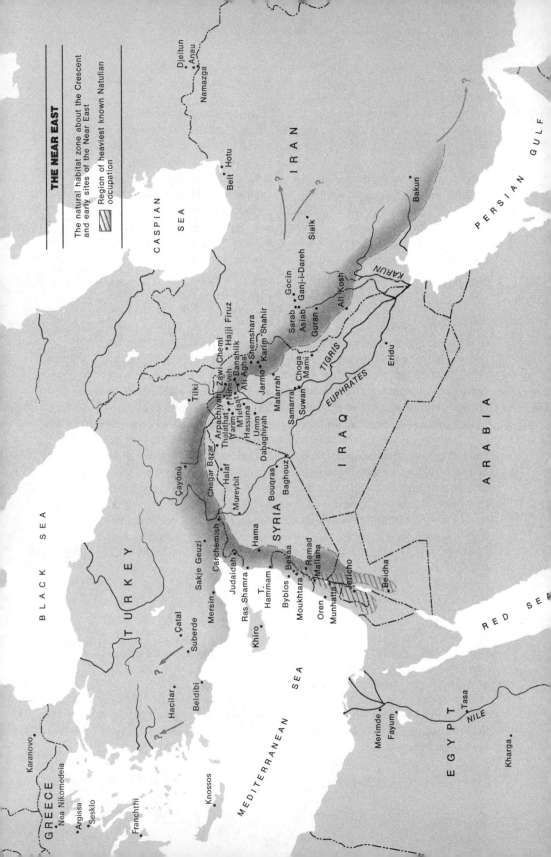

GREECE

Karanovo

Nea Nikomedeia

Argissa

Sesklo

Franchthi

BLACK SEA

TURKEY

Çatal

Suberde

Haçilar

Beldibi

?

CASPIAN SEA

Djeitun

Anau

Namazga

Belt

Hotu

IRAN

Bakun

Sialk

Ganj-i-Dareh

Gocin

Sarab

Asiab

Guran

Ali Kosh

?

?

?

?

Karim Shahir

Jarmo

Ali Aghal

Banahilk

Shemshara

Hajji Firuz

Zawi Chemi

Nineveh

Tilki

Arpachiyah

Thalathat

M'lefat

Yarim

Hassuna

Umm

Dabaghiyah

Matarrah

Samarra

Suwan

Choga Mami

TIGRIS

IRAQ

Eridu

EUPHRATES

KARUN

PERSIAN GULF

ARABIA

Çayönü

Chagar Bazar

Halaf

Mureybit

Baghouz

Bouqras

Carchemish

Sakje Geuzi

Mersin

Judaidah

Ras Shamra

T. Hammam

Khiro

SYRIA

Hama

Byblos

Bekaa

Moukhtara

Ramad

Mallaha

Oren

Munhatta

Jericho

Beidha

MEDITERRANEAN SEA

RED SEA

EGYPT

Merimde

Fayum

NILE

Tasa

Kharga

Knossos

show you a series of Sears Roebuck catalogues, even century by century, for any part of the nuclear area. There is still a great deal of earth to move, and a great mass of material to recover and interpret before we even begin to understand how and why.

Perhaps here, because this kind of archeology is really my specialty, you'll excuse me if I become personal for a moment. I very much look forward to having further part in closing some of the gaps in knowledge of the Near East. This is not, as I've told you, the spectacular range of Near Eastern archeology. There are no royal tombs, no gold, no great buildings or sculpture, no writing, in fact nothing to excite the normal museum at all. Nevertheless, it is a range which, in terms of ideas, gives the archeologist tremendous satisfaction. The country of the hilly flanks is an exciting combination of green grasslands and mountainous ridges. The Kurds, who inhabit the part of the area in which I've worked most recently, are an extremely interesting and hospitable people. Money cannot buy the pleasure of a bright spring morning in the Kurdish hills, on a good site with a happy crew of workmen and an interested and efficient staff. It is probably impossible to convey the full feeling which life on such a dig holds—halcyon days for the body and acute pleasurable stimulation for the mind. Old things coming newly out of the good dirt, and the pieces of the human puzzle fitting into place! I think I am an honest man; I cannot tell you that I am sorry the job is not yet finished and that there are still gaps in this part of the Near Eastern archeological sequence.

Earlier Sites of the Village-Farmers

In the last chapter, we remained undecided as to whether the now available open-air or mound sites (villages?) of the incipient era included the remains of permanent year-around settlements. One or two, especially Mureybit, would tend to suggest permanent settlement. There are also sites which must fall very close to the borderline between incipience and the primary or effective village-farming level. I think of Ganj Dareh high up on the Zagros in Iran, but also of the Bus Mordeh phase of Ali Kosh, low down on the semi-arid Zagros piedmont. Again, rather high on the Tauros piedmont, well north in southeastern Turkey, lies a site called Çayönü. Its lowest levels yield domesticated cereals and pulses, but we have found only the bones of still-wild animals in these lowest levels. I note but cannot explain the lower and semi-arid versus the higher oak-grassland environmental situations involved. Each of these three sites appears to have had reasonably substantial, rectilinear, several-roomed houses; all are at least assumed to have had year-around occupation; all have some radiocarbon age evidence of having been occupied before 7000 B.C.(+)

By about 7000 B.C.(+), we appear to be fully over the threshold into the era of the primary village-farming communities. The first site of this era to be excavated on the Zagros flanks was Jarmo, in a pleasant intermontane valley of Iraqi Kurdistan. We had three seasons of work on Jarmo, from the late 1940s to mid-1950s, before political circumstances interrupted us. Several other Zagros sites (Shemshara in Iraq; Sarab, Guran, and most—if not all—of lower Ali Kosh) have assemblages which are approximate counterparts of Jarmo, although perhaps somewhat further developed. Following Jarmo come a variety of sites and assemblages which lie along the hilly flanks of the crescent and just below it. I am going to describe and illustrate some of these for you.

Since not too much archeological excavation has yet been done on sites of this range of time, I shall have to mention the names of some single sites which now stand alone for an assemblage. This does not mean that I think the individual sites I mention were unique. In the times when their various cultures flourished, there must have been many little villages which shared the same general assemblage. We are only now beginning to locate them. Thus, if I speak of Jarmo, or Jericho, or Sialk as single examples of their particular kinds of assemblages, I don't mean that they were unique at all. I think I could take you to the sites of at least three more Jarmos within twenty miles of the original one. They are there, but they simply haven't yet been excavated. In 1956, a Danish expedition discovered material of Jarmo type at Shemshara, only two dozen miles northeast of Jarmo, and below (hence sealed in by and earlier than) an assemblage of Hassunan type, which I shall describe presently.

Also, I must warn you of how restricted in area are most of our excavations on these sites. Long excavation reports are published, with many pages of speculations and tabulations, but we then find that these all depend on minute exposures (the areas actually excavated) of only 1 or 2 percent of the overall site size. How generally valid, then, are the speculations and tabulations?

The Incomplete Record Between Karim Shahir and Jarmo

As we see the matter now, there are probably still gaps in the available archeological record between the Karim Shahir-M'lefaat-Zawi Chemi group (of the incipient era, see p. 110) and that of Jarmo (of the village-farming era). Possibly the basal or Bus Mordeh phase of Ali Kosh might reach back into this gap, but—being from a lower piedmont environment—it may have its own peculiarities. Although some items of the Jarmo-type materials do reflect traditions which evidently began in the Karim Shahir group, there is not a clear continuity. Moreover, to the degree that we may trust a few radiocarbon determinations, there would appear to be around 2000 years of difference in time. The single available Zawi Chemi radiocarbon determination is 8900 ± 300 B.C.(+); I still believe that the most reasonable group of determinations from Jarmo averages about 6750 ± 200 B.C.(+).

We shall be on firmer ground when more determinations become available, including those on samples from Asiab. The available Sarab determinations cluster at almost 6000 B.C.(+).

Jarmo, in the Kurdish Hills, Iraq

The site of Jarmo has a depth of deposit of about twenty-seven feet, and approximately a dozen layers of architectural renovation and change. Nevertheless it is a "one period" site; its assemblage remains essentially the same throughout, although there are developments in some categories of artifacts and one or two new items are added in later levels. The site covers about four acres of the top of a bluff, below which runs a small stream. It lies in the hill country east of the modern oil town of Kirkuk. The Iraq Directorate General of Antiquities suggested that we look at it in 1948, and we then had three seasons of digging on it before the political situation prevented a return.

The people of Jarmo grew the barley plant and two different kinds of wheat. They made flint sickles with which to reap their grain, mortars or querns on which to crack it, ovens in which it may have been parched, and stone bowls out of which they might eat their porridge. We know that they had domesticated goats, sheep, dogs, and, in the latest levels, pigs, but Professor Reed (the staff zoologist) is not convinced that the bones of the other potentially domesticable animals of Jarmo—cattle and horse—show any signs of domestication. We had first thought that all of these animals were domesticated ones, but Reed feels he must find out much more before he can be sure. As well as their grain and the meat from their animals, the people of Jarmo consumed great quantities of land snails. Botanically, the Jarmo wheat stands about halfway between fully bred wheat and the wild forms.

Architecture: Hallmark of the Village

However we resolve the matter of Jean Perrot's "villages without food production" (see p. 118), my inclination is still to consider ar-

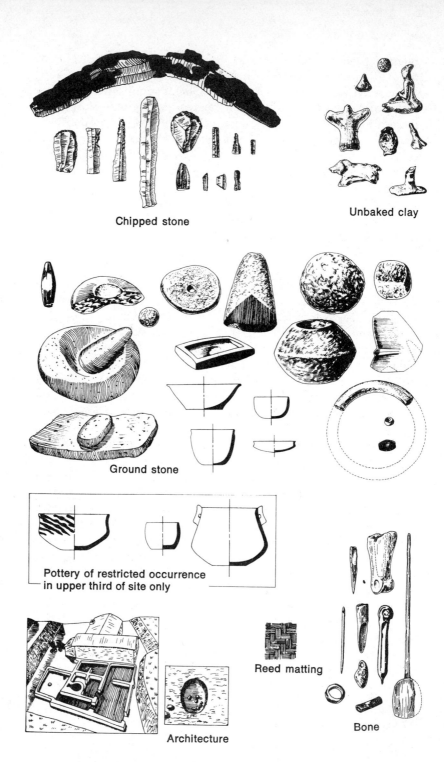

Chipped stone

Unbaked clay

Ground stone

Pottery of restricted occurrence in upper third of site only

Reed matting

Architecture

Bone

Sketch of Jarmo Assemblage

chitectural permanence the sign of a proper village. The houses of Jarmo were only the size of a small cottage by our standards, but each was provided with several rectangular rooms. The walls of the houses were made of puddled mud, often set on crude foundations of stone. (The puddled mud wall, which the Arabs call *touf*, is built by laying a three-to-six-inch course of soft mud, letting this sundry for a day or two, then adding the next course, etc.) The village probably looked much like the simple Kurdish farming village of today, with its mud-walled houses and low mud-on-brush roofs. I doubt that the Jarmo village had more than twenty houses at any one moment of its existence. Today, an average of about seven people live in a comparable Kurdish house; possibly the population of Jarmo was about 150 people.*

It is interesting that portable pottery does not appear until the uppermost or last third of the life of the Jarmo deposit, and even then not over the whole site. Throughout the duration of the village, however, its people had experimented with the plastic qualities of clay. As well as building puddled-mud houses, they modeled little figurines of animals and human beings in clay. One type of human figurine they favored was that of a markedly pregnant woman, probably the expression of some sort of fertility spirit. They provided their house floors with baked-in-place depressions, either as basins or as hearths, and later with domed ovens of clay. As we've noted, the houses themselves were of clay or mud; one could almost say they were built up like a house-sized pot. Then, finally, the idea of making portable pottery itself appeared, although I very much doubt that the people of the Jarmo village discovered the art.

On the other hand, the old tradition of making flint blades and microlithic tools was still very strong at Jarmo. The sickle blade was made in quantities, but so also were many of the much older tool types. Strangely enough, it is within this age-old category of chipped stone tools that we see one of the clearest pointers to a newer age. Many of the Jarmo chipped stone tools—microliths—were made of obsidian, a black volcanic natural glass. The obsidian beds nearest to Jarmo are over three hundred miles to the north. Already a bulk carrying trade had been established, the forerunner of commerce, and the routes were set by which, in later times, the metal trade was to move.

Curiously, our Jarmo-like site in Iran, Sarab, lacks some of the very items which make Jarmo appear settled. Sarab has the flint and obsidian of Jarmo type, also pottery, clay figurines, stone

---

*The proportion of area exposed to the total site area is an important consideration in any such speculation. If I add one third (to account for severe erosion on the north end) to the total present site area, I reckon that we exposed only about 7 percent of the site. This, also, is only for the upper levels; the exposure of the lower levels was still more restricted.

bowls, and bracelets, even goats, sheep, and wheat. But its architectural traces are of wretched reed huts at best. At first we thought that Sarab might have been settled only seasonally. Now the evidence for restricted seasonal settlement is not so clear.

There are now over a dozen radioactive carbon "dates" from Jarmo. As I said earlier, I think the most reasonable cluster of determinations averages to about 6750 ± 200 b.c.(+), although there is a completely unreasonable range of "dates" running from 3250 to 9250 b.c.(+)! *If* I am right in what I take to be "reasonable," the first flush of the food-producing revolution had been achieved almost 9000(+) years ago.

Hassuna, in Upper Mesopotamian Iraq

We are not sure just how soon after Jarmo the next available assemblage of Iraqi material is to be placed. I do not think the time was long, and there are a few hints that detailed habits in the making of pottery and ground stone tools were actually continued from Jarmo times into the time of the next full assemblage. This is named after the site of Hassuna, a few miles to the south and west of modern Mosul. We already have Hassunan-type materials from several other sites in this same general region. We ourselves excavated one, called Matarrah, on the southern fringe of the area; Japanese colleagues are excavating a Hassunan-type site called Thalathat and Russian colleagues another, called Yarim, both near Mosul. Yet another new site, Umm Dabaghiyah, lies well west of the Tigris in now semi-arid desert steppe. It yields the bones of domesticated sheep and goat, as well as large quantities of onager (wild ass) bones. Iraqi colleagues have suggested some Hassunan-type elements in the basal layers of the Tigris riverside site called Suwan. It is probably too soon to make generalizations about it, but the Hassunan sites seem to cluster at slightly lower elevations than do those of the Jarmo type of assemblage.

The catalogue of the Hassuna assemblage is more full and elaborate than that of Jarmo. The Iraqi government's archeologists, who dug Hassuna itself, exposed evidence of increasing architectural know-how. The walls of houses were still formed of puddled mud; sun-dried bricks tend to appear here only in later periods. There were now several different ways of making and decorating pottery vessels. One style of pottery painting, called the Samarran style, is an extremely handsome one and must have required a great deal of concentration and excellence of draftsmanship. On the other hand, the old habits for the preparation of good, chipped stone tools—still apparent at Jarmo—seem to have largely disappeared by Hassunan times. The flint work of the Hassunan catalogue is, by and large, a

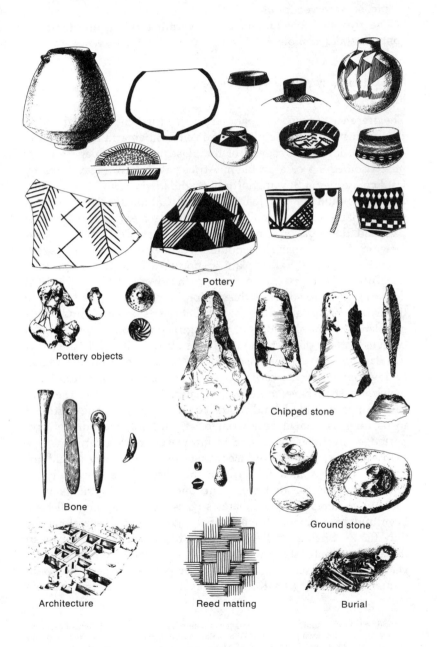

Pottery

Pottery objects

Chipped stone

Bone

Ground stone

Architecture

Reed matting

Burial

Sketch of Hassuna Assemblage

wretched affair. We might guess that the kinesthetic concentration of the Hassunan craftsmen now went into other categories; that is, people discovered they might have more fun working with the newer materials. It's a shame that none of their weaving, for example, is preserved for us.

The two available radiocarbon determinations from Hassunan contexts stand at about 5100 and 5600 B.C. ± 250(+) years.

Two Other Early Village Assemblages in Iraq

The presence of Samarran painted pottery (first encountered within the precincts of the medieval Islamic city of Samarra before World War I) in developed aspects of the Hassunan assemblage initially posed something of a problem. At last, with new excavations by Iraqi colleagues at Suwan, north of Baghdad, on a bluff overlooking the Tigris, and by Dr. Joan Oates of Cambridge University at Choga Mami, on the shoulder of the lower piedmont just east of Baghdad, the situation is becoming more clear. Dr. Oates proposes viewing the Hassunan development as having taken place essentially in the Tigris Valley plain in northern Iraq (the proposition does not seem to extend to the very headwaters of the Tigris in Turkey).* To the south of this region, but evidently restricted to the riverine strips along the middle Euphrates or Tigris, and to the grasslands on the shoulders of the Zagros piedmont, lay the region of an essentially distinct Samarran assemblage. Finally, in the lower alluvial plain itself (classic southern Mesopotamia) lay the region of development of the earliest aspects of the Ubaid assemblage, of which we shall have more to say later. Unfortunately, the very earliest phase of the Ubaid sequence (and hence the one pertinent to us here) is known only from brief, and still inadequately reported, excavations at Eridu, just southwest of ancient Ur.

Insofar as we have radiocarbon determinations, they would appear to support Oates' proposition that these three essentially localized (but *not* isolated from one another) developments were roughly contemporaneous. Oates suggests that they may all have been under way before the end of the Jarmo-like phase along the hilly flanks. She also believes that the beginnings of the Ubaid in the alluvium antedated the beginnings of roughly comparable developments—at least indicated by other painted pottery styles—in Iranian Khuzestan (the Karun Valley plain). She feels the same

---

*I myself have a hunch that the Halafian assemblage (which we will note presently) may have been developing along the Tauros flanks during the sixth millennium, and only reached the known sites in north Iraq at a later time. I cannot yet demonstrate the point, however.

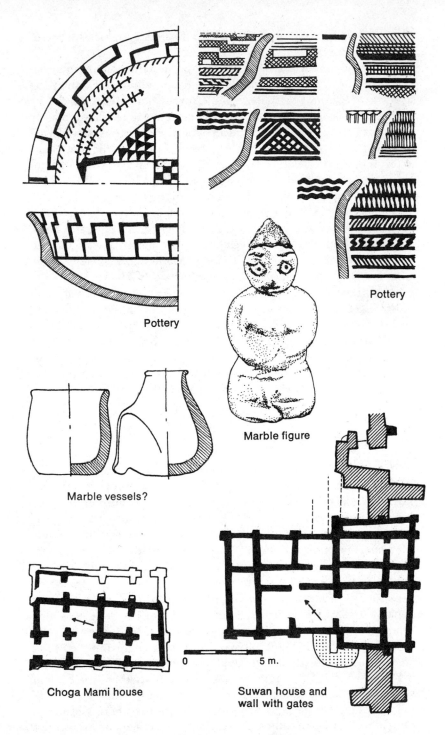

Pottery

Pottery

Marble figure

Marble vessels?

Choga Mami house

Suwan house and
wall with gates

0   5 m.

Sketch of Selected Items of Samarran Assemblage

about Ubaid-type pottery found along the Saudi Arabian littoral of the Arabo-Persian Gulf.

Even though much of the Oates proposition must still remain in the realm of speculation, I find it highly provocative. Further, the yields so far from both Suwan and Choga Mami are by no means inconsiderable, and although we can scarcely dodge talking mainly about painted pottery styles, the level of discussion has moved well beyond that of a sort of philatelist's fascination with the motif repertoires of a generation or two ago. Both Suwan and Choga Mami appear to have had defensive walls and gates, and well-planned, several-roomed, rectilinear houses of mud brick. Emmer and bread wheat, both a naked and a still-hulled barley, lentils, peas, and linseed were grown; and cattle, as well as sheep, goats, pigs, and dogs, were kept. Both the Tigris River flood plain below Suwan and the streams from the nearby hills at Choga Mami make considerations of a simple canalization system perfectly conceivable.

With the riverside sites such as Suwan, and even more so with the sites of the southern alluvium such as Eridu, we are dealing with localities well outside the "natural habitat zone of the potential domesticates." For some time we have been wondering what may have been the earliest aspects of the food-producing way of life, as favorable mutations allowed the early plant and animal domesticates to be moved beyond their original natural habitat zone. It seems to me that we shall very presently find out.

Other Early Village Sites in the Nuclear Area

I'll now name and very briefly describe a few of the other early village assemblages either in or adjacent to the hilly flanks of the crescent. Unfortunately, we do not have radioactive carbon determinations for many of these materials. We may guess that some particular assemblage, roughly comparable to that of Hassuna in the level of technological competence required to produce it, for example, must reflect a culture which existed at about the same time as that of Hassuna. We do this guessing on the basis of the general similarity and degree of complexity of the Sears Roebuck catalogues of the particular assemblage and that of Hassuna. We suppose that for sites near at hand and of a comparable cultural level, as indicated by their generally similar assemblages, the dating must be about the same. We can also tell whether, in a general stratigraphic sense, the sites in question appear at the bottom of the ascending village sequence in their respective areas. Without a number of consistent radioactive carbon determinations, we cannot be precise about priorities.

The ancient mound called Tell es-Sultan at Jericho, in the Dead Sea Valley in Palestine, yields some very interesting materials. At one place where the very basal levels of the mound were exposed, a few artifacts of "Natufian" type were recovered. Next came a phase of development out of this same local "Natufian." This phase (the "hog-backed brick" or "P.P.N.A." phase) included what are said to be the bases of massive stone fortification walls and the general use of formed, sun-dried mud brick.

The houses were round in plan. No pottery was yet being made in this or the next phase. In the next (or "P.P.N.B.") phase, considerable change is apparent. Houses were now rectangular in plan and had plastered floors and walls. A new flint and obsidian industry appeared. Human skulls were modeled over with mud plaster and painted. The P.P.N.B. assemblage is now being exposed in impressive area at Beidha in Jordan, at Munhatta in Israel, and at Ramad in Syria. Following the P.P.N.B. phase, pottery made its appearance in the general region.

Jericho lies in a somewhat strange and tropically lush ecological niche, some 700 feet below sea level; it is geographically within the hilly-flanks zone, but environmentally not part of it. We know as yet very little concerning the basis for its food supply. But in both Beidha and Ramad P.P.N.B. levels, cultivation is evidenced.

The radiocarbon determinations from the Syro-Palestinian region tend to make fairly reasonable clusters. The available Natufian determinations (from Tell es-Sultan) average to ca. 8250 B.C.(+), those of the P.P.N.A. to ca. 7750 B.C.(+), and those of the P.P.N.B. to ca. 6500 B.C.(+). The Ramad material is possibly a somewhat more developed (and slightly later?) form of P.P.N.B. These figures might be taken as reasonable midpoints for probably half-millennia or more in the case of each phase concerned.

Tell es-Sultan contains a remarkably fine sequence, which perhaps does not have the gap we noted in Iraqi-Kurdistan between the Karim Shahir group and Jarmo. While I am not sure that this sequence will prove valid for those parts of Palestine outside the special Dead Sea environmental niche, the sequence does appear to proceed from the local variety of Natufian into that of a very well-settled community.

There is an early village assemblage with strong characteristics of its own in the land bordering the northeast corner of the Mediterranean Sea, where Syria and the Cilician province of Turkey join. This early Syro-Cilician assemblage must represent a general cultural pattern which was at least in part contemporary with that of the Hassuna assemblage. At the base of the coastal site of Ras Shamra, a pre-ceramic phase of the assemblage is reported. The materials from the bases of the mounds at Mersin, and from Judaidah in the Amouq plain, as well as from a few other sites, represent the remains of true villages. The walls of the houses were built of mud, but some of the house foundations were of stone. Several different kinds of pottery were made by the people of these villages. None of it resembles the pottery from Hassuna or from the upper levels of Jarmo or Jericho. The Syro-Cilician people had not lost their touch at working flint. In fact, Perrot believes that the flint tool kits of the Syro-Palestinian P.P.N.B. phase may have been derived from those of this more northerly region. An important southern variation of the Syro-Cilician assemblage has been cleared recently at Byblos, a port town famous in later Phoenician times. There are three radiocarbon determinations which suggest that the time range for these developments was probably in the late seventh to early sixth millennium B.C.(+).

The Tauros Flanks, Anatolia, and the Aegean

Until recently, the great upper basin of the Tigris-Euphrates drainage system on the flanks of the Tauros mountains had remained unknown. Then in 1963–64, Professor Halet Çambel and I joined in forming a University of Istanbul–University of Chicago field project for the examination of the prehistory of southeastern Turkey. Following an extensive surface survey, a low mound north of the walled city of Diyarbakir was chosen for excavation. The site, Çayönü, yielded an early village assemblage without pottery vessels, roughly comparable to that of Jarmo save for its flint and obsidian industry. This industry, while showing some tenuous connections with both the Jarmo flints and those from the Syro-Cilician area, has its own particular characteristics. Only the dog was present as a domesticate at the beginning, when the hunting of wild cattle and deer seems to have been common. Sheep, goats, and probably pigs appeared as domesticates before the prehistoric phase ended. On the other hand, both emmer and einkorn wheat, lentils, peas, and vetch were present as domesticated plants from the beginning. Çayönü also yielded traces of rather surprisingly well built buildings with heavy stone foundations for mud brick walls and a flagstone-paved floor. Another surprise was the appearance of a few pins, a drill point, and a bead of hammered native copper. The available radiocarbon determinations average about 7000 B.C.(+).

These results at Çayönü are most gratifying and further work at the site continues. On the other hand, our 1963–64 survey did not appear to locate any sites we took to be approximately equivalent to either the Karim Shahirian or the Natufian in time or type. More survey and study will be necessary for the location of sites of the incipient era, if indeed they existed, as far north as the Tigris headwaters country. I grow increasingly convinced that such sites are probably to be found farther south in the politically sensitive zone of the Syro-Turkish frontier.

Two sites perhaps of the same general range of time and complexity as Çayönü lie to the west of the Euphrates drainage on the plateau in southwestern Anatolia. The materials in question come from the basal layers of Hacilar, near Lake Burdur, and at Suberde, near Suğla Lake. In these two simple settlements, the plastering of the floors and mud brick walls, taken together with apparent interest in the skulls of the dead at Hacilar, recalls the P.P.N.B. of Syro-Palestine. Cultivated wheat and barley are reported from Hacilar. The study of the Suberde food plant sources is not yet completed, but the animal bones *do not* include any trace of domesticated forms. In fact, the site has been called a hunters' village.

The basal levels of Hacilar and the pertinent material from Suberde appear to have flourished about 6750–6500 B.C.(+). Then, after an interval of still uncertain duration, the remarkable nearby site of Çatal Hüyük was occupied. For some reason not yet clear, the preservation conditions at Çatal Hüyük are exceptionally good. The inventory includes pottery and a flint and obsidian industry somewhat similar to those of early Syro-Cilicia, a variety of small objects in ground stone, metal, and wood, traces of woven stuff, and a fine series of clay or stone figurines. Perhaps most remarkable are the murals and plastic reliefs used as architectural decoration. The excavator, Mr. James Mellaart, is inclined to think of the houses so decorated as shrines and the area so far exposed as a priestly quarter. The situation as far as animal domestication is concerned is confused: the excavator claims sheep and goats; while Dr. Dexter Perkins, a competent zoologist, denies this, but does account for domesticated cattle. Dr. Hans Helbaek has identified three types of cultivated wheat (including bread wheat), as well as naked barley and some variety of legumes, in a preliminary study. The average of the available Çatal Hüyük determinations falls at ca. 5750 B.C.(+). In my judgment, the Çatal Hüyük materials suggest a westerly variant of the assemblage known in the upper Tigris-Euphrates region as the Halafian, which we shall look at presently.

Still more pre-ceramic horizons, on sites on Cyprus and in Thessaly in northern Greece, await their place as our ideas of the general scheme develop. Professor V. Milojcic's site of Argissa in Thessaly appears to be without pottery. Another important site in Macedonia, which does have pottery, is Nea Nikomedeia, with a

single radiocarbon determination of about 6250 b.c. ± 150 years
(+). The Franchthi cave sequence (see p. 120) in southern Greece
also should be recalled here. An early pre-ceramic village has been
reported from the basal levels of Knossos on Crete. On Cyprus, the
site of Khirokitia shows the traces of a substantial, well-built village of round houses, but again evidently without pottery for most
of its duration. Other early village sites on Cyprus are also now under excavation.

The Iranian Plateau

We have already considered sites on the Zagros which lie well up
in elevation toward the Iranian plateau (e.g., Asiab, Ganj Dareh,
Sarab, Guran). The map (p. 124) also shows sites on the plateau itself. From the base of the great mound at Sialk on the Iranian
plateau came an assemblage of early village material, generally
similar in the kinds of things it contained to the catalogues of Hassuna and of Judaidah in the Amouq. The details of how things
were made are different; the Sialk assemblage represents still another cultural pattern. I suspect it appeared a bit later than did that
of Hassuna. Nearer the Zagros, Haji Firuz and the basal layers of
Godin Tepe appear to continue the late Jarmo type of assemblage
of Sarab and upper Guran aspect. A quite different inventory ob-
tains farther to the southeast on the plateau. In the earlier of two
mounds at a place called Bakun, in southwestern Iran, we know
only of coarse and primitive pottery. But next comes the beginning
of a handsome series of painted pottery, often called *buff ware*, as
the paint had been applied on a light buff surface. This decorative
style evidently had its antecedents in lowland Khuzestan, and—if
Joan Oates' proposition is correct—may have originated in Mesopotamia. We shall note the full Mesopotamian aspect in the materials known as Ubaidian in the next chapter.

Unfortunately, much of the excavation done before World War
ii in Iran ignored some of the things which interest us most, such as
plant remains and animal bones, but new excavations by French,
Canadian, and American colleagues are correcting this. The results
of new work at the site of Jaffarabad, near ancient Susa, will be particularly important in this respect.

Beyond the northern frontier of Iran, in Soviet Turkmenistan, an
assemblage resembling that of Sialk was found many years ago by
an American engineer who planned a railroad for the czarist Rus-
sians. The yield of this site, Anau, has since been elaborated at
Namazgah, and Professor V. Masson has excavated a very interesting and still earlier site called Jeitun.

The Nile Valley

The Nile Valley lies beyond the peculiar environmental zone flanking the crescent, and it is certain that the historic village-farming communities in Egypt depended on some form of diffusion of the southwestern Asiatic plant and animal domesticates from the nuclear area. Recently, however, Professor Desmond Clark has argued convincingly for an early Egyptian "process of preadaption using the local animal and plant resources which is most likely to have preceded the introduction of the Asian domesticates." Clark continues that "the appearance of the Asian food plants and animals in the fifth millennium may reflect, therefore, not the beginnings of domestication in Egypt, but the replacement of genetically less suitable local species by more satisfactory exotic forms, a situation made possible between the Nile and the Levant from that time onwards." The earliest trace of the Asiatic domesticates comes from little settlements along the shore of the Fayum lake. The Fayum materials come mainly from grain bins or silos. Another site, Merimde, in the western part of the Nile delta, shows the remains of a true village, but it may be slightly later than the settlement of the Fayum. There are radioactive carbon determinations for the Fayum materials at about 4275 B.C.(+) and from Merimde at about 4100 B.C.(+), which is almost 1500 years later than the determinations suggested for the Hassunan or Syro-Cilician assemblages. I suspect that this is a somewhat overextended indication of the time it took for the generalized cultural pattern of village-farming community life to spread from the nuclear area down into Egypt, but as yet we have no way of testing these matters.

In this same vein, we have two radioactive carbon determinations for an assemblage from sites near Khartoum in the Sudan, best represented by the mound called Shaheinab. The Shaheinab catalogue roughly corresponds to that of the Fayum; the distance between the two places, as the Nile flows, is roughly 1500 miles. This suggests that it took almost a thousand years for the new way of life to be carried as far south into Africa as Khartoum; the two Shaheinab "dates" average about 3300 B.C. $\pm$ 400(+) years.

If the movement was up the Nile (southward), as these dates suggest, then I suspect that the earliest available village material of middle Egypt, the so-called Tasian, is also later than that of the Fayum. The Tasian materials come from a few graves near a village called Deir Tasa, and I have an uncomfortable feeling that the Tasian "assemblage" may be mainly an artificial selection of poor examples of objects which belong in the following range of time.

There might possibly be some surprises in the new materials from the Kom Ombo and Nubian regions, but as regards the effective *production* of food, I'd doubt it. I would not dispute the implications of open-air sites, quantities of milling stones and sickle blades, and other indications of intensive collecting activities. In fact, we *may* be dealing here with an incipient era, based on plant and animal elements which themselves weren't incipiently effective. My notion is that the Nile Valley was *never* a part of the natural habitat for the Asiatic potential domesticates. It may even have taken several millennia before fortunate mutant forms appeared which would tolerate the very special Nile niche.

The same reasoning *may* be at issue in the matter of the first appearance of effective food production in classic southern Mesopotamia, although far less delay seems to have been involved before the domesticates became effective in the south. As matters stand now, these things may not have happened so much later than on the hilly flanks.

Time and Space Developments

There are now two things we can do; in fact, we have already begun to do them. We can watch the spread of the new way of life upward through time in the nuclear area. We can also see how the new way of life spread outward in space from the nuclear area as time went on. There is good archeological evidence that both these processes took place. For the hill country of northeastern Iraq, in the nuclear area, we have already noticed how the succession (still with gaps) from Karim Shahir, through M'lefaat and Jarmo, to Hassuna can be charted (see chart p. 107). In the next chapter, we shall continue this charting and description of what happened in Iraq upward through time. We also watched traces of the new way of life move through space up the Nile into Africa, to reach Khartoum in the Sudan some 3500(+) years later than we had seen it at Jarmo or Jericho. We caught glimpses of it in the Fayum and perhaps at Tasa along the way.

For the remainder of this chapter, I shall try to suggest briefly for you the directions taken by the spread of the new way of life from the nuclear area in the Near East. First, let me make clear again that I *do not* believe that the village-farming community way of life was invented only once and in the Near East alone. It seems to me that the evidence is very clear that a separate experiment arose in the New World. The evidence for independent beginnings in southeastern Asia and China, as well as in sub-Saharan Africa, also seems to mount impressively as we learn more. There are some surprisingly early radiocarbon determinations for the village-like settlements of Japan, called the Jomon. However, it is still unclear whether the earliest phase of the Jomon depended on produced food.

The appearance of the village-farming community in the north-west of India, at least as we now know it, seems to have depended on the earlier development in the Near East. However, as I speculated at a scientific congress in New Delhi in 1961, the same "process of pre-adaption using the local animal and plant resources" which Desmond Clark suggests for Egypt might have been a factor in the case of India, *before* the southwestern Asiatic plant and animal domesticates were diffused to India.

I wish we knew more of how northwestern Africa fit into the whole picture.

The Spread of the Village-Farming Community Way of Life into Europe

How about Europe? I won't give you many details. You can easily imagine that the late prehistoric prelude to European history is a complicated affair. We all know very well how complicated an area Europe is now, with its welter of different languages and cultures. Remember, however, that a great deal of archeology has been done on the late prehistory of Europe, and relatively very little on that of later Asia and Africa. If we knew as much about these areas as we do of Europe, I expect we'd find them just as complicated.

This much is clear for Europe, as far as the spread of the village-community way of life is concerned. The general idea and much of the know-how and basic tools of food production moved from the Near East to Europe. So did the plants and animals which had been domesticated; they were not naturally at home in most of Europe, as they were in western Asia (remember my troubles with definition of the boundaries of the nuclear zone). I do not, of course, mean that there were traveling salesmen who carried these ideas and things to Europe with a commercial gleam in their eyes. The process took time, and the ideas and things must have been passed on from one group of people to the next. There was probably also some actual movement of peoples, but we don't know the size of the groups or how far any one of them moved.

The story of the "colonization" of Europe by the first farmers is thus one of (1) the probable movement from the eastern Mediterranean lands of some people who were farmers; (2) the spread of ideas and things beyond the Near East itself and beyond the paths along which the "colonists" moved; and (3) the adaptations of the ideas and things by the indigenous Forest folk, about whose receptiveness Professor Mathiassen speaks (p. 91). It is important to note that the resulting cultures in the new European environment were European, not Near Eastern. Professor Childe remarked that "the peoples of the West were not slavish imitators; they adapted the gifts from the East . . . into a new and organic whole capable of developing on its own original lines."

The Ways to Europe

Suppose we want to follow the traces of those earliest village-farmers who did travel from western Asia into Europe. Let us start from Syro-Cilicia, that part of the hilly-flanks zone proper which lies in the very northeastern corner of the Mediterranean. Three ways would be open to us. We could go north, or north and slightly east, across Anatolian Turkey, and skirt along either shore of the Black Sea or even to the east of the Caucasus Mountains along either flank of the Caspian Sea, to reach Ukrainian Russia. From here, we could march across eastern Europe to the Baltic and Scandinavia, or even hook back southwestward to Atlantic Europe.

Our second way from Syro-Cilicia would also lie over Anatolia, perhaps past the Hacilar site, to the northwest, where we would have to swim or raft ourselves over the Dardanelles or the Bosphorus to the European shore. Then we could bear left toward Thessaly in Greece. But some of us might turn right again in Macedonia, going up the valley of the Vardar River to its divide and on down the valley of the Morava beyond, to reach the Danube near Belgrade in Yugoslavia. Here we might turn left, following the great river valley of the Danube up into central Europe. We would have a number of tributary valleys to explore, or we could cross the divide and go down the valley of the Rhine to the North Sea.

Our third way from Syro-Cilicia would be by sea. Remember the obsidian in the Franchthi cave and the evidence for boat travel which it provides for at least as early as 7000 B.C.(+)? We would coast along southern Anatolia and visit Cyprus, Crete, and the Aegean islands on our way to Greece, where, in the north, we might meet some of those who had taken the second route. From Greece, we would sail on to Italy and the western isles to reach southern France and the coasts of Spain. Eventually a few of us would sail up the Atlantic coast of Europe to reach western Britain and even Ireland.

Of course none of us could ever take these journeys as the first farmers took them, since the whole course of each journey must have lasted many lifetimes. The radiocarbon determinations for the earliest farmers of the Rhine delta in Holland run at about 4200 B.C.(+). Somewhere before 6000 B.C.(+) would be a safe date to suggest for the first well-developed early village communities of Syro-Cilicia. We suspect that the spread throughout Europe did not proceed at an even rate. Nevertheless, it would appear as if the new way of life was making itself felt along the Atlantic seaboard

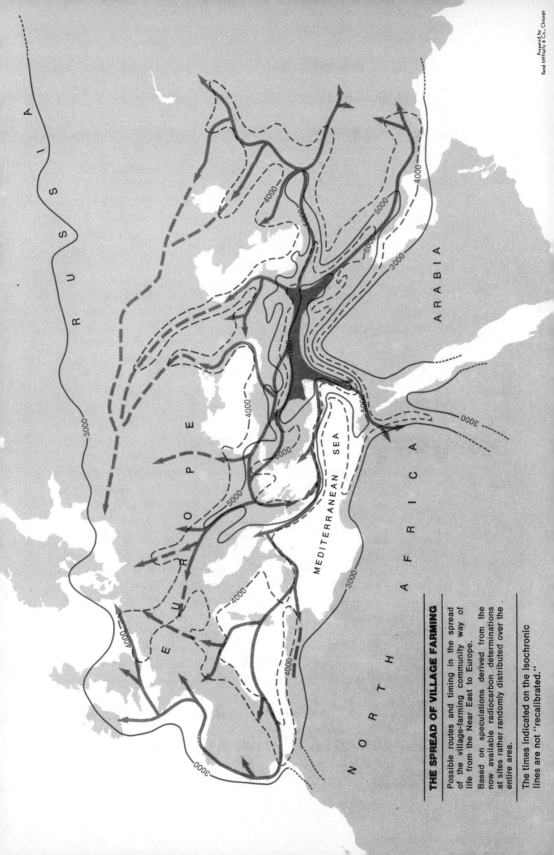

THE SPREAD OF VILLAGE FARMING

Possible routes and timing in the spread of the village-farming community way of life from the Near East to Europe.

Based on speculations derived from the now available radiocarbon determinations at sites rather randomly distributed over the entire area.

The times indicated on the isochronic lines are not "recalibrated."

RUSSIA

ARABIA

EUROPE

MEDITERRANEAN SEA

NORTH AFRICA

3000

4000

5000

6000

Prepared by
Rand McNally & Co., Chicago

of Europe about 2000 years after it was established in Syro-Cilicia.

I offer a highly speculative attempt at charting this spread on a map with isochronic (or time contour) lines (p. 143). The map assumes that village-farming communities had been established in the natural habitat zone in southwestern Asia by about 7000 B.C.(+). We do not know just how soon after this the spread began, but it must have been under way by 6000 B.C.(+). Using the still rather few radiocarbon determinations we now have, I have sketched the way in which I think the time contours may have spread. I warn you that not all prehistorians would accept the implications of this map.

The Earliest Farmers of England

To describe the later prehistory of all Europe for you would take another book and a much larger one than this. Therefore, I have decided to give you only a few impressions of the later prehistory of Britain. Of course the British Isles lie at the other end of Europe from our baseline in western Asia. Also, they received influences along at least two of the three ways in which the new way of life moved into Europe. We will look at more of their late prehistory in a following chapter: here I shall speak only of the first British farmers we now know.

The earliest known British artifacts implying farming are already said to be "in probably a mature and fully extended form." Presumably we have earlier aspects yet to find. The available evidence comes from sites which go back to about 3500 B.C.(+), which are found in regions with surface occurrences of raw flint and which have a narrow flake industry and piercing (rather than broad cutting) arrowheads. The associated pottery may be distinguished into three groups:

1. The east coast and northern or Yorkshire Wold group, with links to the pottery of the Belgian Michelsberg type.
2. The west country group near the Channel coastline, showing traits of the pottery of the French Chassey type.
3. The decorated group, for which Humphrey Case suggests the possibility of a late Danubian ("linear") pottery origin.

As it became well established, the subsistence economy involved emmer and einkorn wheat, barley, the grazing of cattle and pigs, goats, and possibly sheep. Three different types of structures have been encountered. There are roughly circular earthwork enclosures, which some authorities believe may have been seasonal cattle corrals. Secondly, traces of both oblong and round timber-framed houses (presumably sod-covered) have been found, but not within the earthwork enclosures. A third structural type consists of long simple mounds or "unchambered barrows," in one end of which burials were made. There were also pits or mineshafts dug into the chalk beds for extracting flints, and wooden tracks (corduroy roads) were built over marshlands.

A well-known site of the type with great circular earthwork enclosures is Windmill Hill, in Wiltshire, southcentral England. This site name has sometimes been used as a type or period name, but it does not imply all of the now available evidence.

The Megalithic Tradition Begins

The archeological traces of a second early tradition (of one or more cultures?) are to be found first in the west of England, western and northern Scotland, and most of Ireland. The bearers of these materials had come up the Atlantic coast by sea from southern France and Spain. The evidence left for us consists mainly of tombs and the contents of tombs, with only very rare settlement sites. The tombs were of some size and received the bodies of many people. The tombs themselves were built of stones, heaped over with earth; the stones enclosed a passage to a central chamber ("passage graves"), or to a simple long gallery, along the sides of which the bodies were laid ("gallery graves"). The general type of construction is called *megalithic* (great stone), and the whole earth-mounded structure is often called a *barrow*. Since many have proper chambers, in one sense or another, we used the term "unchambered barrow" above to distinguish those of the Windmill Hill type from these megalithic structures. There is some evidence for sacrifice, libations, and ceremonial fires, and it is clear that some form of community ritual was focused on the megalithic tombs.

The cultures of the people who produced the three earliest food-producing assemblages and of those who made the megalithic tombs flourished, at least in part, at the same time. Although the distributions of these different types of archeological traces are in quite different parts of the country, there is pottery of the Windmill Hill and of the other types in some of the megalithic tombs. It has been customary to assume that the megalithic tradition was due to diffusion from the eastern Mediterranean, but Professor Colin Renfrew now vigorously protests this notion on the ground that the recalibration of pertinent radiocarbon determinations indicates that these monuments appeared first in the west.

Further Complications

Until some time after 3000 B.C.(+), evidence of people who may not have been farmers is to be found on sites in southern and eastern England. How these ambiguous traces are now seen to fit with the inventories of the earliest farmers described above is not clear. Stuart Piggott favors the term "secondary Neolithic cultures" (which not all authorities accept) as a descriptive handle for these generalized materials that appear to be the result of the acceptance—by indigenous food-collectors—of some food-producing ways of making and doing things. Some of the pottery, originally called the Peterborough type, is decorated with impressions of cords and was at first believed to be quite different from that of Windmill Hill and the megalithic builders. It is now taken to be an insular evolution of earlier Windmill Hill types. In addition, the distribution of these finds extends into eastern Britain, where the other cultures have left no trace. The makers of this assemblage had villages with semi-subterranean huts, and the bones of oxen, pigs, and sheep have been found in a few of these. On the whole, however, hunting and fishing seem to have been their vital occupations. They also established trade routes especially to acquire the raw material for stone axes.

A probably slightly later culture, whose traces are best known from Skara Brae on Orkney, also had its roots in those cultures of the Baltic area which fused out of the meeting of the Forest folk and the peoples who took the eastern way into Europe. Skara Brae is very well preserved, having been built of thin stone slabs about which dune-sand drifted after the village died. The individual houses, the bedsteads, the shelves, the chests for clothes and oddments—all built of thin stone slabs—may still be seen in place. But the Skara Brae people lived entirely by sheep and cattle breeding, and by catching shellfish. Neither grain nor the instruments of agriculture appeared at Skara Brae.

The list of radiocarbon age determinations for the whole range of the early farmers of Britain, as now available, runs from about 3500 B.C.(+) to about 2250 B.C.(+).

The European Achievement

The above is only a very brief description of what went on in Britain after the arrival of the first farmers. I recommend to you Humphrey Case's essay on the process of the colonization of Britain. There are many interesting details which I have omitted in order to shorten the story.

I believe some of the difficulty we have in understanding the establishment of the first farming communities in Europe is with the word *colonization*. We have a natural tendency to think of colonization as it has happened within the last few centuries. In the case of the colonization of the Americas, for example, the colonists came relatively quickly, and in increasingly vast numbers. They had vastly superior technical, political, and war-making skills, compared with those of the Indians. There was not much mixing with the Indians. The case in Europe 5000 or 6000(+) years ago must have been very different. I wonder if it is even proper to call people colonists who move some miles to a new region, settle down and farm it for some years, then move on again, generation after generation. The ideas and the things which these new people carried were only *potentially* superior. The ideas and things and the people had to prove themselves in their adaptation to each new environment. Once this was done another link to the chain would be added, and then the forest-dwellers and other indigenous folk of Europe along the way might accept the new ideas and things. It is quite reasonable to expect that there must have been much mixture of the migrants and the natives along the way; each of the assemblages we mentioned above would seem to show more or less clear traces of such fused cultures. Sometimes, especially if the migrants were moving by boat, long distances may have been covered in a short time. Remember, however, there seem to be almost 3000 years between the early Syro-Cilician villages and Windmill Hill.

Let me repeat Professor Childe again: "The peoples of the West were not slavish imitators: they adapted the gifts from the East . . . into a new and organic whole capable of developing on its own original lines." Childe was, of course, completely conscious of the fact that his "peoples of the West" were in part the descendants of migrants who came originally from the "East," bringing their "gifts" with them. This was the late prehistoric achievement of Europe—to take new ideas and things and some migrant peoples and, by mixing them with the old in its own environments, to forge a new and unique series of cultures.

During the last several years, following upon the already mentioned suggestion by Colin Renfrew, much-publicized claims have been made for the effects of a "second carbon-14 revolution" (that is, for the effects arising from the recalibration of age determinations to bring them into conformity with the bristlecone pine dendrochronology). Thus we have broad, all-inclusive claims for independent beginnings of European "civilization," and assertions that "the revision of carbon-14 dates for prehistoric Europe has a disastrous effect on the traditional diffusionist chronology."

We need, however, to examine these claims with care. Some of them seem almost intended to suggest complete independence for the more recent prehistory of Europe. This is little more than the revival of a scholarly debate of the turn of this century, the "mirage orientale" response to an extreme "ex oriente lux" notion of Europe's later prehistoric development. The claims do not seriously question the spread of the food-producing way of life from south-western Asia into Europe, however. They focus, rather, on a few selected traits (such as the appearance of monumental passage-grave structures in France). It is indeed true that, with recalibration, these monuments have earlier radiocarbon determinations than the "historically" fixed dates of their supposed eastern Mediterranean antecedents. Well and good, so the passage graves in the West may be earlier, but I cannot, myself, get very upset about this. Given that the elements of the food-producing pattern of the European tradition were derived from the original southwestern Asiatic experiment, I'd think the rest is entirely within the spirit of Childe's "The peoples of the West were not slavish imitators . . ." Indeed, the European variations on the older theme had much originality, and this part of the story must have equal interest for us.

8
The conquest of civilization

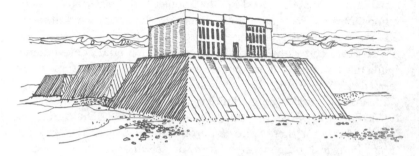

Now we must return to the Near East again. We are coming to the point where written history is about to begin. I am going to stick pretty close to Iraq and Egypt in this chapter. These countries will perhaps be the most interesting to most of us, for the foundations of Western civilization were laid in the river lands of the Tigris and Euphrates and of the Nile. I shall probably stick closest of all to Iraq, because things first happened there and also because I know it best.

There is another interesting thing, too. We have seen that the first experiment in village-farming evidently took place in the Near East. So did the first experiment in civilization. Both experiments "took." The traditions we live by today are based, ultimately, on those ancient beginnings in food production and civilization in the Near East.

What Civilization Means

I shall not try to define *civilization* for you; rather, I shall tell you what the word brings to my mind. To me civilization means urbanization: the fact that there are cities. It means a formal political set-up—that there are kings or governing bodies that the people have set up. It means formal laws, rules of conduct, which the government (if not the people) believes are necessary. It probably means that after things get well established there are formalized projects—

roads, harbors, irrigation canals, and the like—and also some sort of army or police force to protect them. It means quite new and different art forms. It also usually means there is writing. (The people of the Andes—the Incas—had everything which goes to make up a civilization but formal writing. I can see no reason to say they were not civilized.) Finally, as the late Professor Redfield reminded us, civilization seems to bring with it the dawn of a new kind of moral order.

You may quite properly feel that there is a large amount of personal idiosyncrasy involved in the various characterizations or definitions offered for civilization. Recently, I noted the following observation on the matter by Professor Renfrew, "Any distinguishable culture whose institutions and material achievements fulfill the defining criteria which we choose to adopt is properly termed a civilisation." This majestical position leaves the matter wide open; try making a characterization or definition of your own! Or, keeping in mind the things I suggest in my own characterization, note that there were important differences in the way the things I suggest were managed from one civilization to another. In early civilizations, it was usual to find religion very closely tied in with government, law, and so forth. The king might also be a high priest, or he might even be thought of as a god. The laws were usually thought to have been given to the people by the gods. The temples were protected just as carefully as the other projects. But there were important differences in what Professor Henri Frankfort used to call the *form* of doing things from one civilization to another.

Civilization Impossible Without Food Production

Civilizations have to be made up of many people. There is doubtless a population size below which a civilization would not be possible. Some of the people live in the country; some probably live in very large towns or cities. Classes of society have begun. In his thoughtful book *The Evolution of Urban Society,* Professor Adams has considered how new forms of organization of all groups within a society mark off a civilization as something new and different. There are officials and government people; there are priests or religious officials; there are merchants and traders; there are craftsmen, metalworkers, potters, builders, and so on; there are also farmers, and these are the people who produce the food for the whole population. It must be obvious that civilization cannot exist without food production and that food production must also be at a pretty efficient level of village farming before civilization can even begin.

But people can be food producing without being civilized. In many parts of the world this is still the case. When whites first came to America, the Indians in most parts of the hemisphere were food-producers. They grew corn, potatoes, tomatoes, squash, and many other things whites had never eaten before. But only the Aztecs of Mexico, the Mayas of Yucatan and Guatemala, and the Incas of the Andes were civilized.

Why Didn't Civilization Come to All Food-Producers?

Once you have food production, even at a well-advanced level of the village-farming community, what else has to happen before you get civilization? Many have asked this question but have failed to arrive at a full and satisfactory answer. There is probably no *one* answer. We can make an "informed guess" as to one of the reasons why civilization *may* have come about in the Near Eastern instance. Remember, it is only a guess—a putting together of hunches from incomplete evidence. It is *not* necessarily meant to explain how civilization began in any of the other areas—China, southeast Asia, the Americas—where other early experiments in civilization went on. The details in those areas are quite different. Whether certain general principles hold for the appearance of any early civilization is still an open and very interesting question. Professor Adams thinks there are such general principles which hold for the development of any early civilization.

Where Civilization First Appeared in the Near East

You remember that our earliest village-farming communities lay along the hilly flanks of a great crescent and in valley plains above this crescent. (See map on p. 124.) Professor Breasted's "fertile crescent" emphasized the lower and richer alluvial valleys of the Nile and the Tigris-Euphrates Rivers. Our hilly-flanks area of the crescent zone arches up from Egypt through Palestine and Syria, along southern Turkey into northern Iraq, and down along the southwestern fringe of Iran. The earliest fully and effectively food-producing villages of which we now have knowledge already existed in this area by about 7000 B.C.(+).

Now notice again that this hilly-flanks and piedmont zone does not include southern Mesopotamia, the alluvial land of the lower Tigris and Euphrates in Iraq, or the Nile Valley proper. The earliest known villages of classic Mesopotamia and Egypt seem to appear at least a thousand years after those of the hilly-flanks zone. For example, the early Fayum village which lies near a lake west of the Nile Valley proper (see p. 139) has a radiocarbon determination of 4275 B.C. ± 320(+) years. It was in the river lands, however, that the immediate beginnings of civilization were made.

We know that by about 3000 B.C. the Early Dynastic period had begun in southern Mesopotamia. The beginnings of writing go back several hundred years earlier, and we can safely say that civilization had begun in Mesopotamia by 3500 B.C. (I do not add our "(+)" device here, since these time reckonings are made by casting backwards from the written historical sources.) In Egypt, the beginning of the First Dynasty is slightly later, at about 3000 B.C., and writing probably did not appear much earlier. Some authorities have understood the historical chronological evidence to favor later dates (by about 200 years in each case) for the beginnings of civilization in both Egypt and Mesopotamia. The now available radiocarbon evidence—if recalibrated—has so broad a span that it can be claimed to favor either view. But, in round numbers, we may still say that written history and civilization were well under way in both Mesopotamia and Egypt by 3000 B.C.—about 5000 real calendar years ago.

The Hilly-flanks Zone Versus the River Lands

Why did these two civilizations spring up in these two river lands which apparently were not even part of the area where the village-farming community began? Why didn't we have the first civilizations in southern Turkey, Syria, Palestine, north Iraq, or Iran, where we're sure food production had had a long time to develop? I think the probable answer gives a clue to the ways in which civilization began in Egypt and Mesopotamia.

The land in the hilly flanks and in the mountain valley plains beyond is of a sort which people can farm without too much trouble. There is a fairly fertile coastal strip in Palestine and Syria. There are pleasant mountain slopes, streams running out to the sea, and rain, at least in the winter months. The rain belt and the foothills of the Turkish mountains also extend to northern Iraq and on to the Iranian plateau. The Iranian plateau has its mountain valleys, streams, and some rain. These hilly flanks and piedmont of the crescent, through most of its arc, are almost made to order for beginning farmers. The grassy slopes of the higher hills would be pasture for their herds and flocks. As soon as the earliest experiments with agriculture and domestic animals had been successful, a pleasant living could be made without too much trouble. Also, the space available was relatively large, so that an inefficient and soil-exhausting agricultural regime could have been corrected for by simply moving around a bit.

I should add here again that our evidence points increasingly to a climate for those times which was becoming very little different from that for the area today. Wright's cold, dry, artemisia steppe condition was now well past.

Now look at Egypt and southern Mesopotamia. Both are lands with little or no rain, for all intents and purposes. Both are lands with rivers that have laid down very fertile soil—soil certainly superior to that of the piedmont and the hilly flanks. But in both Egypt and Mesopotamia, the rivers are of no great aid without some control.

The ancient Nile (before the time of the great modern dams) flooded its banks once a year, in late September or early October. It not only soaked the narrow fertile strip of land on either side; it also laid down a fresh layer of new soil each year. Beyond the fertile strip on either side rise great cliffs, and behind them is the desert. In its natural, uncontrolled state, the yearly flood of the Nile must have caused short-lived swamps that were full of crocodiles. After a short time, the flood level would have dropped, the water and the crocodiles would have run back into the river, and the swamp plants would have become parched and dry.

The Tigris and the Euphrates of Mesopotamia are less likely to flood regularly than the Nile. The Tigris has a shorter and straighter course than the Euphrates; it is also the more violent river. Its banks are high, and when the snows melt and flow into all of its tributary rivers it is swift and dangerous. The Euphrates has a much longer and more curving course and few important tributaries. Its banks are lower and it is less likely to flood dangerously. The land on either side and between the two rivers is very fertile, south of the modern city of Baghdad. Unlike the Nile Valley, neither the Tigris nor the Euphrates is flanked by cliffs in its lower valleys. The land on either side of the rivers stretches out for miles and is not much rougher than a poor tennis court.

The Rivers Must Be Controlled

The real trick in both Egypt and Mesopotamia was to make the rivers work for you. In Egypt, this was a matter of building dikes and reservoirs that would catch and hold the Nile flood. In this way, the water was held and allowed to run back off over the fields as it was needed. In Mesopotamia, it was a matter of taking advantage of natural river channels and branch channels, and of leading ditches from these onto the fields.

Obviously, we can no longer find the first dikes or reservoirs of the Nile Valley, or the first canals or ditches of Mesopotamia. The same land has been lived on far too long for any traces of the first attempts to be left; especially in Egypt, it has been covered by the yearly deposits of silt dropped by the river floods. But we're pretty sure the first food-producers of Egypt and southern Mesopotamia must have made such dikes, canals, and ditches. In the first place, there couldn't normally have been enough rain for them to grow things otherwise. In the second place, the patterns for such projects seem to have been pretty well set by historic times. And, in the third place, there are at least hints that such practices already existed on the lower shoulder of the nearby piedmont in the Choga Mami and Ali Kosh regions.

Control of the Rivers the Business of Everyone

Here, then, is probably a *part* of the reason why civilization grew in Egypt and Mesopotamia first—not in Palestine, Syria, or Iran. In the latter areas, people could produce their food as individuals. It was neither too hard, nor, of course, was it consciously planned; there were rain and some streams, and good pasturage for the animals even if a crop or two went wrong. In Egypt and Mesopotamia, people had to put in a much greater amount of work, and this work couldn't be individual work. Whole villages or groups of people had to turn out to fix dikes or dig ditches. The dikes had to be repaired and the ditches carefully cleared of silt each year, or they would become useless.

There also had to be hard-and-fast rules. The person who lived nearest the ditch or the reservoir must not be allowed to take all the water and leave none for his neighbors. It was not only a business of learning to control the rivers and of making their waters do the farmer's work. It also meant controlling people. But once these people had managed both kinds of controls, what a wonderful yield they had! The soil was already fertile, and the silt which came in the floods and ditches kept adding fertile soil.

The Germ of Civilization in Egypt and Mesopotamia

This learning to work together for the common good was probably the real germ of the Egyptian and the Mesopotamian civilizations. I am sure that, when enough is learned of all the factors involved, wonderful systems theory diagrams with negative and positive feedbacks and input and output actions will be constructed by coming generations of "new" archeologists! What we can guess at now is that the bare elements of civilization were already there: the need for a governing hand and for laws to see that the communities' work was done and that the water was justly shared.

You may object that there is a sort of chicken and egg paradox in this idea. How could the people set up the rules until they had managed to get a way to live, and how could they manage to get a way to live until they had set up the rules? I think that small groups must have moved down along the mud flats of the river banks quite early, making use of naturally favorable spots, and that the rules grew out of such cases. It would have been like the hand-in-hand growth of automobiles and paved highways in the United States.

Once the rules and the know-how did get going, there must have been a constant interplay of the two. Thus, the more the crops yielded, the richer and better-fed the people would have been, and the more the population would have grown. As the population grew, more land would have needed to be flooded or irrigated, and more complex systems of dikes, reservoirs, canals, and ditches would have been built. The more complex the system, the more necessity for work on new projects and for the control of their use, and so on . . . .

What I have just put down for you is a guess at the manner of growth of some of the formalized systems that go to make up a civilized society. My explanation has been pointed particularly at Egypt and Mesopotamia. The canalization and water-control part of it does not really apply to the development of the Aztecs or the Mayas. But I think that a fair part of the story of Egypt and Mesopotamia must be as I've just told you.

I am particularly anxious that you do *not* understand me to mean that canalization *caused* civilization. I am sure it was not that simple at all. Dr. Adams, whose familiarity with and clear thought on the evidence makes him a trustworthy authority, plays down the role of environment in the formation of early Mesopotamian civilization. He believes that new forms of social organization were much more important. He does not rule environment completely out of the picture, however.

The trouble has been that too many historians and prehistorians (such as Childe) made *irrigation* the cause of civilization. This was clearly a gross oversimplification. For, in fact, a complex and highly engineered irrigation system proper did not come until much later times. Let's say rather that the simple beginnings of irrigation allowed and in fact encouraged a great number of things in the technological, political, social, and moral realms of culture. Another factor of importance—as the population grew larger and the variety of needs of the society tended to encourage more specialization—must have been a gradual enlargement of peoples' interests and loyalties from their relatives or kin-group alone, to include the group of specialists to which they belonged. Simple villages tended to have their interests focused on what the kin-group considered to be most important. In cities, such loyalties and interests tended to be less purely kin-oriented. We do not yet understand what all these things were or how they worked. But without these other aspects of culture, I do not think that urbanization and civilization itself could have come into being.

The Archeological Sequence to Civilization in Iraq

We last spoke of the archeological materials of Iraq on page 130, where I described the village-farming communities of Hassunan and Samarran types. The Hassunan-type villages appear in the hilly-flanks zone and in the rolling land adjacent to the Tigris in northern Iraq. We also noted Joan Oates' suggestion that the Samarran development of the middle river valleys and piedmont-shoulder and the Eridu or Ubaid I phase in alluvial southern Mesopotamia were probably in fair part contemporary with the Hassunan. It is also probable, in my view, that even before the Hassuna pattern of culture lived its course, another new assemblage had been established in the very northernmost corner of Iraq and Syria, and in southeastern Turkey. This assemblage is called Halaf, after a site high on a tributary of the Euphrates, on the Syro-Turkish border. There are radiocarbon determinations for the Halafian which run from about 6000 to 4800 b.c.(+).

The Halafian assemblage is incompletely known. The culture it represents included another remarkably handsome painted pottery, but different from that of the Samarran. Archeologists have tended to be so fascinated with this pottery that they have bothered little with the rest of the Halafian assemblage. We do know that strange stone-founded houses, with plans like those of the popular notion of an Eskimo igloo, were built. As with the pottery of the Samarran style, the Halafian painted pottery implies great concentration and excellence of draftsmanship on the part of the people who painted it.

Classic Southern Mesopotamia First Occupied

Our next step is again into the southland proper. Here, deep in the core of the mound which later became the holy Sumerian city of

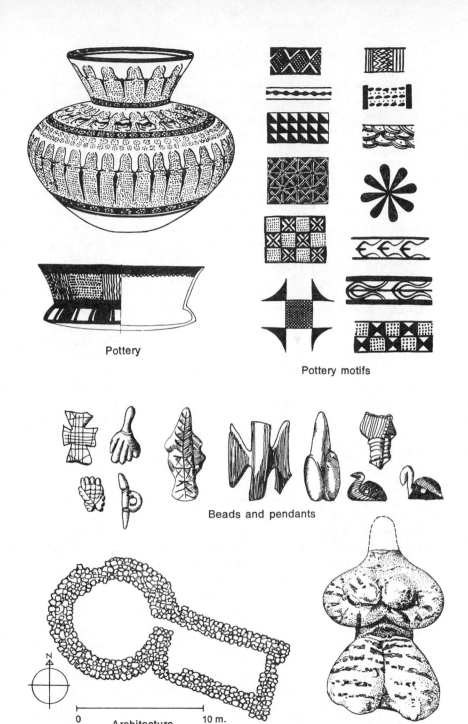

Pottery

Pottery motifs

Beads and pendants

Architecture

0   10 m.

Clay figurine

Sketch of Selected Items of Halafian Assemblage

Eridu, we noted that Iraqi archeologists uncovered another handsome painted pottery. This Eridu pottery, which is about all we have of the assemblage of the people who once produced it, was first seen as a blend of the Samarran and Halafian painted pottery styles. This doubtless (in Oates' view) oversimplifies the case. In another sense, however, the Samarran-type sites of Baghouz, Suwan, and Samarra itself may probably still be seen as way points on the mud flats of the rivers halfway down from the north.

My colleague Robert Adams believes that there were certainly earlier riverine-adapted food-collectors in lower Mesopotamia. The presence of such would explain why the Eridu assemblage is not simply the sum of the Halafian and Samarran assemblages. But the domesticated plants and animals and the basic ways of food production must have come from the hilly-flanks country in the north and east.

Above the basal Eridu (or Ubaid I) levels comes a style of pottery called Haji Mohammed (or Ubaid II), first found by German excavators near Warka and quite recently by the British near Baghdad. Then—as at a number of other sites in the south—comes the full-fledged assemblage called Ubaid (or Ubaid III). Incidentally, there is an aspect of this developed Ubaidian assemblage in the north as well. It seems to move into place before the Halaf manifestation is finished, and the "transitional" motifs of the painted pottery styles look as if they were some kind of blend of the two. The Ubaidian assemblage in the south is by far the more spectacular. The development of the temple has been traced at Eridu from a simple little structure to a monumental building some sixty-two feet long, with a pilaster-decorated façade and an altar in its central chamber. There is painted Ubaidian pottery, but the style is hurried and somewhat careless and gives the *impression* of having been a cheap mass-production means of decoration when compared with the carefully drafted styles of Samarra and Halaf or with the basal Eridu or Haji Mohammed pottery. The Ubaidian people made other items of baked clay: sickles and axes of very hard-baked clay are found. The northern Ubaidian sites have yielded tools of copper, but metal tools of unquestionable Ubaidian find-spots are not yet available from the south. Clay figurines of human beings with monstrous turtle-like faces are another item in the southern Ubaidian assemblage.

There is a large Ubaid cemetery at Eridu, much of it still awaiting excavation. The few skeletons so far tentatively studied reveal a completely modern type of "Mediterraneanoid"; the individuals whom the skeletons represent would undoubtedly blend perfectly into the modern population of southern Iraq. What the full Ubaidian assemblage says to us is that these people had already adapted themselves and their culture to the peculiar riverine environment of classic southern Mesopotamia. For example, hard-baked clay axes will chop bundles of reeds very well, or help a mason dress his unbaked mud bricks, and there were only a few soft and pithy species of trees available. The Ubaidian levels of Eridu yield quantities of date pits; that excellent and characteristically Iraqi fruit was already in use. The excavators also found the clay model of a ship, with the stepping-point for a mast, so that Sindbad the Sailor must have had his antecedents as early as the time of Ubaid. The bones of fish, which must have flourished in the larger canals as well as in the rivers, are common in the Ubaidian levels and thereafter.

The Ubaidian Achievement

On present evidence, my tendency is to see the full Ubaidian assemblage in southern Iraq as the trace of a new era. I wish there were more evidence, but what we have suggests this to me. The culture indicated by the southern Ubaid assemblage soon became a culture of towns—of centrally located towns with some rural villages about them. The town had a temple and there must have been priests. These priests probably had political and economic functions as well as religious ones, if the somewhat later history of Mesopotamia may suggest a pattern for us. It has been thought that presently the temple and its priesthood became the focus of the market; the temple received its due, and may already have had its own lands and herds and flocks. The people of the town, undoubtedly at least in consultation with the temple administration, planned and maintained the simple irrigation ditches. As the system flourished, the community of rural farmers would have produced more than sufficient food.

The evidence used to make this so-called *Tempelwirtschaft* interpretation has been seriously questioned. Certainly by now, however, the tendency for specialized crafts to develop—tentative at best at the cultural level of the earlier village-farming community era—would have been achieved, and probably many other specialists in temple administration, water control, architecture, and trade would also have appeared as the surplus food supply was assured.

Southern Mesopotamia is not a land rich in natural resources other than its fertile soil. Stone, good wood for construction, metal, and innumerable other things would have had to be imported. Grain and dates—although both are bulky and difficult to transport—and wool and woven stuffs must have been some of the mediums of exchange. Over what area did the trading network of Ubaid extend?

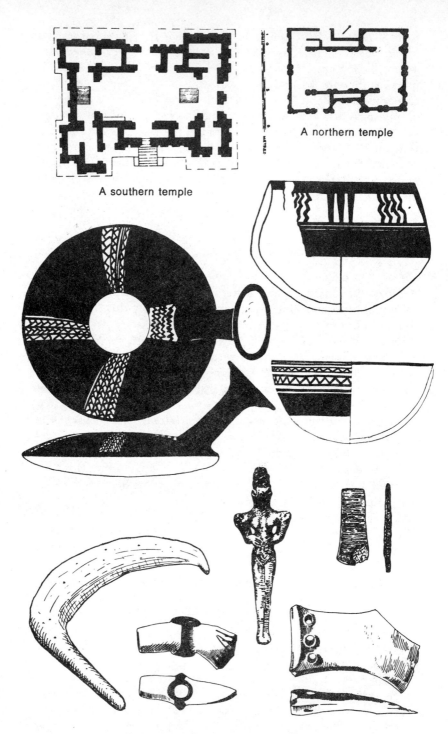

A northern temple

A southern temple

Sketch of Selected Items of Ubaidian Assemblage

We start with the idea that the Ubaidian assemblage is most richly developed in the south. We assume, I think correctly, that it represents a cultural flowering of the south. On the basis of the pottery of the still elusive Eridu people, perhaps some of whom had first followed the rivers into alluvial Mesopotamia, we get the notion that the characteristic painted pottery style of Ubaid was developed in the southland. If this reconstruction is correct, then we may watch with interest where the Ubaid pottery-painting tradition spread. We have already mentioned that there is a substantial (and from the southern point of view, *fairly* pure) assemblage of Ubaidian material in northern Iraq. The pottery appears all along the Iranian flanks, even well east of the Arabo-Persian Gulf (although again the matter of blending with more locally developed styles is at issue), and ends in a later and spectacular flourish in an extremely handsome painted style called the Susa style. Within the last several years, Ubaid potsherds have been encountered on the Saudi Arabian side of the gulf, and new research is being directed toward the meaning of this recent extension of the Ubaid distribution. We've already noted something of this wide distribution area on page 158. Ubaidian pottery has been found in the valleys of both of the great rivers, well north of the Iraqi and Syrian borders on the southern flanks of the Anatolian plateau. It reaches the Mediterranean Sea and the valley of the Orontes in Syria, and it may be faintly reflected in the painted style of a site called Ghassul, on the east bank of the Jordan in the Dead Sea Valley.

Over this vast area—certainly in all of the great basin of the Tigris-Euphrates drainage system and its natural extensions—I believe we may lay our fingers on the traces of the peculiar way of decorating pottery which we call Ubaidian. This cursive and even slapdash decoration, it appears to me, was part of a new cultural tradition which arose from the adjustments which immigrant northern farmers—probably fusing with riverine food-collectors—first made to the new and challenging environment of southern Mesopotamia. But exciting as the idea of the spread of influences of the Ubaid tradition in space may be, I believe you will agree that the consequences of the growth of that tradition in southern Mesopotamia itself, as time passed, are even more important.

The Warka Phase in the South

So far, there are only three radiocarbon determinations for the full Ubaidian assemblage, one from Tepe Gawra in the north and one each from Warka and Uqair in the south. My hunch would be to use the dates 4500 to 3750 B.C.(+), with a plus, or more probably a

Relief on a Proto-Literate Stone Vase, Warka

minus, factor of about 200 years for each, as the time duration of the Ubaid III assemblage in southern Mesopotamia.

Next, much to our annoyance, we have what is almost a temporary blackout. According to the system of terminology I use, our next assemblage after that of Ubaid is called the *Warka* phase, from the Arabic name for the site of Uruk or Erech. We know it only from six or seven levels in a narrow test pit at Warka, and from an even smaller hole at another site. This assemblage so far is known only by its pottery, some of which still bears Ubaidian-style painting. The characteristic Warkan pottery is unpainted, with smoothed red or gray surfaces and peculiar shapes. Unquestionably, there must be a great deal more to say about the Warkan assemblage, but someone will first have to excavate it!

The Dawn of Civilization

After our exasperation with the almost unknown Warka interlude, following the brilliant "false dawn" of Ubaid, we move next to an assemblage which yields traces of a preponderance of those elements which we noted (p. 149) as meaning civilization. This assemblage is that called *Proto-Literate:* it already contains writing. On the somewhat shaky principle that writing, however early, means history—and no longer prehistory—the assemblage is named for the historical implications of its content, and no longer after the name of the site where it was first found. Since some general writings on the subject use site names for this assemblage, I will tell you that the Proto-Literate includes the latter half of what used to be called the "Uruk period" *plus* all of what is otherwise called the "Jemdet Nasr period." It shows a consistent development from beginning to end.

I shall, in fact, leave much of the description and the historic implications of the Proto-Literate assemblage to the conventional historians. Professor Thorkild Jacobsen, reaching backward from the legends he finds in the cuneiform writings of slightly later times, can tell you a more complete story of Proto-Literate culture than I can. It should be enough here if I sum up briefly what the excavated archeological evidence shows.

We have yet to dig a Proto-Literate site in its entirety, but the indications are that the sites cover areas the size of small cities. In architecture, we know of large and monumental temple structures, which were built on elaborate high terraces. The plans and decoration of these temples follow the pattern set in the Ubaid phase; the chief difference is one of size. The German excavators at the site of Warka reckoned that the construction of only one of the Proto-Literate temple complexes must have taken 1500 workers, each working a ten-hour day, five years to build.

Art and Writing

If the architecture, even in its monumental forms, can be seen to stem from Ubaidian developments, this is not so with all our other evidence of Proto-Literate artistic expression. In relief and applied sculpture, in sculpture in the round, and on the engraved cylinder seals—all of which now make their appearance—several completely new artistic principles are apparent. These include the composition of subject matter in groups, commemorative scenes, and especially the ability and apparent desire to render the human form and face. Excellent as the animals of the Franco-Cantabrian art may have been (see p. 80), and however handsome were the carefully drafted geometric designs and conventionalized figures on the pottery of the early farmers, there seems to have been, up to this time, a mental block about the naturalistic drawing of the human figure and especially the human face. We do not yet know what caused this self-consciousness about picturing themselves which seems characteristic of people before the appearance of civilization. We do know that, with civilization, the mental block seems to have been removed.

Clay tablets bearing pictographic signs are the Proto-Literate forerunners of cuneiform writing. The earliest examples are not well understood, but Jacobsen believes they were "devices for making accounts and for remembering accounts." Different from the later case in Egypt, where writing appears fully formed in the earliest examples, the development from simple pictographic signs to proper cuneiform writing may be traced, step by step, in Mesopotamia. It is probable that the full development of writing was connected with the temple and the need for keeping account of the temple's possessions. Professor Jacobsen sees writing as a means for overcoming space, time, and the increasing complications of human affairs: "Literacy, which began with . . . civilization, enhanced mightily those very tendencies in its development which characterize it as a civilization and mark it off as such from other types of culture."

While the new principles in art and the idea of writing are not foreshadowed in the Ubaid phase, or in what little we know of the Warkan, I do not think we need to look outside southern Mesopotamia for their beginnings—or certainly not beyond the adjoining alluvial plain of lowland Khuzestan (the Karun River plain, which is environmentally simply more of Mesopotamia itself). I think we must accept these new principles as completely new discoveries, made by the people who were developing the whole new culture pattern of classic southern Mesopotamia.

The Proto-Literate Achievement

Full description of the art, architecture, and writing of the Proto-Literate phase would call for many details. Scholars such as Professors Jacobsen and Adams can give you these details much better than I can. Nor shall I do more than tell you that the common pottery of the Proto-Literate phase was so well standardized that it looks factory made. There was also some handsome painted pottery, and there were stone bowls with inlaid decoration. Well-made tools in metal had by now become fairly common, and the metallurgist was experimenting with the casting process. Signs for plows have been identified in the early pictographs, and a wheeled chariot is shown on a cylinder seal engraving. But if I were forced to a guess in the matter, I would say that the development of plows and draft animals probably began in the Ubaid period and was another of the great innovations of that time in the Mesopotamian southland. Consider, if you will, the importance of the invention of the wheel and the plow alone for later development.

The Proto-Literate assemblage clearly suggests a highly developed and sophisticated culture. While perhaps not yet fully urban, it was on the threshold of urbanization. There seems to have been a very dense settlement of Proto-Literate sites in classic southern Mesopotamia, many of them newly founded on virgin soil where no earlier settlements had been. When we think for a moment of what all this implies, of the growth of a canalization system which must have existed to allow the flourish of this culture, and of the social and political organization necessary to maintain the canals, I think we will agree that at last we are dealing with civilization proper.

From Prehistory to History

Now it is time for the conventional ancient historians to take over the story from me. You will see that they have a different approach. Their real baseline is with cultures ruled over by later kings and emperors, whose writings describe military campaigns and the administration of laws and fully organized trading ventures. To these historians, the Proto-Literate phase is a simple beginning for what is to follow. If they mention the Ubaid assemblage at all—the one I was so lyrical about—it will be as some dim and fumbling step on the path to the civilized way of life.

I suppose you could say that the difference in the approach is that as a prehistorian I have been looking forward or upward in time, while the conventional ancient historians look backward to glimpse what I've been describing here. My baseline has been several million years ago, with a being who had little more than the capacity to make tools and fire to distinguish him from the animals about him. Thus my point of view and that of the conventional historian are bound to be different. You will need both if you want to understand all of the story of humans, as they lived through time to the present.

9
Other experiments with food production

Although I think we made at least some fair guesses for the time, much has happened since a 1960 symposium, "Courses Toward Urban Life," where the possible beginnings of agriculture were considered, worldwide. It is even more clear now how the evidence is mounting for a number of quite independent beginnings of food production, well removed from the Near Eastern instance. We've already remarked that eastern (and/or?) southeastern Asia, sub-Saharan Africa, and the Mesoamerican and Andean regions of the New World present such cases. Since I myself have no firsthand knowledge of any of these regions or of their excavated materials, I attempt this chapter with some reluctance. I have made very forth-right invitations—as I write—that you consult higher authorities, and I have not attempted to go far beyond the primary level of effective food production in this very brief account. At least, however, this chapter gives me the opportunity again to emphasize that the achievement of effective food production in southwestern Asia was neither unique nor perhaps so much earlier, relatively, than these other instances.

Some Generalities

First, we might note briefly certain generalities. The notion that *vegeculture* instead of *agriculture* (that is, cultivation based on the planting of root, slip, or runner cuttings instead of seeds) may have been an early form of plant manipulation is still current. Were the archeologist's or paleobotanist's attention to be focused entirely on the presence or absence of cereals and pulses and artifacts keyed to their use, for example, foods produced by vegeculture might pass unnoticed. Perhaps this bears on a recent observation by Jack R. Harlan, a top paleobotanist, that "agriculture in the wet tropics and subtropics is difficult and, so far as we now know, rather late in development." In a provocative 1971 paper, Harlan also makes an interesting distinction between agricultural "centers" and "noncenters." In the noncenters, "the number of domesticates is impressive, and the area covered, immense" (in contrast to a center, which is much more compact), and I note that Harlan's noncenters include large portions of tropical and semitropical environments. Harlan lists:

Centers	Noncenters
A1, Southwestern Asia	A2, Sub-Saharan Africa
B1, North China	B2, Southeast Asia–South Pacific
C1, Mesoamerica	C2, South America incl. Amazonia

Interaction between the centers and noncenters is part of Harlan's proposition.

A final generalization could be that there were almost certainly (many?) attempts at manipulating plants and animals in still other regions of the world. Much must have depended, in any given region, on the presence of plants and animals which would make really effective advantageous domesticates (as against what was handily available for the continuance of intensified hunting–food collecting). Here again we return to Desmond Clark's "process of pre-adaption" notion (see p. 139). A case in point would be the very probable and probably early cultivation of such plants as goosefoot or lamb's quarter (*Chenopodium* sp.), pigweed (*Amaranthus* sp.), and sunflower (*Helianthus* sp.) in the otherwise preagricultural eastern woodlands of North America. It is upon such a "pre-adapted" subsistence pattern of intensified hunting–collecting, plus relatively ineffective cultivation, that colleagues such as Melvin Fowler see the subsequent and relatively rapid rise of the cultivation of the diffused Mesoamerican exotics, squash, beans, and maize.

Note also, of course, that this all verges closely on my old notion of incipience, and that I've grown increasingly reluctant to guess at how far back in time incipience itself may go. It would not surprise me greatly were it a very old tendency. We must remember, however, to keep some kind of distinction between levels of incipience and levels of primary and effective food production.

To my way of thinking, these foregoing points suggest something of the kinds of things we need to keep in mind as we consider the various instances of the rise of effective food production. Along with the southwestern Asiatic instance which we've already treated, I select only the other centers and noncenters Harlan lists. For more details than I may give here, there are readings suggested in the bibliography and I urge attention to Flannery's useful 1973 summary.

Southeastern Asia

Speaking as a paleobotanist (with very considerable knowledge of the known archeological and ethnographic situation, but still primarily as a botanist), Jack Harlan includes parts of India, Burma, Indochina, southern China, Indonesia, the Philippines, Borneo, and New Guinea (with perhaps even the Solomons and New Caledonia) in his southeast Asia–Pacific noncenter. On botanical grounds, the banana, breadfruit, some citrus plants, sugarcane, and taro are noncereals identified with the region. Rice would be the major cereal for consideration, but Harlan realizes how meager the archeological evidence for prehistoric rice still is.

According to Kwang-chih Chang, there were hints of three probably loosely related developments in the eastern-southeastern Asiatic region in early post-Pleistocene times. Chang not unreasonably suggests that a general level of incipience was involved here, although lack of evidence prevents demonstrating it. Chang bases this suggestion on the presence—in the assemblages which hint at these developments—of coarse pottery vessels with surfaces decorated by cord impressions, and of certain types of ground stone artifacts. The instances are: (1) the later aspects of the Hoabinhian assemblage, in southeastern Asia, (2) the earliest phases of the Jomon sequence in Japan, and (3) the materials from certain sites in north China. We will have a brief look at each of these developments, but note, to begin with, that none of these three early instances, as given above, has yet produced evidence of food production.

The Hoabinhian, an assemblage known best from Thailand, seems to have begun in late Pleistocene times and to have continued on until 3500 B.C.(+), in the opinion of Chester Gorman, who has worked a key Hoabinhian site. The sites themselves are found either along the coastlines (with meat subsistence sources based on marine animals, shellfish, and fish, as well as rhino, wild pig, and large wild cattle) or in rock shelters in the forested uplands (with wild pig heavily hunted, and with deer, wild cattle, and antelope bones as well). The only available botanical material comes from Gorman's upland rock shelter called Spirit Cave, where various nuts, peas, or beans, the water chestnut, and a cucumber-like plant were recovered. None of these plants have been established as domesticates, nor have the bones of the animals. A hearth in the cave yielded ground stone knives, quadrangular adzes, and some cord-marked pottery, along with a radiocarbon determination of about 6600 ± 200 b.c.(+). There were also earlier (pre-ceramic) Hoabin-hian layers in the cave.

Several thousand years later, a new adaptation, now to the low-land plains, appears to have taken place. At a site called Non Nok Tha, evidence for cultivated rice and pig herding appears some-what before 3000 b.c.(+), but the Hoabinhian patterns of hunting still seem to have obtained. The same type of subsistence appears to characterize the Ban Kao site of about 2000 b.c.(+), and its as-semblage is said to show strong affinities to the Chinese Lungsha-noid materials (which we'll consider presently). From this point on-ward, I sense that events in the whole area soon became as complicated and interrelated (on foundations of many locally ad-justed idiosyncratic developments) as they did in Europe.

China

In the first place, we might note in passing that there seems to be general agreement that "South China" is poorly known arche-ologically. There is also agreement that when it does become known, it will probably show a developmental sequence which links it with southeastern Asia.

What is called north China is really at about the same latitude as is southwestern Asia (Peking is actually a bit south of Istanbul). The climate is much more that of a continental interior, however, and the barely adequate rainfall comes more in summer than in winter (which is dry and severe), in contrast to the Near East. The nuclear area for the beginnings of food production lies in the light soil loesslands of the Wei River and the stretch of the Yellow (Huangho) River just east of the confluence of the two, in Shensi and Honan provinces.

The sites which yield the earliest cord-marked pottery are taken to be the beginning aspect of the so-called Yang-shao village-farm-ing community development. The site which gives its name to this earliest—and, so far as is now known, still preagricultural—aspect is Li-chia-ts'un. It lies just south of the Chinling mountains. Little de-tail is yet available in the West on this assemblage.

The second, or Pan-p'o, aspect of the general Yang-shao phase appears much better known and it seems also to be fully food pro-ducing. The traces of both round and rectilinear, earth-covered, wood-framed houses in evidently only semipermanent villages are known. Both cord-marked and painted pottery, plus the kilns for

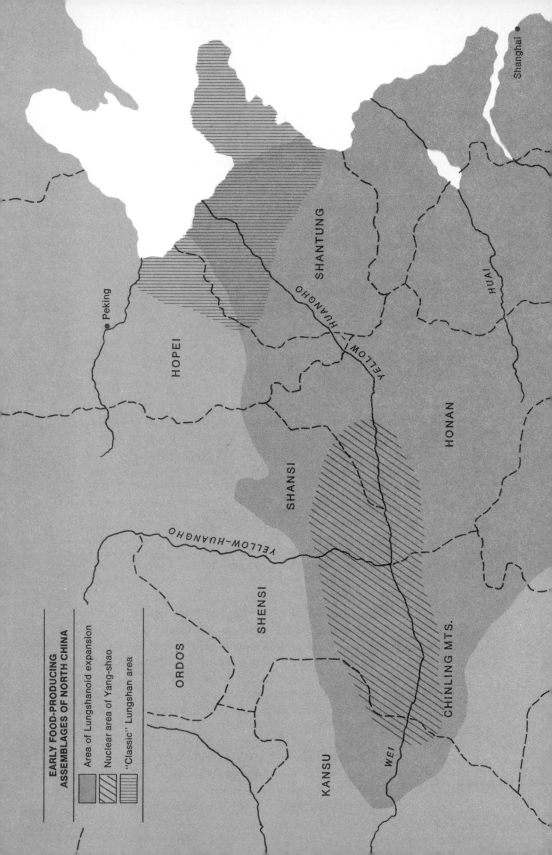

EARLY FOOD-PRODUCING
ASSEMBLAGES OF NORTH CHINA

Area of Lungshanoid expansion

Nuclear area of Yang-shao

"Classic" Lungshan area

Shanghai

Peking

HOPEI

SHANTUNG

HUANGHO

YELLOW

HUAI

HONAN

SHANSI

YELLOW-HUANGHO

SHENSI

ORDOS

CHINLING MTS.

WEI

KANSU

firing pottery, various stone and bone artifacts—including both agricultural tools and projectile points and fishhooks—and fragments
of basketry, have been recovered. A formalized pattern of multiple
burials seems to have obtained. Ping-ti Ho even speaks of arche-
typal Chinese script and numerals. Both dog and domesticated pig
bones are common in the yield, and cattle were probably also domesticated. Foxtail millet was already being extensively grown
(panic millet came later) and silkworms were being kept. A group
of four radiocarbon determinations which average close to 3700 ±
100 B.C.(+) is now available.

A third (or, alternatively, transitional?) aspect of the Yang-shao
phase appears to have been centered somewhat farther toward the
east, in western Honan province. The type name site is now said to
be Maio-ti-kou, although the original name site—Yang-shao-
ts'un—was found in this region, in 1921, by J. C. Andersson, a
Swedish mining engineer and amateur archeologist. In fact, the
Maio-ti-kou appears to be only one of a now increasing number of
regionally adapted assemblages which at the same time have, according to Chang, "a surprising degree of cultural similarity." Since
the details now become too complicated to summarize briefly, I
recommend that you read Chang directly on the matter. His tendency is to group most of these regional assemblages under the
general term *Lungshanoid.* The term comes from a site name, Lung-
shan, also used originally (by older scholars) as the type name for
an assemblage which seemed to represent a second major early-vil-
lage phase of China. The Yang-shao was the other phase and the
two were taken to be equally early and geographically separated.

Rice Cultivation Begins

Before considering Chang's suggested amendment of this old
scheme, we must first note the appearance of rice cultivation. Already in 1921, Andersson's original Yang-shao potsherds yielded
several impressions of rice, but the question of reliability of context
has left the matter troublesome ever since. Following 1949, however, rich finds of rice have been made in sites of the so-called
Lungshanoid group, both near and south of Shanghai, and dating
to the time range 3250 to 2650 B.C.(+). We could note, in passing,
that the degree to which precise time can be reckoned here is not
sufficient to give priority for rice cultivation to either Non Nok Tha
in Thailand or to the Shanghai Lungshanoid group. The general
Lungshanoid inventory, as now available, is more impressive, however. Cattle and sheep were now common domesticates (as well as
dogs and pigs). Settlements appear to have become permanent;

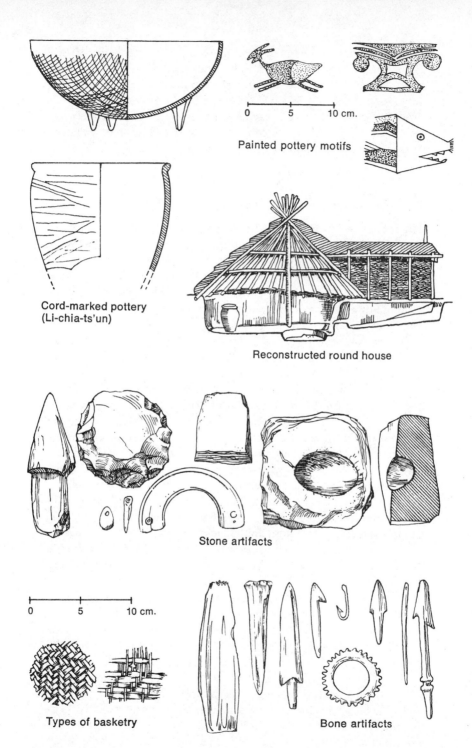

Painted pottery motifs

Cord-marked pottery
(Li-chia-ts'un)

Reconstructed round house

Stone artifacts

0   5   10 cm.

Types of basketry

Bone artifacts

Sketch of Selected Items of Yang-shao (Mainly Pan p'o) Assemblage

pottery was now wheel made and there are other signs of craft specialization. Chang speaks of this Lungshanoid phase as "formative." My hunch would be that the comparable development in southwestern Asia would be that of the Ubaid development. To the limited extent that there is earlier Chinese material available to appraise, I miss seeing levels comparable to the Hassunan-Samarran or to the Jarmoan of southwestern Asia.

The Amended Chinese Sequence

The sequence Kwang-chih Chang suggests, and which Ping-ti Ho also follows, sees the formative Lungshanoid development as based on the general Yang-shao level of culture, but representing a time of expansion out of the original nuclear area of Shensi and western Honan. The various local Lungshanoid developments each had some distinguishing artifactual characteristics, but Chang seems more impressed by that "surprising degree of cultural similarity."

Finally came the so-called Lung-shan level itself, with an inventory significantly different from that of Yang-shao and characterized by black, burnished, wheel-made pottery. It had originally been counted as "oldest" in the more eastern and coastal Shantung and Hopei regions of the lower Yellow River (since in those regions there was nothing stratigraphically below it, the Yang-shao materials not being manifest that far east of their nuclear area). The circumstance that the Lung-shan was stratigraphically oldest in the east, just as Yang-shao was stratigraphically oldest in the northwest, led to a "two culture" notion. Now, with more complete stratigraphic sequences on sites in the middle ground and with radiocarbon determinations, the situation has become more clear. Chang proposes seeing the Lung-shan black, burnished pottery assemblage as a local elaboration upon one of the earlier Lungshanoid developments. And out of this level, with its now distinctive local characteristics, eventually grew the assemblage identified with the Shang dynasty and the beginnings of Chinese history proper.

For a firsthand, well-illustrated account of the brilliance of the Shang assemblage, I pass you on to Kwang-chih Chang's book. Should you fall upon an earlier source dealing with ancient Chinese history, note that the yield from the traditional Shang capital at An-Yang is not the earliest phase of the dynastic assemblage. The An-Yang materials suggest an almost overwhelming contrast with the latest prehistoric assemblages, but more recently excavated earlier aspects of the Shang tend to make this contrast less exaggerated. Chang assesses the beginnings of the Shang at about 1850 B.C., on historical grounds.

Japan

The third instance of very early occurrence of cord-marked pottery in further Asia is that of the Jomon assemblage of Japan. The radiocarbon indications for the whole range of the Jomon development run from about 7500 to 1000 B.C.(+). Save for the dog, however, the case for domestication cannot be made until the Middle Jomon (actually the third) phase, for which the determinations cluster after 3000 B.C.(+). Millet, buckwheat, and beans are mentioned, along with other obviously collected plant food, and there still appears to be some uncertainty as to whether the first three were actually cultivated. By and large, the whole succession of Jomon assemblages reflects a hunting, fishing, and collecting economy, with most sites being near the coastline. In the latter half of the first millennium B.C., a protohistoric phase called the Yayoi began and evidence of rice cultivation appears, but Buddhism and the approach to a literate urban society came about only after approximately 500 A.D.

There is, evidently, no reason to doubt Kwang-chih Chang's observation (see p. 169) that the Jomon development was probably loosely related to both the late Hoabinhian and the earliest Yangshao developments.

India-Pakistan

The situation in India, as I understand it, continues to disturb me. As things now stand, various "late mesolithic and microlithic" assemblages are known over much of the subcontinent and are said to persist until after 3000 B.C.(+) or even later. Then, like a brilliant flash, coming within a very short time, we have the so-called mature aspect of the Harappan or Indus Valley civilization—a literate and monumentally urban one—established by about 2300 B.C.(+). An "early" aspect of the Harappan is said not yet to have been recovered, although we do have what may be partially antecedent inventories on various sites mainly west of the Indus and in eastern Baluchistan.

In his recent paper, Hasmukh Sankalia, the dean of Indian prehistory, is still able to observe that

with regard to the Harappan Culture, its origins are not yet known, but two things are clear; the pottery contains many forms that never recur in later Indian pottery, and which are derived, however distantly, from Western Asia . . . [and] secondly, the Harappan Civilization, wherever it spread in India and Pakistan, introduced most or all of the elements of its culture. Thus there was wholesale colonization in Kutch and Saurashtra, Sind, the Punjab, and into Rajasthan.

Nor do I doubt Sankalia in the least. New information on an Ubaidian-like spread along the littorals of the Arabo-Persian Gulf, as well as in Iran-Baluchistan, makes the matter quite conceivable. What worries me is how the Harappan could have crystallized so suddenly. I still tend to wonder about the possibilities for an as yet unidentified "process of pre-adaption" in the more tropical regions of India. Such might then have preconditioned the continent generally for the rapid acceptance of the southwestern Asian domesticates when Sankalia's "spread" did take place. I note, in passing, the report of V. N. Misra on broad exposures of the large "late mesolithic and microlithic" site of Bagor, in northwestern India. There are radiocarbon determinations for the range from about 5000 to 2800 B.C.(+); no plant materials are reported, but the animal bones are said to include domesticated sheep (and/or) goat and perhaps some cattle.

My hunch is that we still have much to learn about the appearance of food production in the Indian subcontinent.

Sub-Saharan Africa

At a recent symposium, Professors Harlan, de Wet, and Stemler came to some very interesting conclusions regarding the available botanical evidence for agricultural beginnings in sub-Saharan Africa. The noncenter theme (see p. 168) was stressed, along with the idea of agricultural *evolution* rather than agricultural *revolution*. The authors firmly declared that "domestication is a process, not an event." In fact, they observe that

Africa may turn out to be the most useful laboratory of all for developing a fuller understanding of plant domestication and agricultural origins. The African scene is so rich in transitional and intermediate situations. . . . A serious and systematic multidisciplinary study of Africa may give us a much more mature view of what might have gone on in the Near East, the Far East, Oceania, and the Americas. The steps in the evolutionary process appear to be more evident in Africa than elsewhere.

At the same time, the authors warn that such studies are just beginning and are still fragmentary and unsystematic.

The same concern for the incompleteness of the present evidence persists in the writings of Desmond Clark and Thurstan Shaw, both highly competent authorities, on African prehistory. Sub-Saharan Africa in particular has long attracted research on the human paleontology and prehistory of earlier Pleistocene times, but far less work has yet been done on the late Pleistocene-Holocene past. Clark also notes the limited exposures available on excavations already made, the poor conditions for the preservation of materials in sites in the forests, and the difficulty of discerning the exact nature of the subsistence economies from the artifactual finds. Let me add a warning derived from my own readings: an author's use of that troublesome word "neolithic" is in *no* sense a guarantee that there was evidence of food production.

Given the scarcity of evidence, it is probably best to begin with the fact that domesticated sheep and/or goats were certainly present in the Haua Fteah cave in Mediterranean Cyrenaica by 5000 B.C.(+), and domesticated cattle somewhat before that. There is, incidentally, evidence that wild cattle once lived in northern Africa. The Haua Fteah evidence is not only considerably earlier than the available evidence for domestication in the Nile Valley, but it also adds weight to claims for cattle herding—based on rock engravings—in various parts of the Sahara in the sixth millennium B.C.(+). The associated artifacts may include pottery, ground stone and bone tools (including fishhooks and harpoons!) and both microlithic and normal-sized flint tools with many and varied projectile points. The general picture is assumed to be that of a broad band of intensified hunting, collecting, and cattle herding along the north Mediterranean littoral, a pattern which reached well southward over a Sahara which was then grassland. All this could be taken (and indeed has been taken) to mean diffusion from southwestern Asia, but I remind you that Herbert Wright's proposition for a westward refuge of the late Pleistocene flora of southwestern Asia might imply a reverse direction. Indeed, in our 1960 "Courses Toward Urban Life" symposium, northwest Africa remained one of our "areas of perplexity."

It does seem generally agreed that this adaptation—however early and exactly how it happened, spread, and responded to latitudinal climatic and environmental shifts through time—would have stopped short of the heavy tropical rainfall and tsetse zones to the south. Furthermore, the plant domesticates listed by Harlan and his colleagues underline the idea that cattle were the only *introduced* element. The plants which were eventually domesticated were indigenous to the sub-Saharan zones. Harlan et al. list the yam, the oil palm, and the cowpea for the forest-savanna strip, sorghum, voandzeia, and vonio for the savanna itself, and pearl millet for the drier Sahel (the desert margin). The authors believe such crops as tef and possibly finger millet were Ethiopian in origin, and African rice was probably domesticated in the Niger bend.

Unfortunately, we do not yet have archeological evidence to describe the times when the processes of domestication of these plants was taking place. Thurstan Shaw's recent review underlines the unhappy state of the present record. I offer, as a sample, a brief picture of what appears to have been (until very recently?) the rather typical archeological circumstances relating to later sub-Saharan finds. In 1944, in the removal of vast stretches of alluvial soil in the strip-mining of tin in Nigeria, fragments of baked clay sculpture were recovered. There was little if any surface indication of sites. Without the casual interest of the supervisory staff and the fact that twenty to thirty million cubic yards were stripped annually, this so-called Nok sculpture would not have been found. Miners eventually found and reported an essentially undisturbed site, Taruga. Under proper excavation, it yielded more fragments of sculpture, pottery and pottery graters, stone pounders and querns, and also iron fragments, iron slag, and the remains of iron furnaces. Radiocarbon determinations cluster at about 350 B.C.(+).

Exasperatingly incomplete as this Nok assemblage remains, it hardly suggests an early or formative level. Things had been happening for some time, one is bound to feel, and this "iron age" may yet prove to have beginnings as early as the European one. I myself, in face of the incompleteness of the record, would not dream of suggesting whether the Nok development was due to diffusion or was independently achieved. There is, obviously, much more for us to learn about early Africa.

The New World

We noted earlier (see p. 85) that certainly by about 12,000(+) years ago humans had become inhabitants of most of the habitable world. Even the most conservative estimates allow that by that time late Pleistocene hunter-collectors had crossed a then Bering isthmus into the New World. There are, of course, claims for much earlier peoplings of the Americas. Some, including those from the Andes, sound very impressive. Perhaps the earliest current claim is for middle Pleistocene artifacts at the Calico site in Southern California, but—as Vance Haynes shrewdly puts it—the evidence is not compelling. We might also note a proposal of Paul S. Martin that "the disappearance of the native American mammoths, mastodons, ground sloths, horses, and camels coincided very closely with the first appearance of Stone Age hunters around 11,200 years ago." Such "overkill," Martin believes, was possible because these native animals had no "defensive behavior," and this could explain the rapid pace of the spread of the hunting peoples from Alaska to Tierra del Fuego.

Whatever the case may have been—and there is no dearth of theories in these matters—the earliest New World assemblages appear to belong to a *Big-Game Hunting* tradition. Large lancelate flint projectile points (for example, the Clovis point) presently became part of this tradition, and have also been found embedded in bones in "elephant kill sites." Two other groups of assemblages developed, however, the "Old Cordilleran" tradition and the "Desert" tradition. The former consists of groups of assemblages found in western and northwestern North America, with inventories which include bifacially flaked, leaf-shaped projectile points and heavy chopping tools, as well as basketry, matting, and netting—an evident adaptation to hunting, fishing, and collecting activities in the wooded northwestern environments. The "Desert" tradition assemblages appeared in the North American Great Basin and southwest and were of particularly long duration. These inventories are said to be marked by basketry and milling stones in particular, and show every evidence of a subsistence pattern based on cyclic rounds of intensified collecting plus the hunting of desert animals. In South America there appear to have been variations of the Big-Game Hunting theme.

For Europe, following about 8000 B.C.(+), we noted (see p. 141) various traces of cultural readaptation to the succession of post-glacial forested environments made by the Forest folk. A similar phenomenon appears to have taken place, at about the same time, in eastern North America, eventually spreading as far west as the plains. This is known as the *Archaic* tradition; its various assemblages indicate an intensified level of collecting, fishing, and hunting of animals no larger than deer. The experiments with local plant cultivation we noted on page 168 may already have begun at this level, which lasted until about 1000 B.C.(+). It was followed, in the same region, by the *Woodland* tradition assemblages and the appearance (not always simultaneously) of the Mesoamerican plant domesticates and of pottery and impressive burial mounds. Around 1000 A.D., the almost urban establishments which characterize the *Mississippian* tradition began to appear. What is probably the most spectacular sequence of sites and artifacts of North America, however, began in the U.S. southwest around the beginning of our era, and was an extension of the "Desert" tradition. I realize that this is far too brief an account. I can only very strongly urge that you at least scan the text and savor the illustrations in Gordon Willey's two fine volumes on American archeology.

Mesoamerica

In the earlier portions of its prehistoric sequence, the available evidence in Mesoamerica appears to come from the higher and drier valleys, rather than the tropical lowlands. Following the traces of the Big-Game Hunting tradition, the assemblages more or less conform to those of the "Desert" tradition. Already established by 7000 or 8000 B.C.(+), the Indians of this "Desert" tradition appear to have been intensive collectors of wild foods and hunters of small animals. In Flannery's words, ". . . by 5000 B.C., one of their ultimate strategies became the artificial increase of certain edible plants by selection and planting." By 2000 B.C.(+), the *Preclassic* or *Formative* period began, with effective agriculture as well as a meat supplement maintained by hunting. The *Mesoamerican* tradition was now under way.

The plant domesticates which were developed during the food-collecting–incipient-cultivation phase (7000 to 2000 B.C. +) were several varieties of beans, squash, pumpkins, pigweed, chiles, tomatoes, avocados, various New World tropical fruits, and, most importantly, maize. The story began to unfold with Richard Mac-Neish's excavations in dry caves or rock shelters, first in the Tamaulipas mountains in northeastern Mexico and later in the Tehuacán valley in the Mexican heartland. The research has been still further expanded by other colleagues, but so far remains primarily concentrated in the upland valley habitats.

The evolution of these early crops may be watched through three phases of development during the 5000-year range before the Preclassic period began. The details of the botanical story and of the dispute over the origin of maize are covered in Flannery's 1973 essay. MacNeish reminds us that it took at least 2000 years at the beginning of the development before cultivated plants made up even 20 percent of the human diet. I remind you, also, that animal domesticates were not a marked element here, although the dog and turkey were known as domesticates in Mexico. It has long been assumed that the protein-rich beans-squash-maize diet, plus hunting, compensated in this matter.

Comparatively, I have the feeling that the Preclassic inventory has much of the general flavor of the Jarmoan-Hassunan inventories in southwestern Asia. Although the highlands are now the best-known region of all Mesoamerica, local variations always occur, and this was doubtless so over the whole spectrum of environmental diversity from the northeastern highlands to the southern lowlands and tropics. What has become available from early Preclassic sites tends to show well-settled villages in the upland valleys. House remains are of wattle-and-daub, and there is evidence of a growing population. Pottery was by this time (2000 B.C. +) well established; some of it had impressed decoration and some had simple painted decoration. At Zacatenco, in the Valley of Mexico itself, for example, there were numbers of clay figurines of human females. Obsidian was commonly knapped into knife blades and projectile points, and a variety of ground stone tools, including querns, were made. Deer and smaller animals and water fowl were hunted and a new maize hybrid appeared.

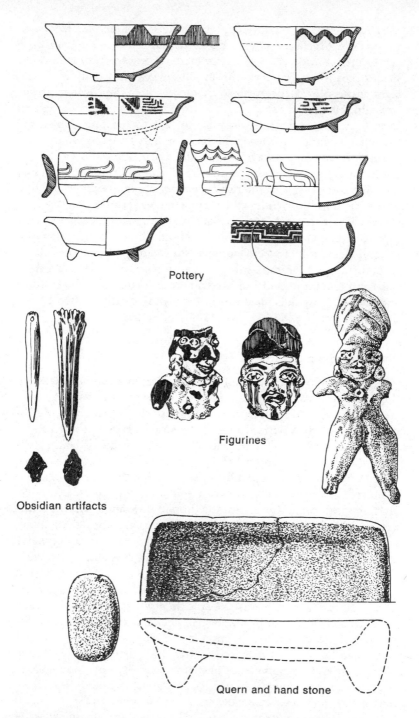

Pottery

Figurines

Obsidian artifacts

Quern and hand stone

Sketch of Selected Items of Mesoamerican Early Preclassic Assemblage

The next step in the development of the Mesoamerican tradition, the middle Preclassic phase, began about 1000 B.C.(+). With it came the first indications of the ceremonial center, and—as Gordon Willey sees it—the transition from village to a "larger order of villages-and-center" henceforth so characteristic of the Mesoamerican tradition. Here, comparatively, the level of the inventory suggests to me something generally similar to that of the later-Ubaid-to-Protoliterate range in Mesopotamia, although in Mesopotamia the distinction between village and center does not seem to obtain. Furthermore, we cannot claim for the Ubaidian-Protoliterate range anything comparable to the rise of the monumental Olmec art style of the Veracruz lowlands, which appeared within the middle Preclassic. The earliest Mesoamerican hieroglyphs appear on stelae (upright stone slabs) during this phase, and in this sense, also, the cultural level of the two developments is roughly comparable.

Again I urge that you sample more of Gordon Willey's descriptions and illustrations of the Mesoamerican materials, which led to another of the world's instances of independent, urban, literate civilization.

Andean America

We have already seen (p. 168) that Jack Harlan and his colleagues think of South America as a noncenter in terms of agricultural origins. Certainly the great urban climax of pre-Columbian development in South America came in the Andean region, but Harlan's position reminds us that the situation may not be so completely neat. Furthermore, intensive archeological attention to pre-agricultural and early agricultural sites in South America is even more recent than for Mesoamerica and, as in sub-Saharan Africa, archeological preservation in the humid lowlands on the Amazonian side is wretched. Most work, so far, has been done along the very arid Pacific coastal strip, where sites cluster along water courses which head in the Andes, thus implying some elemental form of irrigation. Here preservation is normally excellent. At the moment, it seems that—various earlier and still current suggestions to the contrary—there was considerable independence between Mesoamerica and South America in the matter of plant domestications. Indeed, plant cultivation in the Andean highlands might have been as early as in Mesoamerica, and there may well have been independent domestications of essentially the same plants (e.g., the common wild bean, *Phaseolus vulgaris*) in both areas. However, maize does seem to have come from Mesoamerica.

The plants which Flannery lists for Peru, without qualification as to context or cultivated state, are several species of beans, maize, squash, cotton, chile, potato, and three plants of the Amazonian slopes, guava, manioc, and peanut. To this we must add a few animal domesticates: the dog, llamas and alpacas, muscovy ducks, and guinea pigs—only the latter two (and occasionally the llama) being normal sources of tame meat. Fish and shellfish were also of great importance from the beginning on the coastal strip (by Inca times, fish were delivered upmountain by runners!).

The oldest now available South American plant domesticates are beans, which appeared in Thomas Lynch's excavations in Guitarrero cave, in the northern Peruvian highlands, at about 6000 B.C.(+). The cave sequence begins even earlier, and projectile points, bone and antler tools, plant fiber cordage, and probable basket fragments appeared. Another long cave sequence is available from Richard MacNeish's work at the Rosamachay and other caves in the Ayacucho province in the southcentral highlands. Here maize is evidenced at least as early as 2500 B.C.(+); it is not yet known from coastal sites earlier than about 2000 B.C.(+). By the time of the *Jaywa* phase (about 6500 B.C. +), MacNeish believes he sees "hints of the domestication of the llama and guinea pig as well as plants." In the following *Piki* phase (about 5500 to 4300 B.C. +), the evidence increases and so do resemblances to the early coastal inventories.

The above materials are newly excavated and are still being analyzed. How much they eventually will further change the more conventional picture, based primarily on the sequence from the coastal sites, remains to be seen. Visualize again a long, thin, and *very dry* coastal strip cut by the mouths of occasional rivers from the mountains, and a seashore teeming with fish, shellfish, and marine animals. This "conventional sequence" was first taken to begin at the base of the deep deposit in a north coastal and riverside mound, Huaca Prieta, shortly before 2000 B.C.(+). Indeed, however, a long preface has now been appended to this sequence. Beginning about 5000 B.C.(+), and with at least 2000 years of "villages" without agriculture, there were either self-sufficient hunting, collecting, and heavily fishing establishments at the mouths of some rivers, or there were pairs of alternate winter-summer encampments in localities without both advantages perennially. By about 2500 B.C.(+), increased population and the introduction of cultivation from the highlands are evidenced; settlements grew in size, but the largest were those with both coastline and arable land together. By the time of Huaca Prieta, or about 2000 B.C.(+), cultivated foods had become much more important, hamlets appeared along the middle and upper river courses, and fishing settlements were still flourishing, but the largest settlements were still those situated on arable lands with river mouths.

At about 2000 B.C.(+), the "Initial" period began on some portions of the Peruvian coast, and with it came the appearance of pottery vessels, the full spectrum of the Peruvian plant domesticates, the heddle loom, hints of ceremonial centers, and the beginnings of monumental architecture. Gordon Willey's descriptions and illustrations again make me think, comparatively, of approximately the Samarran of Mesopotamia, or even of the developed Ubaidian.

As in Mesoamerica with the Olmec manifestation, the next step in Peru includes another great art and architectural style, the *Chavin*. Such materials need to be seen in many clear illustrations—if not in the original—and again I heartily recommend Willey to you. It has been suggested that the Chavin style represents the rapid spread of some kind of cultic activity soon after 1000 B.C. The general period called the "Early Horizon" also saw the appearance of metallurgy in both copper and gold and the flowering of textiles. I shall not take you further myself, suggesting rather that you use Willey's bibliography for more competent accounts that I can give. Note, however, that the "Early Horizon" ends at about 250 B.C.(+), while the Inca historians themselves do not count the beginning of their kingdom to have come until 1438 A.D., with their defeat of the Chancas! This means that there is much of Andean culture-history I have not accounted for.

10
The end of prehistory

You'll doubtless easily recall your general course in ancient history: how the Sumerian dynasties of Mesopotamia were supplanted by those of Babylonia, how the Hittite kingdom appeared in Anatolian Turkey, and about the three great phases of Egyptian history. The literate kingdom of Crete arose, and by 1500 B.C. there were splendid fortified Mycenaean towns on the mainland of Greece. This was the time—about the whole eastern end of the Mediterranean—of what Professor Breasted called the "first great internationalism," with flourishing trade, international treaties, and royal marriages between Egyptians, Babylonians, and Hittites. By 1200 B.C., the whole thing had fragmented; "the peoples of the sea were restless in their isles," and the great ancient centers in Egypt, Mesopotamia, and Anatolia were eclipsed. Numerous smaller states arose—Assyria, Phoenicia, Israel—and the Trojan War was fought. Finally Assyria became the paramount power of all the Near East, presently to be replaced by Persia.

A new culture, partaking of older west Asiatic and Egyptian elements, but casting them with its own tradition into a new mold, arose in mainland Greece and along the Ionian coast of Anatolia.

I once shocked my Classical colleagues to the core by referring to Greece as "a second-degree derived civilization," but there is much truth in this. The principles of bronzeworking and then of ironworking, of the alphabet, and of many other elements in Greek culture were borrowed from western Asia. Our debt to the Greeks is too well known for me even to mention it, beyond recalling to you that it is to Greece we owe the beginnings of rational or empirical science and thought in general. But Greece fell in its turn to Rome, and in 55 B.C. Caesar invaded Britain.

I last spoke of Britain on page 146. I had chosen it as my single example for telling you something of how the earliest farming communities were established in Europe. Now I will continue with Britain's later prehistory, so you may sense something of the end of prehistory itself. Remember that Britain is simply a single example we select; the same thing could be done for all the other countries of Europe, and will be possible also, some day, for further Asia and Africa. Remember, too, that prehistory in most of Europe runs on for 3000 or more years *after* conventional ancient history begins in the Near East. Britain is a good example to use in showing how prehistory ended in Europe. As we said earlier, it lies at the opposite end of Europe from the area of highest cultural achievement in those times, and should you care to read more of the story in detail, you may do so in English. In fact, in Professor Stuart Piggott's book *Ancient Europe* you may learn what happened in late prehistoric and proto-historic times (to the expansion of Rome) over the whole continent.

Metal-Users Reach England

We left the story of Britain with the peoples who made several different but in part related assemblages—the Windmill Hill people, the megalith-builders, and Professor Piggott's generalized "Secondary Neolithic cultures"—making adjustments to their environments, to the original inhabitants of the island, and to each other. They had first arrived at least by 3500 B.C.(+), and were simple pastoralists and hoe cultivators who lived in village communities. Some of them planted little if any grain. By 2000 B.C.(+), they were well settled in. Then, somewhere in the range from about 1900 to 1800 B.C.(+), the traces of the invasion of a new series of peoples begin to appear.

The first newcomers are called the *Beaker folk,* after the name of a peculiar form of pottery they made. Some authorities believe the beaker type of pottery occurred first in Portugal, where it is found with great collective tombs of megalithic construction and with copper tools somewhat before 2500 B.C.(+); others believe it derived from eastern Europe. As Piggott points out, there was precocious copperworking in both areas. But the Beaker folk who reached England seem already to have moved up through Spain and Brittany to the Rhineland and Holland. While in the Rhineland, and before leaving for England, the Beaker folk seem to have mixed with the local population and also with incomers from

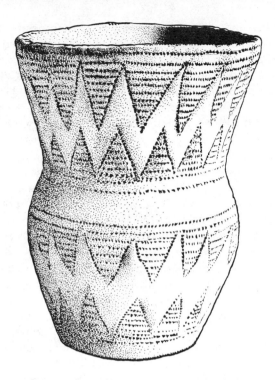

Beaker

northeastern Europe whose culture included elements brought originally from the Near East by the eastern way through the steppes. This last group has also been named for one or another of the peculiar articles in its assemblage; the group is called the *Battle-axe,* or *Corded-ware, folk.* A few Battle-axe elements, including, in fact, stone battle-axes and corded beakers, reached England with the earliest Beaker folk,* coming from the Rhineland.

The Beaker folk settled earliest in the agriculturally fertile south and east. There seem to have been several phases of Beaker folk invasions, and it is not clear whether these all came strictly from the Rhineland or Holland. We do know that their copper daggers and awls and armlets are more of Irish or Atlantic European than of Rhineland origin. A few simple habitation sites and many burials

---

*The British authors use the term "Beaker folk" to mean both archeological assemblage and human physical type. They speak of a "tall, heavy-boned, rugged, and round-headed" strain which they take to have developed, apparently in the Rhineland, by a mixture of the original (Portuguese?) beakermakers and the northeast European battle-axe makers. However, since the science of physical anthropology is very much in flux at the moment, and since I am not able to assess the evidence for these physical types, I *do not* use the term "folk" in this book with its usual meaning of standardized physical type. When I use "folk" here, I mean simply *the makers of a given archeological assemblage.* The difficulty only comes when assemblages are named for some item in them; it is too clumsy to make an adjective of the item and refer to a "beakerian" assemblage.

of the Beaker folk are known. They buried their dead singly, some-times in conspicuous individual barrows with the dead warrior in his full trappings. The spectacular element in the assemblage of the Beaker folk is a group of large circular monuments with ditches and with uprights of wood or stone. These *henges* became truly monumental several hundred years later; while they were occasion-ally dedicated with a burial, they were not primarily tombs. The ef-fect of the invasion of the Beaker folk seems to have cut across the whole fabric of life in Britain. There is at least a suggestion, how-ever, that the very earliest of the henges may have been started during Piggott's "Secondary Neolithic culture" phase.

There was, furthermore, a second major element in British life at this time. It shows itself in the less well understood traces of a group again called after one of the items in their catalogue, the *Food-vessel folk*. There are many burials in "food-vessel" pots in northern England, Scotland, and Ireland, and the pottery itself seems to link back to that of the Peterborough type. Like some of the earlier so-called Secondary Neolithic people in the highland zone before them, the makers of the food-vessels seem to have been heavily involved in trade. It is quite proper to wonder whether the food-vessel pottery itself was made by local women who were married to traders who were middlemen in the transmis-sion of Irish metal objects to north Germany and Scandinavia. The belt of high, relatively woodless country, from southwest to north-east, was already established as a natural route for inland trade.

Although instances of plow use are rare, Piggott remarks that traces of cross-plowed fields are known from Cornwall in the ear-lier half of the second millennium B.C. Plowing was evidently done with the *ard*, or simple pointed plow. Heavy earth-throwing plows did not reach England until Roman times.

More Invasions?

Sometime during the earlier half of the second millennium B.C. (I am being imprecise on purpose), spectacular burials of aristocratic "heroes" or "chieftains" were made in the Wessex region of south-ern England. As the editors of *Current Archaeology* put it, this "Wes-sex culture" has been conceived of as "a sort of European Common Market in which the amber of Scandinavia and the gold of Ireland were traded for the faience beads of Egypt, with the princes of Wessex acting as the middlemen, taking the profits and building Stonehenge with the proceeds." Together with the Egyptian bead types, the burials were believed to be fixed to about 1500 B.C. by Mycenaean bronze dagger types, and by carvings of these latter on the stones of Stonehenge.

In 1968, however, realizing that radiocarbon determinations needed recalibration to fit the bristlecone pine dendrochronology, Colin Renfrew announced that the Wessex burials must have been earlier than the Mycenaean age by several hundred years. This led to blasts of publicity, in the Sunday supplement press, for independent origins of European "civilization." The only trouble was that there were no direct Wessex radiocarbon determinations—only those for "associated cultures." Now direct Wessex age determinations are available and they run about 1200–1250 B.C.(+), which recalibrates to about 1400–1500 B.C., and this coincides nicely with the historically fixed dates of the Egyptian beads and for Mycenae.

This is where the Wessex matter stands at the moment, but there is still a high head of steam of archeological argument. To the degree that I can pick my way through the finer points of this argument, I still understand that the final form of the spectacular sanctuary at Stonehenge is considered to be part of the Wessex achievement. A wooden henge or circular monument was first made several hundred years earlier, but the site now received its great circles of stone uprights and lintels. The diameter of the surrounding ditch at Stonehenge is about 350 feet, the diameter of the inner circle of large stones is about 100 feet, and the tallest stone of the innermost horseshoe-shaped enclosure is 29 feet 8 inches high. One circle is made of blue stones which must have been transported from Pembrokeshire, 145 miles away as the crow flies. Carvings representing the profile of a standard type of bronze axe of the time, and several profiles of bronze daggers—one of which (as we noted above) has been called Mycenaean-Greek in type—have been found carved in the stones. Even more recently, an American astronomer, Professor G. S. Hawkins, has presented a case that the stones of Stonehenge are set in such a way that they *could* have been used for astronomical calculation and prediction. We cannot, of course, describe the details of such religious or astronomical (or both) activities as may well have been staged in Stonehenge, but we can certainly imagine the well-integrated and smoothly working culture which must have been necessary before such a great monument could have been built. Professor Piggott remarks,

The monument bespeaks unified and indeed personal authority, not only in concept and realization as an architectural entity, but in the prestige and power that could draw on the actual labour force and technical skills required, if only for relatively short or seasonal occasions, over many years: the continuity of building and rebuilding on the site over probably five centuries argues for a similar continuity of tradition and authority.

The range from 1900 to about 1400 B.C.(+) includes the time of development of the archeological features usually called the "Early Bronze Age" in Britain. The main regions of the island were populated, and the adjustments to the highland and lowland zones were distinct and well marked. The different aspects of the assemblages of the Beaker folk and the clearly expressed activities of the Food-vessel folk and the Wessex warriors show that Britain was already taking on her characteristic trading role, separated from the European continent but conveniently adjacent to it. The tin of Cornwall—so important in the production of good bronze—as well as the copper of the west and of Ireland, taken with the gold of Ireland and the general excellence of Irish metalwork, assured Britain a trader's place in the then known world. Contacts with the eastern Mediterranean may have been by sea, with Cornish tin as the attraction, or may have been made by the Food-vessel middlemen on their trips to the Baltic coast. There they would have encountered traders who traveled the great north-south European road, by which Baltic amber moved southward to Greece and the Levant, and ideas and things moved northward again.

There was, however, the Channel between England and Europe, and this relative isolation gave some peace and also gave time for a leveling and further fusion of culture. The separate cultural traditions began to have more in common. The growing of barley, the herding of sheep and cattle, and the production of woollen garments were already features common to all Britain's inhabitants save a few in the remote highlands, the far north, and the distant islands not yet fully touched by food production. The "personality of Britain" was being formed.

Cremation Burials Begin

Along with people of certain religious faiths, archeologists are against cremation (for other people!). Individuals to be cremated seem in past times to have been dressed in their trappings and put upon a large pyre; it takes a lot of wood and a very hot fire for a thorough cremation. When the burning had been completed, the few fragile scraps of bone and such odd beads of stone or other rare items as had resisted the great heat seem to have been whisked into a pot and the pot buried. The archeologist is left with the pot and the unsatisfactory scraps in it.

Tentatively, after about 1400 B.C.(+) and almost completely over the whole island by 1200 B.C.(+), Britain became the scene of cremation burials in urns. We know very little of the people themselves. None of their settlements have been identified, although there is evidence that they grew barley and made enclosures for cattle. The urns used for the burials seem to have antecedents in the pottery of the Food-vessel folk, and there are some other links with earlier British traditions. In Lancashire, a wooden circle seems to have been built about a grave with cremated burials in urns. Even occasional instances of cremation may be noticed earlier in Britain, and it is not clear what, if any, connection the British cremation burials in urns have with the classic *Urnfields* which were now beginning in the east Mediterranean and which we shall mention below. Certainly there are hints of European contact through metallurgy. Axes with proper socketholes and long swords designed for slashing—good European types—now appeared for the first time.

The British cremation–burial-urn folk survived a long time in the highland zone. In the general British scheme, they make up what is called the "Middle Bronze Age," but in the highland zone they last until after 900 B.C.(+) and are considered to be a specialized highland "Late Bronze Age." In the highland zone, these later cremation-burial folk seem to have continued the older Food-vessel tradition of being middlemen in the metal market.

Granting that our knowledge of this phase of British prehistory is very restricted because the cremations have left so little for the archeologist, it does not appear that the cremation–burial-urn folk can be sharply set off from their immediate predecessors. But change on a grander scale was on the way.

Reverberations from Central Europe

In the centuries immediately following 1000 B.C., we see with fair clarity two phases of a cultural process which must have been going on for some time. Certainly several of the invasions we have already described in this chapter were due to earlier phases of the same cultural process, but we could not see the details.

Around 1200 B.C., central Europe was upset by the spread of the so-called Urnfield folk, who practiced cremation burial in urns and whom we know to have been possessors of the long, slashing swords and the horse. I told you above that we have no idea that the Urnfield folk proper were in any way connected with the people who made cremation–burial-urn cemeteries a century or so earlier in Britain. It has been supposed that the Urnfield folk themselves may have shared ideas with the people who sacked Troy. We know that the Urnfield pressure from central Europe displaced other people in northern France, and perhaps in northwestern Germany, and that this reverberated into Britain about 1000 B.C.

Soon after 750 B.C., the same thing happened again. This time, the pressure from central Europe came from the Hallstatt folk, who were iron tool-makers; the reverberation brought people from the western Alpine region across the Channel into Britain.

At first it is possible to see the separate results of these folk movements, but the developing cultures soon fused with each other and with earlier British elements. Presently there were also strains of other northern and western European pottery and traces of Urnfield practices themselves which appeared in the finished British product. I hope you will sense that I am vastly over-simplifying the details.

The result seems to have been—among other things—a new kind of agricultural system. The land was marked off by ditched divisions. Rectangular fields imply the plow rather than hoe cultivation. We seem to get a picture of estate or tribal boundaries which included village communities; we find a variety of tools in bronze, and even whetstones which show that iron had been honed on them (although the scarce iron has not been found). Let me give you the picture in Professor Piggott's words: "The . . . Late Bronze Age of southern England was but the forerunner of the earliest Iron Age in the same region, not only in the techniques of agriculture, but almost certainly in terms of ethnic kinship. . . . We can with some assurance talk of the Celts. . . . The great early Celtic expansion of the Continent is recognized to be that of the Urnfield people."

Thus, certainly by 500 B.C. there were people in Britain some of whose descendants we may recognize today in name or language in remote parts of Wales, Scotland, and the Hebrides.

The Coming of Iron

Iron—once the know-how of reducing it from its ore in a very hot, closed fire has been achieved—produces a far cheaper and much more efficient set of tools than does bronze. Iron tools seem to have been made in quantity first in Hittite Anatolia about 1500 B.C. In continental Europe, the earliest, so-called Hallstatt, iron-using cultures appeared in Germany soon after 750 B.C. Somewhat later, Greek and especially Etruscan exports of *objets d'art*—which moved with a flourishing trans-Alpine wine trade—influenced the Hallstatt iron-working tradition. Still later, new classical motifs, together with older Hallstatt, oriental, and northern nomad motifs, gave rise to a new style in metal decoration which characterizes the so-called La Tène phase.

A few iron-users reached Britain a little before 400 B.C. Not long after that, a number of allied groups appeared in southern and southeastern England. They came over the Channel from France and must have been Celts with dialects related to those already in England. A second wave of Celts arrived from the Marne district in France about 250 B.C. Finally, in the second quarter of the first century B.C., there were several groups of newcomers, some of whom were Belgae of a mixed Teutonic-Celtic confederacy of tribes in northern France and Belgium. The Belgae preceded the Romans by only a few years.

Hill-forts and Farms

The earliest iron-users seem to have entrenched themselves temporarily within hill-top forts, mainly in the south. Gradually they moved inland, establishing *individual* farm sites with extensive systems of rectangular fields. We recognize these fields by the *lynchets,* or lines of soil-creep which plowing left on the slopes of hills. New crops appeared; there were now bread wheat, oats, and rye, as well as barley.

At Little Woodbury, near the town of Salisbury, a farmstead has been rather completely excavated. The rustic buildings were within a palisade, the round house itself was built of wood, and there were various outbuildings and pits for the storage of grain. Weaving was done on the farm, but not blacksmithing, which must have been a specialized trade. Save for the lack of firearms, the place might almost be taken for a farmstead on the American frontier in the early 1800s.

Toward 250 B.C. there seems to have been a hasty attempt to repair the hill-forts and to build new ones, evidently in response to signs of restlessness being shown by remote relatives in France.

The Second Phase

Perhaps the hill-forts were not entirely effective or perhaps a compromise was reached. In any case, the newcomers from the Marne district did establish themselves, first in the southeast and then to the north and west. They brought iron with decoration of the La Tène type, and also the two-wheeled chariot. Like the Wessex warriors of over a thousand years earlier, they made "heroes' " graves, with their warriors buried in the war-chariots and dressed in full trappings.

The metalwork of these Marnian newcomers is excellent. The peculiar Celtic art style, based originally on the classic tendril motif, is colorful and virile, and fits with Greek and Roman descriptions of Celtic love of color in dress. There is a strong trace of these newcomers northward in Yorkshire, linked by Ptolemy's descrip-

Slashing Sword

Celtic Buckle

tion to the Parisii, doubtless part of the Celtic tribe which originally gave its name to Paris on the Seine. Near Glastonbury, in Somerset, two villages in swamps have been excavated. They seem to date toward the middle of the first century B.C., which was a troubled time in Britain. The circular houses were built on timber platforms surrounded with palisades. The preservation of antiquities by the waterlogged peat of the swamp has yielded us a long catalogue of the materials of these villagers.

In Scotland, which yields its first iron tools at a date of about 100 B.C., and in northern Ireland even slightly earlier, the effects of the two phases of newcomers tend especially to blend. Hill-forts, *brochs* (stone-built round towers), and a variety of other strange structures seem to appear as the new ideas develop in the comparative isolation of northern Britain.

The Third Phase

For the time of about the middle of the first century B.C., we again see traces of frantic hill-fort construction. This simple military architecture now took some new forms. Its multiple ramparts must reflect the use of slings as missiles, rather than spears. We probably know the reason. In 56 B.C., Julius Caesar chastised the Veneti of Britanny for outraging the dignity of Roman ambassadors. The Veneti were famous slingers, and doubtless the reverberations of escaping Veneti were felt across the Channel. The military architecture suggests that some Veneti did escape to Britain.

Also, through Caesar, we learn the names of newcomers who arrived in two waves, about 75 B.C. and about 50 B.C. These were the Belgae. Now, at last, we can even begin to speak of dynasties and individuals. Some time before 55 B.C., the Catuvellauni, originally from the Marne district in France, had possessed themselves of a large part of southeastern England. They evidently sailed up the Thames and built a town of over a hundred acres in area. Here ruled Cassivellaunus, "the first man in England whose name we know," and whose town Caesar sacked. The town sprang up elsewhere again, however.

The End of Prehistory

Prehistory, strictly speaking, was now over in southern Britain. Claudius' effective invasion took place in 43 A.D.; by 83 A.D., a raid had been made as far north as Aberdeen in Scotland. But by 127 A.D., Hadrian had completed his wall from the Solway to the Tyne, and the Romans settled behind it. In Scotland, Romanization can have affected the countryside very little. Professor Piggott adds that "it is when the pressure of Romanization is relaxed by the break-up of the Dark Ages that we see again the Celtic metal-smiths handling their material with the same consummate skill as they had before the Roman Conquest, and with traditional styles that had not even then forgotten their Marnian and Belgic heritage."

In fact, many centuries go by, in Britain as well as in the rest of Europe, before the archeologist's task is complete and the historian on his own is able to describe the ways of men and women in the past.

Britain As a Sample of the General Course
of Prehistory in Europe

In giving this very brief outline of the later prehistory of Britain, you will have noticed how often I had to refer to the European continent itself. Britain, beyond the English Channel for all of her later prehistory, had a much simpler course of events than did most of the rest of Europe in later prehistoric times. This holds, in spite of all the "invasions" and "reverberations" from the continent. Most of Europe was the scene of an even more complicated ebb and flow of cultural change, save in some of its more remote mountain valleys and peninsulas.

The whole course of later prehistory in Europe is, in fact, so very complicated that there has been, until recently, no single good book to cover it all. Now, fortunately, we have Professor Piggott's book, and in English. Writing it must have been a difficult and complicated task, as the book shows. I suspect that the difficulty of making a good book that covers all of its later prehistory is another aspect of what makes Europe so very complicated a continent today. The prehistoric foundations for Europe's very complicated set of civilizations, cultures, and subcultures—which begin to appear as history proceeds—were in themselves very complicated.

Hence, I selected the case of Britain as a single example of how prehistory ended in Europe. It would have been more complicated had I chosen a continental region. Even in the subject matter on Britain in Chapter 8, we saw only little direct trace of the effect on Britain of the very important developments which took place in the Danubian way from the Near East. Britain received the impulses which brought copper, bronze, and iron tools from an original east Mediterranean homeland into Europe, almost at the ends of their journeys. But by the same token, they had time en route to take on their characteristic European aspects.

Some time ago, Sir Cyril Fox wrote a famous book called *The Personality of Britain*, subtitled "Its Influence on Inhabitant and Invader in Prehistoric and Early Historic Times." We have not gone into the post-Roman, early historic period here; there are still the Anglo-Saxons and Normans to account for, as well as the effects of the Romans. But what I have tried to do was to begin the story of how the personality of Britain was formed. The principles that Fox used in trying to balance cultural and environmental factors and interrelationships (long before "ecology" became such a fashionable word among archeologists!) would not be greatly different for other lands.

Summary

In the pages you have read so far, you have been brought through the earliest 99 percent of the story of human life on this planet. I have left only 1 percent for the historians to tell.

The Drama of the Past

In ancestors first became human-like when evolution had carried them to the point where the eye-hand-brain coordination was good enough so that tools could be made. When tools began to be made according to sets of standardized or lasting habits, we know that real humans were on the way. This happened at least two million years ago. The stage for the play—at the very beginning—seems to have been a broad middle belt of African and doubtless Asian savanna grassland. At least, it seems unlikely that only one little region saw the beginning of the drama.

Glaciers and different climates came and went, to change the settings. But the play went on in the same first act for a very long time. The people who were the players had simple roles at first. They had to feed themselves and protect themselves as best they could. They did this by hunting, catching, and finding food wherever they could, and by taking such protection as caves, fire, and their simple tools would give them. Before the first act was over, however, the last of the glaciers was melting away, and the players had become culturally adept at adjusting their ways of life to almost all of the habitable niches of the world's environmental spectrum. Oceania and the New World had been added to the stage. If we want a special name for the first act, we could call it *The Food-Gatherers*.

There were not many climaxes in the first act, so far as we can see. But I think there may have been a few. Certainly the pace of the first act accelerated with the swing from simple gathering to more intensified collecting. The great cave art of France and Spain was probably an expression of a climax. Even the ideas of burying the dead and of the "Venus" figurines must also point to levels of human thought and activity that were over and above pure food getting.

The Second Act

The second act began only about 10,000 years ago. A few of the players started it by themselves near the center of the Old World part of the stage, in the Near East. It began as a plant and animal act, but it soon became much more complicated.

But the players in this one part of the stage—in the Near East— were not the only ones to start off on the second act by themselves. Other players, possibly in several places in the Far East, in sub-Saharan Africa, and certainly in the New World, also started second acts that began as plant (but not always animal) acts, and then became complicated. We can call the whole second act *The Food-Producers.*

The First Great Climax of the Second Act

In the Near East, the first marked climax of the second act happened in Mesopotamia and Egypt. The play and the players reached that great climax that we call civilization. This seems to have come less than 5000 years after the second act began. But it could never have happened in the first act at all.

There is another curious thing about the first act. Many of the players didn't know it was over and they kept on with their roles long after the second act had begun. On the edges of the stage there are today some players who are still going on with the first act. The Eskimos, and the native Australians, and certain tribes in the Amazon jungle are some of these players. They seem perfectly happy to keep on with the first act.

The second act moved from climax to climax. The civilizations of Mesopotamia and Egypt were only the earliest of these climaxes. The players to the west caught the spirit of the thing, and climaxes followed there. So, too, did climaxes come in the Far Eastern and New World portions of the stage, and we await more news from Africa in the matter.

The greater part of the second act should really be described to you by a historian. Although it was a very short act when compared to the first one, the climaxes complicate it a great deal. I, a prehistorian, have told you only about the first act and the very beginning of the second.

The Third Act

Also, as a prehistorian I probably should not even mention the third act—it began so recently. The third act is *The Industrialization*. It is the one in which we ourselves are players. If the pace of the second act was so much faster than that of the first, the pace of the third act is terrific. The danger is that it may wear down the players completely. This is part of the theme of Alvin Toffler's interesting book *Future Shock*, written—incidentally—before the full impact of our present energy problem. And, to anyone born as I was in the first decade of this century, Toffler's quotation from the economist Kenneth Boulding is very telling. Boulding says, "The world of today . . . is as different from the world in which I was born as that world was from Julius Caesar's. I was born in the middle of human history. . . . Almost as much has happened since I was born as happened before." Incidentally, Boulding is three years younger than I am.

What sort of climaxes will the third act have, and are we not already deeply in one? You have seen by now that the acts of my play are given in terms of modes or basic patterns of human economy—ways in which people get food and protection and safety. The climaxes involve more than human economy. Economics and technological factors may be part of the climaxes, but they are not all. The climaxes may be revolutions in their own way, intellectual and social revolutions if you like.

If the third act follows the pattern of the second act, a climax should come soon after the act begins. We may be due for one soon if we are not already in it. Remember the terrific pace of this third act.

Why Bother with Prehistory?

Why do we bother about prehistory? A main reason is surely our curiosity about ourselves. But a second main reason is that we think it may point to useful ideas for the present. We are in the troublesome beginnings of the third act of the play. The beginnings of the second act may have lessons for us and give depth to our thinking. I know there are at least *some* lessons, even in the present incomplete state of our knowledge. The players who began the second act—that of food production—separately, in different parts of the world, were not all of one "pure race," nor did they have "pure" cultural traditions. Some apparently quite mixed Mediterraneans got off to the first start on the second act and brought it to its first two climaxes as well. Peoples of quite different physical type achieved the first climaxes in China and in the New World and had one at least well along the way in Africa.

In our British example of how the late prehistory of Europe worked, we listed an almost continuous series of "invasions" and "reverberations." After each of these came fusion. Even though the Channel protected Britain from some of the extreme complications of the mixture and fusion of continental Europe, you can see how silly it would be to refer to a "pure" British race or a "pure" British culture. We speak of the United States as a "melting pot." But this is nothing new. Actually, Britain and all the rest of the world have been "melting pots" at one time or another.

By the time the written records of Mesopotamia and Egypt begin to turn up in number, the climaxes there are well under way. To understand the beginnings of the climaxes, and the real beginnings of the second act itself, we are thrown back on prehistoric archeology. And this is as true for China, India, Africa, Middle America, and the Andes as it is for the Near East.

There are lessons to be learned from all of the human past, not simply lessons of how to fight battles or win peace conferences, but of how human society evolves from one stage to another. Many of these lessons can be looked for only in the prehistoric past. In no other way can the processes of long-range change be understood. So far, we have made only a beginning. There is much still to do, and many gaps in the story are yet to be filled. The prehistorian's job is to find the evidence, to fill the gaps, and to discover the lessons people have learned in the past. As I see it, this is not only an exciting but a very practical goal for which to strive.

For Further Reading

This is obviously an abbreviated bibliography. Most of the general works cited have useful bibliographies, as do many of the papers. I have tried to select titles for breadth of coverage, for differences in points of view, and (especially with some of the shorter papers) for provocative items of interest.

Books of General Interest

Childe, V. Gordon. *What Happened in History*. Baltimore: Penguin, 1954.
——. *Man Makes Himself*. New York: Mentor, 1955.
——. *The Dawn of European Civilization*. New York: Vintage, 1957.
Clark, Grahame. *Archaeology and Society*. Cambridge: Harvard, 1957.
——. *Aspects of Prehistory*. Berkeley: University of California, 1970.
Franksfort, Henri, H. A. Franksfort, Thorkild Jacobsen, and John A. Wilson. *Before Philosophy*. Baltimore: Penguin, 1954.
Howell, F. Clark. *Early Man*. New York: Time-Life, 1965.
Pfeiffer, John. *The Emergence of Man*. New York: Harper & Row, 1969.
Redfield, Robert. *The Primitive World and Its Transformations*. Ithaca: Cornell, 1953.
Washburn, Sherwood L., and Ruth Moore. *Ape into Man: A Study of Human Evolution*. Boston: Little, Brown, 1974.

The History of Prehistory

Two accounts of the development of ideas in prehistoric archeology and a collection of essays by excavators, looking back over their previous work.

Daniel, Glyn E. *The Idea of Prehistory*. New York: Watts, 1962.
Willey, Gordon C. *Archaeological Researches in Retrospect*. Cambridge: Winthrop, 1974.
———, and Jeremy Sabloff. *A History of American Archaeology*. San Francisco: Freeman, 1974.

A selection of current views on where prehistoric archeology has been and is going. I have tried to include some of the extremes of the spectrum, "new" vs. "old" archeology. My personal views run closer to those of Finley and Trigger than to those of Binford.

Binford, Lewis R. *An Archaeological Perspective*. New York: Seminar, 1972.
Finley, M. I. "Archaeology and History." *Daedalus*, 100(1), 1971, 168.
Redman, Charles L., ed. *Research and Theory in Current Archeology*. New York: Wiley, 1973. (See particularly Adams' "Discussion" and Flannery's "Archeology with a Capital 'S.' ")
Sabloff, Jeremy, Thomas W. Beale, and Anthony M. Kurland, Jr. "Recent Developments in Archaeology." *Annals of the American Academy of Political and Social Science*, 408, 1973, 103.
Trigger, Bruce. "Archeology and Ecology." *World Archeology*, 2, 1971, 321.
Watson, Patty Jo, Steven A. LeBlanc, and Charles L. Redman. *Explanation in Archeology: An Explicitly Scientific Approach*. New York: Columbia, 1971.

Geochronology and the Ice Age

Three general books and a paper setting forth Wright's position.

Butzer, Karl W. *Environment and Archaeology*. Chicago: Aldine, 1971.
Flint, Richard F. *Glacial and Quaternary Geology*. New York: Wiley, 1971.
Kurtén, Björn. *Pleistocene Mammals of Europe*. Chicago: Aldine, 1968.
Wright, Herbert E., Jr. "Natural Environment of Early Food Production North of Mesopotamia." *Science*, 161, 1968, 334.

Fossil Humans and Race

The points of view of physical anthropologists and human paleontologists are changing quickly. Different views are represented here.

Campbell, Bernard. *Human Evolution*. Chicago: Aldine, 1974.
Lasker, Gabriel W. *Physical Anthropology*. New York: Holt, Rinehart & Winston, 1973.
Pilbeam, David. *The Ascent of Man: An Introduction to Human Evolution*. New York: Macmillan, 1972.
Poirier, Frank E. *Fossil Man: An Evolutionary Journey*. St. Louis: Mosby, 1973.

General Prehistory

An account of stone tool knapping, two very general outlines of the prehistoric sequences through time and worldwide, and a collection of articles on a broad range of Old World prehistory.

Bordaz, Jacques. *Tools of the Old and New Stone Age.* New York: Natural History, 1970.

Clark, Grahame. *World Prehistory: A New Outline.* Cambridge: Cambridge, 1969.

Coles, J. M., and E. S. Higgs. *The Archaeology of Early Man.* London: Faber & Faber, 1969.

Lamberg-Karlovsky, C. C., ed. *Old World Archaeology: Foundations of Civilization.* San Francisco: Freeman, 1972.

Mainly on Europe, either dealing with all of prehistoric time or concentrating on the Pleistocene time range.

Bordes, François. *The Old Stone Age.* New York: McGraw-Hill, 1968.

——. *A Tale of Two Caves.* New York: Harper & Row, 1972.

Clark, Grahame, and Stuart Piggott. *Prehistoric Societies.* New York: Random House, 1965.

Clark, J. G. D. *Prehistoric Europe: The Economic Basis.* London: Methuen, 1952.

Klein, Richard G. *Man and Culture in the Late Pleistocene.* San Francisco: Chandler, 1969.

Leroi-Gourhan, A. *The Art of Prehistoric Man in Western Europe.* London: Thames & Hudson, 1968.

Marschack, Alexander. *The Roots of Civilization.* New York: McGraw-Hill, 1972.

Ucko, Peter J., and A. Rosenfeld. *Palaeolithic Cave Art.* New York: McGraw-Hill, 1967.

General treatments of African, Asian, and Australian prehistory, through time.

Chang, Kwang-chih. *The Archaeology of Ancient China.* New Haven: Yale, 1968.

Clark, J. Desmond. *The Prehistory of Africa.* New York: Praeger, 1970.

Fairservis, Walter A., Jr. *The Roots of Ancient India.* New York: Macmillan, 1971.

Gould, Richard A. *Australian Archaeology in Ecological and Ethnographic Perspective.* Andover, Maine: Warner Modular Publications, 1973.

General treatments of New World prehistory.

Archaeology, 24(4), October 1971. Entire issue.

MacNeish, Richard S., ed. *Early Man in America.* San Francisco: Freeman, 1973.

Meggers, Betty J. *Prehistoric America.* Chicago: Aldine, 1972.

Patterson, Thomas C. *America's Past: A New World Archaeology.* Glenview, Ill.: Scott, Foresman, 1973.

Willey, Gordon R. *An Introduction to American Archaeology.* 2 vols. Englewood Cliffs: Prentice-Hall, 1966, 1971.

Speculations on how life must have been lived in prehistory, with reference to ethnographic accounts of simpler societies.

Clark, Grahame. *The Stone Age Hunters.* London: Thames & Hudson, 1967.

Lee, Richard B., and Irwen De Vore. *Man the Hunter.* Chicago: Aldine, 1968.

Sahlins, Marshall. *Stone Age Economics.* Chicago: Aldine, 1972.

Watson, Richard A., and Patty Jo Watson. *Man and Nature: An Anthropological Essay in Human Ecology.* New York: Harcourt Brace Jovanovich, 1969.

Post-Pleistocene Prehistory

A variety of interesting readings on Old and New World situations.

Braidwood, Robert J., and Gordon R. Willey, eds. *Courses Toward Urban Life.* Chicago: Aldine, 1962.

Flannery, Kent V. "The Origins of Agriculture." In Bernard J. Siegel, ed., *Annual Review of Anthropology,* 2, 1973, 271.

Harlan, Jack R. "Agricultural Origins: Centers and Noncenters." *Science,* 174, 1971, 468.

Harlan, Jack R., ed. *Origins of African Plant Domestication.* The Hague: Mouton, in press.

Reed, Charles A., ed. *The Origins of Agriculture.* The Hague: Mouton, in press.

Stuever, Stuart, ed. *Prehistoric Agriculture.* New York: Natural History, 1971.

Tringham, Ruth, ed. *Ecology and Agricultural Settlements: An Ethnographic and Archaeological Perspective.* Andover, Maine: Warner Modular Publications, 1973.

Ucko, Peter J., and G. W. Dimbleby. *The Domestication and Exploitation of Plants and Animals.* Chicago: Aldine, 1969.

Résumés of late pre- and protohistory in the Near East.

Clark, J. Desmond. "A Reexamination of the Evidence for Agricultural Origins in the Nile Valley." *Proceedings of the Prehistoric Society,* 37(2), 1971, 34.

Oates, Joan. "The Background and Development of Early Farming Communities in Mesopotamia and the Zagros." *Proceedings of the Prehistoric Society,* 39, 1973, 147.

The later pre- and protohistory of Europe, including useful general treatments and a selection of interesting papers.

Burgess, Colin. "The Bronze Age." *Current Archaeology,* 19, 1970, 208.

Case, Humphrey. "Neolithic Explanations." *Antiquity,* 43, 1969, 176.

Coles, John, and Joan Taylor. "The Wessex Culture: A Minimal View." *Antiquity*, 45, 1971, 6.

Piggott, Stuart. *Ancient Europe*. Chicago: Aldine, 1965.

Renfrew, Colin. "Wessex as a Social Question." *Antiquity*, 47, 1973, 221.

——. *Before Civilization: The Radiocarbon Revolution and Prehistoric Europe*. London: Jonathan Cape, 1973.

Selkirk, Andrew. "Wessex with Mycenae: The Wessex Culture." *Current Archaeology*, 32, 1972, 225 & 241.

Tringham, Ruth. *Hunters, Fishers, and Farmers of Eastern Europe, 6000–3000 B.C.* New York: Hutchinson, 1971.

Wainwright, G. J. "The Excavation of a Neolithic Settlement on Broome Heath, Ditchingham, Norfolk." *Proceedings of the Prehistoric Society*, 38, 1972, 1.

Papers on Africa and Asia.

Fogg, Bernard. "Recent Work in West Africa: New Light on the Nok Culture." *World Archaeology*, 1, 1969, 41.

Gorman, Chester. "The Hoabinhian and After." *World Archaeology*, 2, 1971, 300.

Kidder, J. Edward, Jr. "Agriculture and Ritual in the Middle Jomon Period." *Asian Perspectives*, 11, 1968, 19.

Misra, V. N. "Bagor—A Late Mesolithic Settlement in Northwest India." *World Archaeology*, 5, 1973, 92.

Sankalia, H. D. "Prehistoric Colonization in India." *World Archaeology*, 5, 1973, 86.

Shaw, Thurstan. "Early Agriculture in Africa." *Journal of the Historical Society of Nigeria*, 6, 1972, 143.

A sampling of recent, interesting New World papers.

Asch, Nancy C., Richard I. Ford, and David L. Asch. "Paleoethnobotany of the Koster Site." *Illinois State Museum Reports of Investigations*, 24, 1972.

Haynes, Vance. "The Calico Site: Artifacts or Geofacts?" *Science*, 181, 1973, 305.

Martin, Paul S. "The Discovery of America." *Science*, 179, 1973, 969.

The Dawn of Civilization

A distinguished comparative study and a volume of papers given at a London symposium.

Adams, Robert McC. *The Evolution of Urban Society*. Chicago: Aldine, 1966.

Ucko, Peter J., Ruth Tringham, and G. W. Dimbleby. *Man, Settlement and Urbanism*. London: Duckworth, 1973.

Digging, Methodology, and Procedures

In addition to the following readings, the journal *Archaeometry* covers the science/archeology field.

Braidwood, Linda. *Digging Beyond the Tigris.* New York: Schuman, 1953.

Braidwood, Robert J. *Archeologists and What They Do.* New York: Watts, 1960.

Burleigh, Richard, V. R. Switsur, and Colin Renfrew. "The Radiocarbon Calendar Recalibrated Too Soon?" *Antiquity,* 47, 1973, 309.

Hole, Frank, and Robert F. Heizer. *An Introduction to Prehistoric Archaeology.* New York: Holt, Rinehart & Winston, 1973.

Michaels, Joseph W. *Dating Methods in Archaeology.* New York: Seminar, 1973.

Rouse, Irving. *Introduction to Prehistory: A Systematic Approach.* New York: McGraw-Hill, 1972.

Semenov, S. A. *Prehistoric Technology.* Bath, England: Adams and Dart, 1973.

Waterbolk, H. T. "Working with Radiocarbon Dates." *Proceedings of the Prehistoric Society,* 37, 1971, 15.

Index

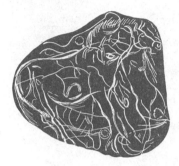

Numbers in italics indicate pages on which terms are defined.

Battle-axe (corded-ware) folk, 187
Beaker folk, 186–88, 190
Beans, 168, 169, 175, 180, 182, 183
Bear cult, 60, 61
Beidha, 135
Beldibi, 110
Bering Strait, 30, 85, 92, 178
Bifacial tool, 42, 45n, 58
Binford, Lewis, 59, 97
Binford, Sally, 59
Blade tool, 58, 66; special types of, 72–76
Bökönyi, Sandor, 115
Bordes, François, 47, 59, 69
Boskop skull, 30
Bostanci, Enver, 110
Boulding, Kenneth, 199
Bouqras, 116
Breasted, James Henry, 102, 151, 185
Bricker, Harvey, 54
Bricks, mud, 5, 6, 130, 134, 135, 136, 137
Bronze, 188, 189, 190, 192
Burials, 59, 60, 61, 81, 112, 145, 172, 179, 188, 190–91
Bushmen, 30
Butzer, Karl, 11n
Byblos, 136

Calico, 178
Çambel, Halet, 136
Canals, 134, 153–54, 155, 165
Cannibalism, 52
Carbon dating. See Radiocarbon method of dating
Case, Humphrey, 144, 146
Çatal Hüyük, 137
Cattle: domestic, 101, 134, 137, 144, 146, 172, 176, 177, 190, 191; wild, 80, 103, 115, 116, 127, 136, 169
Caucasoid, 30
Cave art. See Art
Caves, 35–36
Çayönü, 119, 125, 136, 137
Celts, 192, 193, 195
Chang, Kwang-chih, 169, 172, 174, 175
Chariots, 165, 193
Chavin art style, 184
Childe, V. Gordon, 2, 81, 88, 90, 93, 117, 118, 122, 123, 141, 147, 148, 155

Chimpanzee, 17–18, 38–39
Choga Mami, 132, 134, 154
Chopper tool, 42
Choukoutien, 30, 52
Civilization: beginnings of in Near East, 151–65; characteristics of, 149–51
Clactonian, 53, 56, 59
Clark, Desmond, 61, 84, 139, 141, 168, 176
Cleaver, 45
Combe Capelle-Brunn man, 30
Coon, Carleton S., 90, 113
Copper, 136, 158, 184, 186, 187, 190
Core tool, 41
Craft-specialization, 122–23, 159, 174
Cremation, 190–91
Cro-Magnon man, 30
Culture, characteristics of, 33–34, 54–56, 61–62, 99

Dabban, 68, 83
Dart, Raymond, 22
David, Nicholas, 72
Deir Tasa, 139, 140
Dendrochronology, 4, 86, 147, 189
"Desert" assemblage, 179–80
De Wet, J. M. J., 176
Discoidal core, 57, 83
Dog, domestic, 90, 100, 104, 113, 127, 134, 136, 172, 175, 180, 183
Dordogne sequence, 70–80
Dubois, Eugene, 24

"Early Horizon" period, 184
East Rudolf, 16
Ehringsdorf, 27
Emiran, 68, 83
Engis, 28
Eoliths, 39
Eras, 99
Eridu, 132, 134, 156, 158, 159, 161
Euphrates, irrigation and flood control, 153–54

Fauresmith industry, 61
Fayum, 139, 140, 152

Figurines, 115, 129, 137, 158, 180, 198; "Venus," 79, 129, 198
Fire, 25, 26, 49, 50, 52, 81, 197
Flake tool, 41
Flannery, Kent, 97, 98, 100, 122, 169, 180, 182
Folk, 187n
Fontéchevade, 27, 32, 53
Food collecting, 98–99, 122–23
Food-producing revolution, causes of, 93–98
Food-producing stages: incipient cultivation, animal domestication era, 100–120; village-farming era, 121–48
Food production (village-farming): in China, 170–75; in Europe, 141–48; in India, 175–76; in Japan, 175; in Mediterranean area, 125–39, 151–63; in New World, 178–84; in southeast Asia, 169–70; in sub-Saharan Africa, 176–78
Food-vessel folk, 188, 190, 191
Forest folk, 88–92, 99, 100, 105, 141, 146, 179
Fort Ternan, 39
Fowler, Melvin, 168
Fox, Sir Cyril, 196
Franchthi, 120, 138
Frankfort, Henri, 150
Freeman, Leslie, 59

Ganj Dareh, 113, 125, 138
Garrod, Dorothy A., 68
Geleen, 105n
Geological method of dating, 63, 70–72
Geologist, 2
Ghassul, 161
Gibraltar, 28
Glaciers, 11–14, 27, 37–38, 81, 87, 95–96, 197
Glastonbury, 194
Goat: domestic, 103, 105n, 115, 117, 127, 130, 134, 136, 137, 144, 176, 177; wild, 115
Godin Tepe, 138
Gorman, Chester, 169
Ground stone tools, 88, 110, 115, 116, 130, 137, 169, 170, 177, 180
Guitarrero, 183
Guran, 126, 138

Hacilar, 137
Haji Firuz, 138
Halafian, 132n, 137, 156, 158
Hallstat folk, 192, 193
Hand adze, 50
Hand axe, 45, 50
Harappan (Indus Valley) culture, 175, 176
Harlan, Jack R., 101, 118–19, 168, 169, 176, 177, 182
Hassuna, 130–32, 134, 136, 138, 139, 156
Haua Fteah, 29, 66, 83, 177
Hawkins, G. S., 189
Haynes, Vance, 178
Heidelberg, 25, 27, 32
Helbaek, Hans, 137
Henges, 188, 189
High Lodge, 53
Hill-forts, 193–94
Ho, Ping-ti, 101, 172, 174
Hoabinhian, 169, 170, 175
Hole, Frank, 115
Hominids (Hominidae), 16, 18–26, 32, 54
Homo erectus, 24–26, 28, 32
Homo erectus pekinesis. See Peking man
Homo "habilis," 16, 22, 24, 25, 54
Homo sapiens, 21, 27, 28, 30, 32, 57, 60
Homo sapiens neaderthalenis. See Neandertal
Horse: domestic, 191; wild, 49, 52, 60, 80, 81, 109, 115, 127, 178
Houses, 110, 116, 125, 129, 130, 134, 135, 136, 137, 138, 144, 156, 170, 180, 193. See also Huts
Howe, Bruce, 68, 113
Howell, F. Clark, 20, 22, 27, 49
Huaca Prieta, 183
Human paleontologist. See Physical anthropologist
Humans: earliest dates for, 10, 15–16, 19–20, 32; characteristics of, 13, 20–21, 33, 54, 197; geographical origin of, 16; relationship to apes, 15–18, 19–20
Huts, 50, 60, 81, 93, 115, 122, 130, 146

Ice Age. See Pleistocene
Incas, 150, 151, 184
Indians, American, 30, 81, 85, 88,

Mousterian, 47, 57–60, 66, 68
Movius, Hallam, 50, 69, 90
Mugharet es-Skhul, 29
Munhatta, 135
Mureybit, 116, 117, 118, 120, 125

Nahal Oren, 120
Namazgah, 138
Natufian, 109–13, 116, 117, 120, 135, 136
Neandertal, 26, 27–28, 32, 57, 68
Nea Nikomedeia, 137
Negroes, 30
Nile, irrigation and flood control, 153–54
Noallian, 70, 72
Nok assemblage, sculpture, 178
Non Nok Tha, 170, 172
Nuclear area (food-producing), *101*

Oates, Joan, 132, 134, 138, 156, 158
Obsidian, *66*, 129
"Old Cordilleran" tradition, 179
Oldowan, 25, 40, 41, 42–44, 50, 51, 52–53, 56, 61
Olduvai Gorge, 16, 22, 25, 32, 40, 43, 44, 49
Olmec art, 182
Olorgesailie, 49
Omo Basin, 16, 22, 23, 29, 40, 43
Ovens, 129

Paleobotanist, *3*
Paleoclimatologist, *3*
Paleontologist, *2–3*
Pan p'o, 170
Patjitanian, 51
Pebble tools, *42*
Pech de l'Azé II, 47, 49
Peking man, 25, 30, 32, 34, 52
Perigordian, 68, 70, 72, 74, 78, 81, 83
Perkins, Dexter, 137
Perrot, Jean, 110, 116, 118, 119, 127, 136
Petrolona, 26
Physical anthropologist, *1*
Pig: domestic, 101, 103, 127, 134, 136, 144, 146, 170, 172; wild, 49, 103, 169
Piggot, Stuart, 146, 186, 188, 189,

192, 195, 196
Piki phase, 183
Pithecanthropus, 24
Pleistocene (Ice Age): characteristics and duration of, 11–14, 37, 87, 96, 97
Pliocene, 16
Plow, 123, 165, 188, 192
Potassium-argon method of dating, 3
Pottery, pottery styles: Africa, 84, 177, 178; America, 179, 180, 184; Britain, 144, 145, 146, 186, 188, 191, 192; China, 170, 172, 174; India, 175; Japan, 175; Near East, 129–38 and 156–65 passim; southeast Asia, 169
Pre-Aurignacian, 66
Preclassic (Formative) phase, 180, 182
Prehistory, *1, 9*, 166, 199–200
Pre-neandertaloids, 27, 28, 29
Primates: relationship to humans, 17; use of tools by, 38. *See also* Apes
"Proto-Australoid" skulls, 30
Proto-Literate, 163–65, 182
Protomagdalenian, 70
Puddled mud, 129, 130

Rabat, 25
Race, 30, 55, 199–200
Radiocarbon method of dating, 3, 4, 63, 86, 147–48
Ramad, 135
Ramapithecus, 19–20, 39
Ras Shamra, 135
Redfield, Robert, 33, 150
Reed, Charles A., 127
Religious activity, 61, 123, 137, 145, 150, 158, 159, 189. *See also* Temples
Renfrew, Colin, 145, 147, 150, 189
Retouching, *41–42*
Rhodesian man, 29
Rice, 101, 169, 170, 172, 175, 177
Rosamachay, 183

Saccopastore, 27
Samarran, 130, 132, 156, 158
Sangoan, 61
Sankalia, Hasmukh, 175, 176
Sarab, 126, 127, 129, 130, 138
Sarich, Vincent, 18

1 2 3 4 5 6 7 8 9 10 –DB– 80 79 78 77 76 75 74